PRAISE FOR *WHEN GOD DOESN'T FIX IT*

This book is a must-read. ..., Carol, and I have had the privilege of witnessing much of what is described in this book. I will assure you, it is the real story. Get ready to be encouraged, challenged, and taught well when you read *When God Doesn't Fix It*.

—RANDY POPE
PASTOR OF PERIMETER CHURCH

I've sat on stage and watched Laura minister with song to those who were hurting, and I know the story of her life will help to heal many more who are struggling with their own brokenness. Together, our family has been ministered to by her vulnerability and willingness to walk in the valley and still say "God, I Trust You."

—STEVEN CURTIS AND MARY BETH CHAPMAN
GRAMMY AWARD-WINNING ARTIST AND *NEW YORK TIMES*
BESTSELLING AUTHOR

Laura is one of my heroes when it comes to trusting God. She's joyful, genuine, and faithful even though her story includes messy chapters that haven't necessarily been "fixed." This book will be on my nightstand for a long time!

—LISA HARPER
AUTHOR AND BIBLE TEACHER

WHEN GOD
DOESN'T FIX IT

WHEN GOD DOESN'T FIX IT

LESSONS YOU NEVER WANTED TO LEARN,
TRUTHS YOU CAN'T LIVE WITHOUT

LAURA STORY
WITH JENNIFER SCHUCHMANN

W PUBLISHING GROUP

AN IMPRINT OF THOMAS NELSON

Published in Nashville, Tennessee, by W Publishing Group, an imprint of Thomas Nelson. W Publishing Group and Thomas Nelson are registered trademarks of HarperCollins Christian Publishing, Inc.

Published in association with Creative Trust, www.creativetrust.com.

Thomas Nelson, Inc., titles may be purchased in bulk for educational, business, fund-raising, or sales promotional use. For information, please e-mail SpecialMarkets@ThomasNelson.com.

Direct quotations from *The NIV Application Commentary* in chapter 10 are taken from Gary M. Burge, *John, The NIV Application Commentary* (Grand Rapids, MI: Zondervan, 2000), 272–73.

Library of Congress Control Number: 2015908304

ISBN 978-0-7180-3697-3

Printed in the United States of America

17 18 19 RRD 12

To Martin
You are still my dream come true

"My grace is sufficient for you, for my power is made perfect in weakness."

—2 CORINTHIANS 12:9

CONTENTS

UNEXPECTED CALLS

THE CALL THAT CHANGED MY LIFE HAPPENED AROUND noon in February 2006. I was in St. Louis attending a conference with two of my coworkers. They sat in the front seat of the rental car with the radio on; I was in the backseat checking my phone messages. As we headed to Panera Bread for lunch, I noticed a voice mail from my husband, Martin, and I called him back. That's when he gave me the news that dramatically changed the course of our lives and the lives of those closest to us.

We're all just one phone call away from learning the results of a test or the news of an affair, the death of a loved one, the loss of a job, or a thousand other ways our hope can be shattered.

In that moment, we think life as we know it is over.

The truth is, life, as we've yet to know it, has just begun.

C

In the summer of 2005, Martin and I had been married a year. We lived rent free in Greenville, South Carolina, near a church where we were working for the summer. We'd just packed up our belongings and sold our house, intending to move to Savannah, Georgia, in the fall so Martin could attend Savannah College of Art and Design (SCAD). For years, Martin had been the campus director of a college ministry where he led a Bible study and also did graphic design and web development work for Wofford College. I'd graduated from Bible college and had dabbled in music, ministry, and helping Martin with the Bible study—none of which paid well. We planned to get jobs in Savannah, and then once Martin was finished with school, we'd move back to Spartanburg, South Carolina, to be near our parents. The SCAD degree would help Martin get a well-paying job in the graphic design field, which would allow me to stay home and raise the kids we both wanted to have someday.

That was our plan for a perfect life.

The first detour came when Martin's friend John Roland called us from Atlanta. "Hey, I know this is crazy," John said to Martin, "but I have a job for Laura at my church if you guys are interested in moving to Atlanta."

John worked at Perimeter Church, located in the northern suburbs of Atlanta. The church was seeking a worship leader. In addition, John told us that SCAD had just opened an Atlanta campus. If we moved to Atlanta, Martin could continue school and I would have a job. My last job had been playing bass in a bluegrass band in a Mexican restaurant. In other words, I had no marketable skills, so a position at a church in Atlanta sounded much better than a waitressing job in Savannah.

Martin handed me the phone. "Tell me about the job," I said.

John described the duties, which included choosing music for the congregation, leading volunteers, and developing worshippers. But I had never done any of those things. Sure, I'd majored in music and played bass in a touring band that had performed at retreats and youth groups, but the only time I ever sang was under duress when our female singer was gone or ill. I didn't know a thing about leading worship.

"And the church is looking for somebody who can write worship songs," John continued.

That's why John is calling me!

In an effort to avoid paying performance fees for the music our touring band covered, everyone in the band was asked to write songs. I'd written a few, including one called "Indescribable." A year earlier, an executive from a record company called to ask if they could use my song on the CD of a worship leader from Texas—a guy named Chris Tomlin. I'd agreed, and Tomlin's label released "Indescribable" as a single. The song had just started getting a lot of radio play.

Other than my friends and family (and John), no one knew that the song had been written by the blonde girl who played bass at the Mexican restaurant on Thursdays. Until someone else called it a *worship* song, I didn't even think of it that way because of all of the five-syllable words in the chorus. Regardless of how the song was doing, neither songwriting nor playing bass in a bluegrass band qualified me to lead a congregation in singing.

"John, I've written a few songs, but when it comes to leading worship . . . ," I said as I prepared to decline his offer.

"We offer a steady salary and health insurance," he added.

"Wait, you said health insurance?" I asked.

"Yes, and retirement benefits."

I wasn't a math major, but it didn't take me long to calculate the salary, benefits, and retirement numbers, and compare the total to what I was making at the Mexican restaurant—free burritos and all the chips and salsa I could eat.

"Like I was saying, when it comes to leading worship, I'm so glad you asked me. I'd love to be your church's worship leader," I said.

After praying about it with Martin, that's how the detour began. Martin would go to school in Atlanta, and I would start at Perimeter Church in the fall.

ℐ

During June and July, Martin and I made several trips to Atlanta to look for a condo. My boss-to-be, Randy Schlichting, one of the pastors at Perimeter, along with the other staff members, did everything they could to reach out and make us feel welcome. Though I didn't know what I was doing, I couldn't wait to get started.

But something else was going on, and I wasn't sure if I should mention it to anyone. As July turned to August and my September 1 start date loomed nearer, I realized I couldn't go through with the move. I closed the door to the church office where I was working and called Randy. Like every other time I called, he seemed delighted to hear from me.

"Are you excited about coming?" he asked.

"Um, I need to talk to you about something," I stammered, unsure of how much to say. "I don't know if it's the best thing for Martin and me to move to Atlanta and for me to take this job."

For several months, Martin had been experiencing some unusual symptoms. He'd been more forgetful than usual. Some days he wanted to do nothing but sleep followed by days where he wouldn't sleep at all. His heart would race, and he'd get sweaty and nauseous as if he was having a panic attack, but none of the doctors we saw could determine what was wrong with him. The symptoms had started in March and then subsided; but by August, they had returned. Though he'd seen four different doctors, we still hadn't discovered the cause of his symptoms.

I paused, searching for the right words. "There's something wrong with my husband. We don't know whether it is physical, emotional, or psychiatric. We just know that something is wrong with him—" That's all Randy let me get out before he interrupted me.

"Well, here's what I think you need to do. You need to get your belongings into a U-Haul and come straight to Atlanta. We'll take care of whatever is wrong with your husband once you get here. We're not having you move to Atlanta just so you can be a worship leader; we're having you move to Atlanta because you are part of Perimeter Church now. You and Martin come down, and we'll take care of your family."

"Okay, we'll come," I said, choking back my tears. I hung up and let them stream down my face as I slumped my head into the back of the chair. *It's going to be okay.*

And it was.

For a while.

C

We moved to Atlanta in August so I could start my job and Martin could start school. Everything was great in our marriage, and Martin's symptoms seemed to disappear with the move. I fell in love with my job, my coworkers, and the people of Perimeter Church. I started reading books on how to be a worship leader and spent a lot of time learning from the pastors at Perimeter, but there was still a lot I didn't know. Perimeter was generous with their training and encouraged me to attend a couple of upcoming conferences in February.

That holiday season was the first Martin and I had spent away from our parents, but they came to Atlanta and we traveled to South Carolina as much as our schedules allowed. Once the holidays were over, Martin seemed to be perpetually exhausted. At first I thought he was just working too much. Not only was he going to school, but he also had a job in a coffee shop. *He's just tired*, I thought.

But soon he started falling asleep during Bible study or, worse, during the worship services. I was embarrassed, and when we got home on Sunday afternoons, I'd let him know.

"I know you're tired, but you can't sleep while I'm leading the music, and especially not when my boss is preaching!"

He'd apologize and promise to do better.

Then it started happening at social events. We'd be at someone's house, and he'd fall asleep while the host was telling a story. A few weeks later, he failed to show up for a party because he fell asleep. One night, we'd planned to meet for dinner, and he didn't show. I tried calling his cell phone. When he finally answered, he said, "I sat down on the couch for ten minutes, but I fell asleep."

I was frustrated. "It's been two hours. If you were going to take a nap, why didn't you set an alarm?"

"I wasn't planning to take a nap. I just fell asleep."

After that night, I turned down invitations because I got tired of making excuses for him.

When we first got married, we used to lie awake in bed at night, talk about our days, and pray for each other. Now, though, it seemed as soon as Martin was horizontal, he was out. I'd be telling him about my day, and next thing I knew, I would hear him snoring.

"Martin! You're not even listening to me!" I'd say, poking him.

"I'm sorry. I'm so sorry. Go ahead, tell me one more time."

Before I could get another word out, he'd be snoring again.

Martin had been a real go-getter with tons of energy. He'd been an athlete, an honor student, and on academic scholarship to college. I couldn't remember a time when he didn't work hard. But now he'd become someone I didn't recognize.

Occasionally, I'd tell a close friend or family member that Martin wasn't at all who he was before we got married. "He sleeps constantly," I'd complain. "I ask him to do one little thing, like unload the dishwasher, and the next morning he tells me he forgot. Last Sunday he fell asleep watching football!"

They'd laugh and say something like, "All men are like that."

But Martin never had been like other men.

His first semester at SCAD he'd made As in all of his classes. But now, he was struggling. After getting home from his coffee shop job around eight o'clock, he'd start his homework and then fall asleep at the table. Soon I was staying up at night force-feeding him cup after cup of coffee as I helped him study for tests. But nothing I did could keep him awake. He started getting Fs on his quizzes and then on his tests. He wasn't only failing in his classes; he was also failing at life.

My dad and brother took him skiing. When they got back my dad said, "Martin fell asleep on the ski lift."

Other weird things were happening. Martin was twenty-four years old, but he was going through another growth spurt. He grew an inch and a half in nine months.

We'd been to four physicians in South Carolina, and my dad was a doctor. None of them could find anything wrong. Where Martin had once been sharp and quick, now he was lethargic.

Some of our closest friends began noticing and offered their own opinions.

"He's just lazy," one man said.

"He needs some counseling," one of the wives said.

One day, a church member sat me down and said, "I know you've only been married a short time, and no newlywed wants to hear this, but I think your husband might have a mental illness."

Before we moved to Atlanta, I'd told a close friend or two about some of Martin's earlier symptoms. They'd try to comfort me with stories of their own. "That sounds like my sister's husband. He has schizophrenia!" Or, "I have a friend whose dad has been diagnosed with bipolar disorder!" I began to think perhaps Martin had a mental problem, and the thought scared me.

Perimeter Church is a large church with an amazing counseling department, so whether Martin needed help with his laziness, counseling, or something more serious, we agreed we needed to talk to someone. Martin knew things weren't right, and he wasn't happy about it. Both he and I became concerned that he may be depressed.

Psychologist Clay Coffee spent an hour and a half asking Martin questions while I readied myself for the worst. But Clay didn't think Martin suffered from a mental illness.

"I think it's simple," Clay said. "You're depressed because you can't stay awake and you're having trouble remembering things. I know you're expecting me to tell you it's something mental, but it sounds like something physical. I think you need to see a medical doctor."

On one hand, we were relieved Clay didn't think it was something worse. On the other hand, we had both hoped antidepressants would fix whatever needed fixing with Martin.

He'd already seen four doctors and now a counselor, and none of them could find anything wrong. Could it be this was just who Martin was?

Before Martin and I got engaged, a spiritual mentor wisely told me, "If you tell Martin you love him and that you want to spend the rest of your life with him, you have to be prepared to see it through even if the fluffy feelings disappear, because marriage isn't just about fluffy feelings." Somehow I thought it would take three to five years for that to happen, not twelve to eighteen months, but I'd made a commitment. I would still love and serve my husband even if the fluffy feelings were gone.

I began praying more and having conversations with God. *I get it, God. He's the man I married, and I'm in it for the long haul. But boy, is he different than I thought he was when we first married. I can still see glimpses of the man I loved back then, and I am hanging on to those. We're going to press on through this, but God, you've got to help me. Something has to change!*

C

Martin's sleepiness continued into February 2006. He started missing classes because he overslept. I grew concerned because I was scheduled to attend two worship conferences that month. The first was in North Carolina, where I was asked to lead worship. The second was in St. Louis, where I would learn how to lead worship. (The irony of the conference order wasn't lost on me.)

I wasn't sure if I should attend either conference. I was worried about leaving Martin home alone. *How will he get up in time for class by himself? How will he get his homework done?* I couldn't imagine what would happen when I wasn't there.

But Martin encouraged me to go. "I'll be fine."

While in North Carolina at the first conference, I called him between sessions. He sounded like he'd just woken up. "What are you doing?"

"Oh, I'm just resting."

In the background, I could hear *ding, ding, ding.* It didn't take a professional musician to know that was the sound the car made when someone opened the door and left the key in the ignition.

"Were you sleeping in the car?" I asked.

"Yeah, I had some trouble staying awake on my way home."

"What do you mean you had trouble staying awake?"

"I fell asleep and hit a guardrail. I'm okay, but the car is a little scratched. So when I got home, I parked the car and took a nap."

I couldn't believe what he was telling me. As soon as we hung up, I called his friend John Roland, who was now my coworker and our next-door neighbor. I told John what Martin had done. "You've got to take the keys away from him," I said. "He can't drive anymore, and I think he should stay home from class until I get back to Atlanta."

When I got home, I could see how tired Martin was. I was also convinced I finally knew what his problem was—narcolepsy. I made a mental note to schedule an appointment with a doctor when I got home from my upcoming trip to St. Louis.

The next morning when the alarm went off, Martin rolled over and asked me a really odd question. "Are we going to the airport today?"

"No. Why would we go to the airport?"

"Okay."

It was such a strange question that alarm bells went off in my head.

"Why don't you go fix us some coffee, Martin? I'll be down in a second," I said.

As soon as Martin left our bedroom, I reached for the phone and then slithered down my side of the bed until I was sitting on the floor. I called my boss.

"Martin just asked if we were going to the airport today. Something is really wrong," I whispered. "I'm going to take the day off and take him to the doctor."

That afternoon, Martin and I met with a general practitioner who was highly recommended by a friend. The doctor ran a lot of tests that day and then had us come back for the results later.

On the second visit she said, "For the most part everything looks good, but your hormone levels are low." She mentioned a number of potential causes, including Martin's thyroid and something to do with a testicle.

"It's not that!" Martin said defensively.

"I'm not saying it is," she chuckled. "In fact, I think everything points to the pituitary gland. I'd like to get a CT scan and an MRI of your pituitary to see if there is anything going on there."

Relieved they weren't investigating more private parts, we scheduled the tests for the following Tuesday. I would be in St. Louis at the conference, but John agreed that Martin could stay with him and he would drive Martin to get his scans.

I attended the conference with Jeff Wreyford and Eric Gilbert, two of my coworkers. I'd looked forward to this conference since I'd first signed up. I'd only been at the church for six months, and I still had a lot to learn about leading worship.

The first presenter was Pastor Scotty Smith from Nashville. He promised the entire first session would be on worship—not picking songs, not choosing music styles, not leading or directing. We'd focus solely on what it meant for us to worship, and to worship regardless of our circumstances.

During the session, he reminded us that our first ministry was not to our churches but to our families. "Don't let the job fool you. Your number-one ministry will always be your family. These churches will take your life if you let them, but your greatest serving opportunity isn't in the church; it's in your home."

That's great, I thought, *but it really doesn't apply to me. Martin and*

I don't have kids, and once we do, I'll stay at home with them. I was hopeful the afternoon sessions would contain more practical teaching.

My coworkers and I headed to the parking lot to get lunch. I got into the backseat of the rental car, and that's when I noticed there was a voice mail on my phone from Martin, asking me to call him as soon as possible. I called his cell. "What's going on?"

"Hey, I've got some news. I have a brain tumor."

"What?"

"Yeah, the doctor said the scans show I have a brain tumor. It's pressing against my pituitary gland, which is why my hormones have been messed up. That's why I've been so sleepy. I have no adrenaline being released."

He sounded nonchalant, almost as if it was a relief to know it was a brain tumor. I was shaken. I couldn't concentrate on what he was saying. I just kept hearing *brain tumor* over and over in my head. I needed to process what was happening, but my mind was racing.

"Hey, can you guys turn down the radio?" I asked Jeff and Eric. We were pulling into the parking lot and I needed a moment to get ahold of my thoughts.

"Um, Martin, let me call you back in a second. We just pulled into Panera."

"What's up?" Jeff asked, concerned.

"Martin has a brain tumor." My voice shook as I spoke. "You guys go in. I'll call him back and then I'll come in when I'm done."

"Are you okay?" Eric asked.

I started to cry.

"What can we do?" Jeff wanted to know.

"I'm not sure yet. Let me just call him back."

"We'll wait for you," Jeff said as he opened his door.

"And we'll be praying," Eric added.

The numbers on my phone were blurred as I called Martin again. "Are you okay?" I asked him, trying to control the shakiness in my voice.

"Yeah. They said I needed to set up an appointment with a neurosurgeon to talk about having it removed. I wanted to wait until you got back. I thought you might want to go with me."

Finding out that Martin had a brain tumor flooded my heart with compassion and love for him. I felt stupid for being angry and embarrassed by his behavior when the whole time he had been suffering from a brain tumor.

"Martin, I am so sorry," I said, letting the tears flow.

Although it was a scary, huge diagnosis and I was very worried, I also felt a sense of relief. I'd been praying for something to change. Martin had been praying to figure out what was wrong; he thought he was losing his mind. Finally we had an answer. Though it wasn't a *good* answer, at least it gave us hope that it could be fixed. I could hear the relief and hope in Martin's voice as we cried together on the phone.

"When will you be home?" Martin asked.

"I'm not sure. I'll call Randy and then I'll call you back."

I hung up and slumped back into the seat, trying to breathe deeply. I wanted to slow down my tears and racing heart before I called my boss. After a good cry and a few deep breaths, I called Randy—my boss and the pastor who had encouraged us to move to Atlanta and had promised the church would take care of us. He had no idea what he was getting into when he made that promise.

"Martin has a brain tumor—"

Before I could finish my sentence, Randy took charge. "Okay, we'll get you home on the first flight we can and have someone meet you at the airport."

I called Martin back and we talked briefly. His calm acceptance of the diagnosis encouraged me. He was determined to take that sucker out so we could get on with our lives. We'd already wasted a year not knowing what was wrong, and now it was time for action. Our plan was to fix it and move on.

Eric and Jeff drove me to the hotel, where the three of us threw my things into a suitcase and raced to the airport. I was in a daze as I made it through security and walked to my gate. I arrived with ninety minutes to spare.

I should call Mom and Dad, I thought, reaching for my phone. But it wasn't in my pocket. In my purse? I swallowed hard, realizing I'd left it in the rental car. It was the worst time ever for me to be left alone without my phone. My mind was spinning. There were so many people to tell, and I wanted to talk to Martin. But in that moment, there was someone even more important I needed to talk to. *God, where are you in all of this? Couldn't you have helped the doctors find the tumor earlier? Why did Martin and I have to go through all this before finally getting a diagnosis?*

Mixed in with the sadness, relief, and fear, I felt angry that it had taken a year for the doctors to find the tumor. And I was tempted to be angry with God, who could have directed them to the proper diagnosis. But then I had another thought.

Am I going to let my circumstances determine my view of God, or am I going to let God determine how I view my circumstances?

It was a bigger question than I realized at the time. But I answered it in prayer. *God, I want you.* Though I had accepted Christ as my Lord and Savior years earlier, as I sat in the faux leather seats in the busy airport and looked out at the tarmac, I knew Martin and I were about to embark on a new journey. As soon as the plane landed in Atlanta, everything would be different. I would hit the ground running—searching for answers, the best doctor, and the cure to whatever had caused the tumor in the first place. But in that airport, at that moment, I wanted God to know once again that he came first and that I was grateful for so many things.

Thank you for hearing my prayer. I prayed for a change, and you have given it to us. Thank you, God, for a diagnosis. For this diagnosis.

An operable brain tumor seemed much better than having to endure a lifetime of the unknowns of a mental illness.

Thank you that there is a tumor the doctors can go in and remove.

Yes, it was scary, and it was certainly a detour on the life plan we had laid out, but I was confident we quickly would return to our normal life. Martin would be a semester or two behind in school, but he'd still graduate and get a job in graphic design. In a few years, we'd move closer to my parents' home in Spartanburg. I'd quit my job and be a stay-at-home mom just like my mom. In the future, the brain tumor would be a great story to tell of how God brought us through it all, and we would all live happily ever after.

I couldn't have been more naive.

TWO

INNER ENCOUNTER IN OUTER MONGOLIA

MARTIN AND I MET AT A FELLOWSHIP OF CHRISTIAN Athletes barbecue in August 1994. He was an athlete, and I was trying to fellowship with one. It was the first FCA event I ever attended, and I went only because it was in my girlfriend's backyard. Otherwise I would have been much too insecure to go.

Although I was a tomboy, I wasn't into sports. I enjoyed artsy things like playing the piano and being in the orchestra or as Martin's athlete friends called it, the "dork-estra." As a scrawny, quirky kid, I was a free spirit with bits of a tree hugger and hippie thrown in the mix. Apparently I was also fashion-challenged. Case in point: I wore overalls to the barbecue. Not just any overalls, but moose-covered overalls. So you can imagine how swept off my Birkenstocks I was when this six-foot-three, blond, blue-eyed, gorgeous baseball player sat down next to me. I nearly choked on my hot dog!

It was the weekend before the start of high school classes. I was a senior and Martin was a junior. I found out later he was the best player on the baseball team. (He went on to play in college.) He was extremely outgoing, and did I mention good-looking? But what really attracted me was that he was so goofy. Despite my insecurities, that was something I could relate to.

Somehow, the artsy girl and the athletic boy made a love

connection. We dated on and off for a year until I went to college. Even in college, I'd come home on the weekends to hang out with him. It was a comfortable and familiar relationship. We were best friends despite the distance.

After attending Calvin College for a semester, I attended the University of South Carolina on a music scholarship. I started playing piano when I was seven and string bass when I was ten. From middle school through college, I was always part of a musical ensemble. I played in an orchestra and a bluegrass band, and anything in between that required a string bass. I hung out with other musical people, who were usually impressed that I could play piano by ear. For years I found my identity in my music. People would ask me to play a song, and I could. It was my niche. It was one of the reasons people paid attention to me.

Other things helped prop up my self-esteem, like the cute 300ZX sports car I drove to college. Then there was my boyfriend, the good-looking baseball player. Among my peers I was recognized for my musical talents, and rewarded for my hard work with a music scholarship.

Looking back, it's easy to see that all the arrows in my life pointed to me, not to God. I'd chosen to follow Christ when I was ten, but at college my faith didn't mean all that much. It was hard to tell those of us who were believers from those who weren't when we all went to the same parties and drank the same drinks. I didn't give my faith a lot of thought. I was finally cool, and I felt good about myself (though for all the wrong reasons). It was the first time I'd ever felt that way, and I enjoyed every minute of it.

Until it all ended.

C

One spring day during my freshman year, I went home to Spartanburg for the weekend. Martin and I were tossing the football at a local park. We were messing around as he tried to yank the ball from me. I hung on, but I tumbled to the ground and Martin crashed on top of me. I heard a really loud *pop*. As an excruciating pain radiated up and down my right arm, I realized something had snapped.

"Ow! That hurts!"

"Oh, shake it off. You'll be fine," Martin said.

But my arm was really aching. I asked him to take me home.

By the time he dropped me off, my elbow had swelled to three times its normal size. My dad, a doctor, examined my arm. "You need to have that looked at," he said immediately.

When Martin came over later that evening, my arm was in a cast and I was livid. He was apologetic, but I didn't care. "You have no idea what this means! I'm a music major, and I can't play anything with a broken arm!" I was so mad at Martin I said, "We're done!"

I broke up with him for breaking my arm.

Sunday, on the way back to college, instead of driving my cute sports car with the stick that I could no longer shift, I rode in my parents' sedan. Dad had to carry my books and laundry to my dorm room. On Monday, I dropped half my classes because I could no longer play bass.

But that wasn't all. The next week was Valentine's Day. I could hear squeals from the girls who received flowers, candy, and perfume from their boyfriends. Beautiful bouquets filled my friends' dorm rooms, and the hall never smelled better.

I never felt worse.

Alone in my dorm room, I lay on my bed, the cast weighing heavily against my stomach. I didn't have a boyfriend, a car, or a class in my major. Music was the whole reason I'd gone to college. Now it was as absent as my cute former boyfriend. Everything that made me cool, everything that brought me attention and fed my ego was suddenly missing.

For the first time I began to wonder, *What's life all about anyway? Do I have a purpose? Is this all that life has to offer?* The things that mattered in my world had been stripped away, and all I had left was a question mark. If everything that brought me joy or significance was so fleeting it could disappear with the snap of an elbow, then what's the point?

A friend in my dorm had been praying for me. One day, she invited me to a Christian campus meeting. I'd only been to church a handful of times since I started college, and I figured if there was ever a time to go back, this was it.

While there, I heard a message reminding me how much God loves me. I had nothing to offer him in return. In fact, I couldn't even put on my own deodorant—I had to ask my roommate for help. But the speaker said God didn't want anything *from* me; he had something *for* me. I was God's child, and he wanted me to stop running so he could love me. The speaker was so inspiring that when he announced a mission trip to Mongolia, my friend and I signed up. Since I wasn't of any use to anyone else, I thought, *If God can use me, I might as well go.*

I had no idea what I was getting into.

I grew up with a lot of material objects. Though my parents were frugal, my dad was a cardiologist and made a good living. We had a country club membership, so I could order whatever I wanted and just sign the ticket. When I was in high school, my parents surprised me with an expensive instrument—my very own bass. In short, I was spoiled.

When I got to Mongolia, I had the culture shock of my life.

✒

We landed in Ulaanbaatar, the capital city. Located between China and Russia, the country had been under Soviet influence until 1990, when it had its own democratic revolution. Six years later, I could still see the influence. The apartment complexes were identical buildings in dire need of maintenance. Everything was dirty.

We spent our first four days meeting with local church leaders. They took us to a pizza restaurant, where the menu revealed three kinds of pizza—mutton, cheese, and American. The American pizza was topped with ham, corn, and mutton. Apparently they didn't know we like pepperoni.

But it got worse when we went to the countryside.

On the fifth day, our group paired up with translators and hit the road in five Jeeps. We had two huge round tents, called yurts: one for the guys and one for the girls. We drove to the middle of nowhere, where *nowhere* actually had a name—Outer Mongolia.

We were in a region with small hills and nothing but grass for miles. Our plan was to minister to the Buddhist nomads who grazed their herds in nearby meadows.

Each morning we would eat breakfast and then pray. Afterward, we'd break into groups of three or four, plus a translator and a Jeep driver, and head out in different directions. When we came across a yurt, we'd stop and the translator would introduce us and tell the family who lived there we were from America. We'd ask if they'd like to see a movie about God. They almost always said yes; most had never seen a movie before. The translator would set up the generator and film equipment and project the *JESUS* film onto the walls of their tent. The rest of our team would stay at the campsite, do laundry in the river, and cook dinner so it would be ready when we returned. Every night, dinner was the same—mutton stew with carrots. Occasionally, we'd get bread with jam, and when that happened, we thought it was Christmas!

When we ate with the locals we had to be mindful of their traditions. For example, the nomads didn't use toilet paper. Instead they wore robes and to keep things sanitary, they kept their left hand—the one they used to wipe—inside their robe. When they handed us food or we handed them something, we had to be careful not to use our left hands. Fortunately, my cast had come off my right arm before I left; otherwise, I would not have been able to eat in public!

Everything in Outer Mongolia smelled like sweat and manure—including us.

My only possessions were my backpack with a change of clothes, a toothbrush, and my Bible. During our downtime, I'd often sit for hours on the side of a hill and read my Bible. As I read the Scriptures, I began to pray differently. Instead of being self-absorbed and miserable, I became grateful for my time in Mongolia. God had taken me out of my self-centered life and dropped me in the middle of nowhere so I could get alone with him. I started to see him differently than I had before.

Every day during our month in Mongolia I watched the *JESUS* film, a cinematic portrayal of the Gospel of Luke, two or three times. For me, it was a daily encounter with Jesus. Seeing it over and over again, I was struck by how he had lived a perfect life and died a death he didn't deserve, just for me. I wasn't the only one who encountered Jesus. As the Mongolian people heard the message of the film—that God loved them, sent Jesus to die for them, and had a purpose for their lives—their eyes would widen and tears would well up.

"Why did Jesus go to the cross *for me*?" they asked. "Why did he have to die? Why me?"

Hearing their questions shook me. Two months earlier, I was asking a lot of "Why me?" questions. But mine were out of selfish pride. "Why am I not getting flowers?" "Why do I have a broken arm?" "Why can't I drive my sports car?" I had such a sense of entitlement. I thought I *deserved* a music scholarship, a sports car, and a boyfriend. Sitting on the side of the hill in Mongolia, after reading the Scriptures, I realized there was only one thing I deserved—hell.

I started asking the same question as the locals: "Why did Jesus come to save me?" God knew me inside and out. The good, the bad, and the really ugly. Yet he was still willing to send his Son to die for me. Why he did it was beyond my comprehension.

Two weeks into our trip, it was my turn to stay at camp to help with laundry and cooking. As I completed my chores, I did a lot of thinking. I was washing other people's clothes in a cold river. I had almost no material goods. But I was happier than I had ever been. When I finished, I took my Bible and sat on a hill looking out at a brilliant-blue, dazzling sky above a carpet of green. I felt more alive than ever.

Everything felt so real. God felt so real.

In that moment, I no longer needed the stuff I once thought I couldn't live without. I didn't need to play in the orchestra. I didn't need a boyfriend. I didn't need material comforts. What I needed was more of God. My thoughts turned to prayers. *It's not stuff that makes me happy. It's not even recognition or achievements that make me happy. It's you who makes me happy, God. I want to give my life to you and to telling other people about you.*

I'd prayed a prayer when I was ten, but that day when I was nineteen and warmed by the Outer Mongolian sun, I encountered Jesus. Nothing in my life has been the same since.

On the plane ride home, I sat with Adrian Despres, the man who led the trip. "What are you going to do when you get home?" he asked.

"I have no idea," I responded honestly. "I just want to tell people about Jesus. I don't care about music anymore; the drive I had for it is completely gone. Maybe I should join the Peace Corps or something."

"Laura," he said gently, "you should use your music to tell people about Jesus."

I chuckled at the thought. Who ever heard of a string-bass-playing evangelist? Playing bass was perfect for insecure people like me who had a good ear for music. In a symphony or an orchestra, bass players stand in the back with an enormous wooden instrument in front of them. It was hard to imagine them talking about Jesus.

"How would I even start to do that?"

Adrian told me about the Bible college he graduated from—Columbia International University. He said the school trained people like me to use our talents in ministry. "They'll help you figure out how to use your musical gifts for God's glory."

The location was certainly convenient. I'd already signed a lease in Columbia. However, I was unsure. But during the flight home, Adrian convinced me that God could do anything, and with the right training, I could lead people to Jesus through music. Pastor Despres then admitted that when he interviewed me for the mission trip, he wasn't sure if he should take me.

He told me, "I prayed, 'God, I don't know anything she can offer our team.' But the more I prayed, the more I sensed God saying you needed to go. This trip proved to me that God is doing something inside you."

Apparently God was. I was convinced.

I got home in July, and classes started in late August. My parents agreed I could go as long as the school was accredited. Check. I requested application forms and filled them out. Another check.

Before the admissions interview, Pastor Despres reminded me that it was a conservative institution. But I didn't care what their political beliefs were; I just wanted to use my talents to tell people about Jesus. I took the application paperwork and went to the interview.

"Tell us about your background," the admissions officer said.

I filled him in on my background, the mission trip, and how Pastor Despres had recommended the school.

"Have you drunk any alcohol in the past year?"

"Oh, yeah, I've drunk a lot of alcohol in the past year. I was a freshman at the University of South Carolina."

He arched an eyebrow and wrote something on his pad. "Have you smoked a cigarette?"

"Yep."

"How many times have you been to church in the last year?"

"Including the times I went in Mongolia?"

By now, he was furiously scribbling on his pad. I wondered why he was asking all these questions. I called Adrian when I left and told him about the interview. I could hear him laugh. "Laura, when I said conservative, I wasn't talking about the politics."

In August 1996, I started classes at CIU. Somehow, they decided to let me in.

Much later, I found out Adrian had made a phone call and said, "I know she's not your ideal candidate, but I really think God is going to do something with her."

There are times when we all feel unsure of what we should do next. We feel insignificant and ill equipped. Adrian was reminding me that God had a plan for my life.

I hoped and prayed that what he said was true.

⌀

Growing up, my family was beyond frugal. While other families bought their shoes at a mall, we shopped at Gilbert's, a warehouse shoe store. Inside, there were bins filled with mismatched shoes. We would search through them to find a pair. Most shoes had something wrong with them. They were factory rejects and irregulars. They would be missing a tongue, or there were holes in the soles. Some of them were old, they'd sat in a store until they discolored, the laces had gone missing, or they couldn't be sold.

I would dig through bin after bin until I found a shoe that had all of its parts, was approximately my size, and wasn't too discolored. But that was only half of the pair. The other shoe could be in any other bin in the store. For whatever reason, the two shoes that made up the pair were never together in the same place. It was like lightning striking twice—the odds were always against it.

For much of my childhood, I felt like a shoe at Gilbert's. I had a sense that when I was pushed out of the heavenly assembly line onto this earth, I had a few major parts missing or discolored. It was as if I was formed without certain pieces—I lacked life skills or coping mechanisms, and I was always one shoe short of a pair.

But in the Bible, the apostle Paul tells us something very different:

For we are God's handiwork, created in Christ Jesus to do good works, which God prepared in advance for us to do. (Eph. 2:10)

Paul said we were created *by* God, *for* God. We are his "handiwork"— his *masterpiece*.

I learned what following meant when I was twelve. My dad took our family snow skiing for a week. Because he was frugal, he decided to save the cost of a rental car by getting a ski-in, ski-out hotel near the slopes. The problem is that most of them are expensive—*really* expensive. So being cheap, my father looked hard to find an inexpensive one and he did. It was only fifty feet from the slope.

Fifty feet straight up.

Our first morning there, it had snowed a couple of feet overnight. Fresh powder is great for skiing. But I was a twelve-year-old girl in puffy ski bibs and ski boots, looking at an uphill climb. My dad could not carry my gear, and there was no way I could make it to the top on my own. I wanted to cry but was afraid the tears would freeze on my face and my goggles would fog.

Then my father stepped in—literally.

"Let me go first, and I want you to walk in my steps. Put your foot down where I lift mine up. That way the snow will be packed underneath you, and you can make it to the top of the hill."

Just put your feet exactly where I put my feet.

I think of that image every time I think of God preparing good works in advance for us. All we have to do is follow him, our feet stepping where his feet have already made a path. The hard work has been done. We don't have to blaze a trail; we just have to put our feet exactly where our Father leads us.

Breaking my arm was the first major trial I experienced in life. But out of that trial, I had an opportunity to follow God and do good works that glorify him. God loved me so much, he was willing to strip everyone and everything away from me so I could receive the "incomparable riches of his grace" (Eph. 2:7). Paul tells us the grace that saves us isn't something we have done or can ever do. It is a gift from God that comes from having life-trusting faith in him.

I no longer believe the myth that trials are a curse. Trials are an opportunity. They are an invitation to do good works to glorify our Father in heaven, to transform our lives from the inside out, and to drive us into the arms and footsteps of Jesus.

ℐ

Years after that mission trip, as I sat in the St. Louis airport, worried about Martin and waiting for my plane to arrive, I prayed. *God, I know this trial is an opportunity for Martin and for me. I know we are on a scary new adventure and I have no idea where it will take us, but I am willing to go. I believe I am your masterpiece, not because I feel it but because you say it. Though I can obsess about my deficiencies and my insecurities, I know you designed me perfectly for the good works you set before me. Help me in this time of trial to follow in your footsteps, so that I may complete those works for your glory.*

MYTH: TRIALS ARE A CURSE.

TRUTH: TRIALS ARE AN OPPORTUNITY.

THREE

WHEN GOD DOESN'T FIX WHAT WE WANT FIXED

MARTIN SAT ON THE EXAM TABLE, HIS LONG LEGS dangling uncomfortably off the side. After a week of referrals, tests, more referrals, and many prayers that God would fix whatever was wrong with Martin, we'd finally been sent to the neurosurgeon who had literally written the book on the surgery Martin needed. He greeted us when he entered the room and began looking through Martin's medical history and test results.

"It's malignant," he said, flipping the page.

I felt a cold, tingling sensation start at the back of my neck and spread down my spine. My heart raced, but my mind raced faster as a million questions formed. I fought against blurting them out. I glanced at Martin. His jaws were clenched as he stared at the floor.

After a long pause, the doctor flipped another page and said, "But I don't think it's cancerous."

My mouth dropped open. *Doesn't malignant mean cancerous?*

"Of course, I won't know for sure until I get in there," the surgeon added as he put the file down. "But I'm pretty confident it's not cancer."

"So what does that mean?" Martin asked.

"It means that some patients can live their whole life with a benign tumor as long as it isn't causing any trouble. The problem with yours is that it's still growing."

Using his hands to demonstrate, he explained that the tumor had a cystlike structure that expanded and contracted. Each time it expanded, it pushed against the adrenal gland, stopping the flow of hormones. "That's why you've been tired," he said to Martin. "You don't have any adrenaline when the adrenal gland is being compressed. But when the mass contracts, your body receives a surge of hormones. That's what makes you sweat and your heart rate increase. It's also why you can go without sleep for three or four days—your body is flooded with adrenaline. Taking out the tumor will fix all that."

The surgeon described how he would go in through Martin's nose to remove the tumor. "Once it's out, we'll take some fat from your waistline to plug the hole where we removed it. Your nose will be bandaged and we'll pack it to keep the plug in place. You'll have a couple of days in the ICU and one night in a regular hospital room. If we do the surgery on Monday, you'll be home from the hospital by the weekend."

Then the surgeon paused and let out a deep breath.

"I want you to know that while I am confident I can remove it, the surgery isn't without complications." He went on to describe a long list, everything from recurring headaches to allergic reactions to death. "The percentage of any one of these happening is very small. But the biggest risk is that you might not wake up from the surgery."

Though the doctor reassured us the likelihood of death was infinitely small, the thought of losing Martin was unbearable.

"What if he doesn't have the surgery?" I asked.

"We'll continue to monitor him, but the symptoms he's experiencing will continue. What concerns me most, though, is the tumor is so close to the optic nerve that as it grows and expands, he could lose his sight."

I glanced at Martin, and we both knew what we had to do.

"Okay. Then let's get it out," Martin said.

The doctor went through all of the surgery details, explaining how Martin would be loopy when he woke up and that the effects would linger. "He might not recognize you. For a few weeks he might be confused, but as the swelling goes down, he'll get better." The doctor reassured us that the procedure wasn't an emergency; we could take a couple of weeks to get everything lined up.

We set the date for late April to give our parents enough notice to be in town for the week. Then we left the surgeon's office with a handful of paperwork and a pamphlet that promised to answer all our questions. The pamphlet was reassuring and confirmed what the doctor said. Day one they would do the surgery. Martin would spend days two and three in the ICU, day four in a regular bed, and be released on day five. After that, he'd spend a few weeks recovering. It was reassuring to think that five days after surgery, our life would begin returning to normal.

I felt relieved, almost happy. *God is going to fix this.*

If this had happened a few years earlier or later, we would have been living in South Carolina. Instead, in his incredible timing, God had worked through circumstances to move us to Atlanta, the home of the neurosurgeon who wrote the textbook on Martin's surgery. Martin would get it fixed, delaying his graduation from SCAD by only a semester or two. Then we'd move back to South Carolina to be near family—and to start one of our own. The tumor was merely a hurdle we needed to clear on the path to our future, and we were in the right place at the right time to do it.

The night before the surgery, we had a big dinner with Martin's family. They were always a party. We met at his brother's house, where we had Martin's favorite foods: crab legs and steak. Before eating, Martin's dad, Cary, said a blessing and prayed for Martin.

"Lord, as Martin goes through this surgery, we want you to keep in mind everything that Martin has done for you . . ." He chuckled and then continued with the prayer.

Though I knew his words were tongue in cheek, they struck me because I knew what he meant. Martin was the most religious person in his family. His parents had been shocked when they found out he had a brain tumor. I think they had a sense of, *How could God let this happen to Martin after all our son has done for him?* But God doesn't work that way. And I knew that. In any other situation, I might have laughed. But that night, even though I knew better, I understood his plea. And at some deep level, I shared it. I also wanted to remind God of all the good things Martin and I had done for him—leading college Bible studies, taking students on mission trips, and working at a church. *Doesn't God owe us something for all we've done?*

℘

The next morning we arrived at the hospital at six. Both of our parents were there, along with our friend John and my boss, Randy Schlichting. Before they took Martin back, we gathered to pray for him. The neurosurgeon told us he expected the surgery to take three to four hours.

"I'll be out to talk to you once Martin is in recovery," he said.

His confidence was reassuring.

The first three hours of waiting were fairly upbeat. As scary as it was, everyone in the waiting room had been through the events of the past year with us, and we were all glad that Martin was having the tumor removed.

Four hours into the surgery, each of us was lost in our own thoughts and prayers, but whenever someone entered the room, we all looked up expectantly.

Four hours and forty-five minutes after the surgery started, the neurosurgeon entered the room and, using my married name, said, "Mrs. Elvington?" Before I could respond he saw me, came over, and pulled up a chair.

"The surgery went great. It took longer than I thought, but everything went fine."

I let out a sigh, and I could feel the relief from the others.

"The tumor ended up being bigger than we could see on the CT scan. It was behind his pituitary, so we had to go through the pituitary gland to reach it. As a result his pituitary is no longer functioning, which means he'll have to take supplements to replace the hormones he no longer produces. In addition, parts of the tumor were wrapped around his optic nerve. He might have some damage to his eyesight, but we won't know for sure until the swelling goes down."

At the time, I didn't fully understand the ramifications of what he was telling me. All I knew was that while it stunk that Martin would have to be on medication the rest of his life, it wasn't the worst thing that could have happened. Martin was organized, responsible, and one of the most methodical men I knew. I wasn't worried about him taking daily pills. He'd handle it just fine.

"His vitals are great. He's in recovery and, in the next hour or so, he'll be moved to the ICU. You'll be able to see him once he gets there." When the doctor left, the room erupted into hugs and high fives. *Thank you, Jesus!* The surgery had been successful. Martin was fixed. We were going to be fine. God had answered all of our prayers.

ℒ

Ninety minutes later, the nurse came for me and walked me down to his room. I could see through the glass window that Martin was hooked up to several machines. There was a big patch over his nose and an incision where they'd done a kind of liposuction to make the "fat pad" skin graft that plugged the hole in his nose. As I rounded the corner to his room, his eyes were open. When I walked in, they lit up as soon as he saw me. It was such a relief to see that he recognized me after the doctor's warning that he might not.

"How are you feeling?" I asked, reaching out to take his hand.

"Laura Story!" he said.

That's odd. After the success of "Indescribable," I continued to use my maiden name when I performed, but after we got married, Martin had always called me by my legal married name—Laura Elvington.

"What are *you* doing here?" he asked.

I laughed. The doctor had warned me that Martin would be a little loopy. He asked me about people from our high school, and I answered his questions the best I could even though it had been years since we'd seen most of them. It seemed odd until I had a sudden realization. *He knows who I am. He knows we went to high school together. But does he know we're married?*

How do you break that to someone who's just had brain surgery? As gently as possible I said, "Do you know why I'm here?"

"No."

"It's because we're married. I'm your wife."

It was an awkward thing to say, but even more awkward to stand there through a long pause, watching confusion cross his face.

Slowly he asked, "We're mar-ri-ed?"

"Yes, we're married."

His eyes grew wide and his face broke out into the most beautiful smile I'd ever seen. He raised his left arm into a fist, pumped it, and loudly said, "Yes!" The nurse outside his room heard him and looked up to see what was happening. It was the sweetest moment ever. If you're going to break that kind of news to your spouse, that's the best way for it to go. I leaned over and kissed him. "I love you." It didn't bother me that he was loopy; the victory was that he'd had a successful surgery and that what had been broken was now fixed.

✐

Because his body had stopped producing hormones, Martin needed to stay in the hospital longer than the five days we expected. There were issues trying to regulate his hormones, his sodium, and his water intake and output. He needed other medications to replace his pituitary and thyroid. This required blood work every few hours.

Martin continued to be confused. He asked many of the same questions over and over. One day, he saw the ring on my hand and said, "So you're married?"

"Yes, I am," I said, trying not to giggle. "Do you know who I am married to?"

"Is it Ward?"

Ward was Martin's friend from college. "No, it's you."

"It's me? It's me!"

He was so sweet. He had the same excitement each time I told him I was his wife.

Occasionally, he'd get up to use the bathroom, and then one of us would notice he'd been in there a long time. I'd open the door, and he would be picking at the plug in his nose.

"Martin, the doctor told you not to pick your nose!" It was dangerous because he could mess up the packing that held the plug in place.

"Laura," he'd say, "that is the very thing the doctor told me *to* do."

It was two and a half weeks before he was finally released. As I drove him home, I thanked God for the miracle of Martin making it through the surgery. Though he was still a little confused, he could walk and talk. I was so happy for him and for us.

At home that afternoon, it soon became clear that I couldn't leave Martin alone even while he was sleeping. He woke up from a nap forgetting that he'd had brain surgery. "There's something in my nose," he said, trying to pull it out again. I had to watch him carefully.

That night, when I climbed into bed with Martin, his eyes opened wide. He was obviously very uncomfortable and pulled the sheets up under his chin, attempting to hide or protect himself.

"What's wrong?" I asked.

"Laura, I appreciate your wanting to look after me, but this is not appropriate," he said.

I tried not to laugh because he sounded so sincere. Martin had always been a man of integrity. He didn't want to go to bed with anyone other than his wife. He didn't know that I *was* his wife!

℘

The first few days at home were busy getting Martin settled and arranging his therapy appointments for the following week. Since I'd taken a couple of weeks off work before the surgery (and our extended stay at the hospital meant I'd had to take a couple more), I called my boss and told him I'd be happy to jump back in and lead worship the following weekend. I missed being at church. So many people were asking about Martin, I felt this would be an opportune time to update them on how God had answered their prayers.

On Monday, Martin started rehabilitation. Mom and Dad were there to help me navigate him down the long flight of stairs outside of our condo and get him into the car. This was the first time we'd left the condo since we'd gotten home almost a week earlier. Martin did a great job at rehab, and he fell asleep on the way home. Tuesday was much like Monday. But on Wednesday, Martin seemed lethargic. He could walk, but his energy seemed low. When we arrived at the hospital, my dad grabbed a wheelchair and put him in it, and I pushed him inside.

"I have a headache," he said.

I looked at his face and noticed his nose was running—something the doctors had warned us to watch for. It continued to run while he did his therapy. I mentioned it to my dad, who has been a cardiologist for more than thirty years.

"Has it been coming out both sides, or just one?" he asked.

"Just one."

Dad took his finger, swiped it under Martin's nose, and after touching it said, "I think that's spinal fluid."

The physical therapist recommended that we take Martin to the emergency room and get someone to look at him. After a brief wait and a thorough examination, the doctor found the hole inside his nose had opened up. He added some temporary packing and said they would have to do surgery to repair the hole.

"We'll go ahead and admit him," the ER doctor said. "That way we can keep an eye on him until his surgery."

The surgery was scheduled for Monday, so Martin would spend four more days in the hospital. No one sounded an alarm; the whole thing was very laid back. It was as if he'd torn a few stitches on a lacerated arm, and they wanted to make sure everything was good before they sutured him up again.

The next three days in the hospital were uneventful, almost casual. I was still scheduled to lead worship at our Saturday night and Sunday morning services. I thought about getting a replacement, but Martin's parents were in town for the surgery on Monday, so they would stay with him in case he needed anything. Everyone thought it would be good for me to have a break from spending so many nights at the hospital.

"We've got this," said the nurse who'd been encouraging me to go home for a night. "We won't bother you unless it's an emergency."

It had been a month since I'd last been in church, and it was like coming home to be in the presence of God and his people. I loved being with my worship team and getting hugs from so many friends in the hallways. So many of these people had been praying for Martin, and they all wanted an update on how he was doing. It was encouraging to be able to tell them how God had brought Martin through the surgery and sustained me during the long month that followed. I thanked God for everything. Though Martin had a temporary setback, it was minor. They would repair the hole on Monday. Everything would be fixed, and we'd be back on track.

Eric, the other worship leader at Perimeter, and his wife, Shea, invited me to stay with them after the Saturday service since we all had to be back early the next morning. I was happy and relaxed as I fell asleep in their guest bed that night. With no one to worry about, I slept soundly.

Around three thirty in the morning, I woke to the ring of my phone. At first I thought it was my alarm, but as I picked it up I could see it was a call from Martin's mom. Cary and Mary had spent the night at the hospital with Martin. As any mother would, Mary worried about her son so, frankly, I wasn't surprised that she was calling. *Martin probably tried to get out of bed to use the bathroom. I should have warned her about that.*

"Hel-lo?" I said, yawning into the phone.

"Laura! Martin is . . . the doctor . . . I was sleeping . . . That's my son! . . . they said . . . hospital ICU—"

"Mary, slow down. I can't understand what you're saying." She was so upset she was sobbing and gasping for air. I couldn't make out anything she said.

"He stopped breathing . . . machine and tubes . . . ICU . . . coded."

By now, I was wide-awake. But she wasn't making any sense.

"Come . . . hospital . . . he's coded!"

"Okay, okay, I'm on my way," I said, zipping my jeans.

I quickly hung up with Mary, pulled on a T-shirt, and then woke Eric and Shea.

"Hey, I have to go to the hospital. Something's going on with Martin."

"Is he okay?" Shea asked, while I threw my stuff into a bag.

"I think so," I said as I stepped into my shoes. "Mary just called. He was fine when I left a few hours ago, but she's upset and said something about him not breathing. I'm hoping she's exaggerating, but I'd better go. Eric, do you think you can cover for me this morning?"

"Of course."

"Are you okay to drive?" Shea asked as I ran out the door.

I waved them off. "I'm fine."

While I fumbled for my keys and started the motor, I tried to make sense of what Mary said. *Did he really stop breathing? Could he have coded?* None of it made sense. I needed to get there and find out for myself.

Speeding through the dark and eerily empty Atlanta highways, I called my parents, who had returned to Spartanburg, and then our friend John. I was also worried about Martin waking up and wondering why I wasn't there.

I arrived and headed straight to the ICU. As I entered, I could see my husband through the glass, lying lifeless on his back. It was alarming to see he wasn't breathing on his own. Tubes connected to a life support machine were doing all the work. With the rise and fall of his chest, his body seemed to convulse as each breath was pumped into him. I was stunned. *What had gone wrong?*

Cary and Mary were standing outside his room.

"What's going on?" I asked.

Mary sobbed while Cary filled me in. "Around 3 a.m., Mary was in the lobby and I was sitting next to Martin. I couldn't sleep, so I was watching him. Then without warning, it looked like he wasn't moving. I got up to take a closer look, and I could see he wasn't breathing. I was so scared, I ran out and yelled for the nurse. They came in with one of those carts and the paddles and . . ." He broke down and couldn't finish.

Fear grabbed my chest and squeezed it like a vise. Panic spread throughout my body, but I refused to let it control me. There was no time for grief or hysteria; there were decisions to be made. This was the biggest, most frightening thing I'd ever faced in my life. I needed to be strong for whatever happened next.

A nurse approached. "Are you Mrs. Elvington?" she asked.

"Yes, I'm Laura."

She essentially repeated everything Cary had just said. Then she added, "The doctor will be in soon and he can tell you more."

When she said the doctor would be there shortly, I assumed she meant Martin's neurosurgeon, but a resident showed up instead. He was so young; it was hard to take him seriously.

"It looks like he has contracted meningitis. We think the infection may have entered through the hole in his nose," the resident said. "As a result, he's experiencing hydrocephalus—swelling of the brain. The way we relieve this is by drilling one, maybe two holes in his skull to release the pressure. You'll need to sign some forms . . ."

That didn't make any sense. "So you're saying he contracted an infection from the hole in his nose and now you want to drill one in his head?"

"Yes, ma'am. That's the protocol."

I wanted to shake him and say, "What do you know? You're just a resident. Last week you were reading textbooks and taking quizzes!"

Instead, I took a deep breath.

"I need to see a doctor. And not just any doctor. I want to see *our* neurosurgeon or someone from *his* practice." There was no way I was going to let a resident with a shiny new drill experiment on my husband's head. "I want him to explain this to me, because our surgeon had a treatment plan and this is not part of his plan."

"I understand," the resident said. "He's on his way, and I'll have him come talk to you. But we're going to go ahead and prep your husband for surgery because we can't wait any longer." He paused to look at the three of us. "I need you to know there is no guarantee he will make it through the night or through the surgery. If there are friends and family who want to see him, I suggest you call them now."

As he walked away, he took my breath with him.

I reached for the counter for support. I felt dizzy and shaky. I didn't know whether to be scared or angry.

Martin's parents began sobbing. I didn't know what to say.

The nurse suggested we wait outside, so the three of us dutifully found our way to the ICU waiting room and sat down. Martin's parents called his brother. I reached for my phone to make a few calls to people who would want to know. I'm sure I didn't make any sense on the phone. I was lost in my own thoughts, and I had no answers for their questions.

How could things have changed so quickly? We had a plan. Martin was supposed to have surgery to fix the hole on Monday morning. If it was serious, why didn't they tell us? Why didn't they repair the hole earlier?

We had seen all of the doctors they told us to see. We had every test done they requested. We followed all of the neurosurgeon's directions before and after surgery. There had been a thousand action points that kept me busy and gave me a false sense of control—even security—that things could be fixed. But now the medical map was missing. We no longer had a road to follow. No signposts marked the way back to the path we'd so carefully planned. We were off-roading into the darkest abyss I'd ever faced and there was nothing I could do.

My mom arrived around six, and I met her in the lobby. John came in at the same time. The three of us clung to one another and cried. It was the first time I had cried since I was in St. Louis and received the call from Martin telling me he had a brain tumor.

As word of Martin's condition spread, the ICU waiting room began to fill with friends and family praying and preparing to say good-bye to Martin. We took turns going in to see him until the surgeon arrived.

Pulling me aside, the neurosurgeon said, "It's not looking good. This is one of those complications we talked about. We *have* to drill a hole to relieve the pressure. It's the only chance he has and it isn't much of a chance."

There was nothing I could do. I was powerless to fix this. And worse, it appeared the doctor might not be able to fix it either.

C

Our desire is for God to fix broken things.

But God's desire for us is to fix our relationship with him.

There is a troubling passage in the first chapter of the Gospel of Mark that illustrates this. Jesus had the opportunity to heal people, but instead he seemed to turn his back on them. It happened not long after Jesus started his ministry with his disciples. They were in Capernaum, Peter and Andrew's hometown, where Jesus had healed Peter's mother-in-law along with many others. Mark said, "The whole town gathered at the door, and Jesus healed many who had various diseases" (Mark 1:33–34).

The news of Jesus' healing had spread outside Capernaum. Early the next morning, ailing travelers streamed into town and headed toward Simon's house, as the disciples rubbed their hands in expectation of what the day would bring.

Then someone noticed that Jesus was missing. They set off in a search party. Where was he? They had to find him! The crowds were growing restless. They wanted to be healed.

The disciples found him and exclaimed, "Everyone is looking for you!" (v. 37). They expected that Jesus would return with them. But his response was not at all what they predicted. Jesus replied, "Let us go somewhere else—to the nearby villages—so I can preach there also. That is why I have come" (v. 38).

It's hard to understand why sometimes Jesus heals and sometimes he doesn't. When it feels as though he's turned his back and walked the other way, it's hard not to be disappointed. Maybe even angry.

But while we're focused on the unhealed sickness, hurt, and pain in our lives, God is focused on a bigger picture. Something else is broken, and it has eternal consequences if it doesn't get fixed.

It's our relationship with our Creator.

While doctors can heal physical ailments, emotional wounds can be soothed, and grief lessens with time, our broken relationship with God continues to cause us pain even when our life is going well. God wants to restore our relationship with him more than anything else. Though he loves us, he'll allow us to feel the pain of this world's unhealed hurts if it brings us closer to him.

I want Martin to be healthy and tumor free.

God wants that too. But more than healing us physically, God wants my relationship with him to be healthy. Jesus came to heal, but he doesn't always fix the broken things I want fixed. But if I allow him to, God will always heal my broken relationship with him.

Understanding that doesn't lessen my desire for Martin to be healthy, but it does change everything else.

MYTH: GOD'S PRIMARY DESIRE IS
TO FIX BROKEN THINGS.

TRUTH: GOD'S PRIMARY DESIRE IS TO FIX
MY BROKEN RELATIONSHIP WITH HIM.

FOUR

DON'T BE SURPRISED
BY TROUBLE

IT WAS THE GREATEST TEST OF MY LIFE, BUT IT WAS
Martin's life that hung in the balance.

Have you ever felt bewildered, disappointed, or angry that you
didn't get what you thought you deserved? Looking around, you see
others have gotten what you wanted, and you don't understand why
you can't get it too. Someone else received your cure, your fix, your
apology, the life you wanted, or the baby you prayed for. What you
had hoped for, what you earned, what you thought would be mended,
what you were waiting on, is now gone. That one thing that was
almost in your hands, that you rearranged your schedule for, that you
stood in line to receive, and that you made an appointment to get, can
no longer take place. Though someone else may have been involved, it
still feels as though God has turned his back on you.

Imagine the disappointment those sick and hurting travelers
from the surrounding villages and towns must have felt when they
arrived in Capernaum that morning and heard that their hope for
healing had snuck away under the cover of darkness.

What kind of God-man leaves town so he doesn't have to heal
those who need it most? Jesus didn't say good-bye or promise he'd
be back soon. He didn't even tell his friends that he was leaving; they

had to go out into the countryside and hunt him down. When he said he wasn't coming back, his disciples were as shocked as the crowds. When he left town, the hope of healing departed with him.

If there is anything to learn from the Mark 1 passage, it's that God's ways aren't our ways.

A God who leaves physically sick people to preach the good news to spiritually sick people is a God who cares more about our soul than our body. That is who our God is.

Maybe you're wondering, *Why can't God just heal everyone physically and then do whatever he wants with us spiritually?* At least he could heal the good people, or the people who deserve it. People like Martin. And *you*, or the person you're thinking about right now.

I had a twinge of that feeling as I watched them wheel Martin off for this second surgery. I'd been mostly good. Martin had been mostly good. And like Martin's father had prayed before Martin's first surgery, I wanted God to remember the good things we'd done for him.

It's tempting to think that what we do for God will bring the favor of God. We think if we've done enough for God—gone to church on Sunday, dropped some money in the collection plate, read our Bibles, and said our prayers—then he will repay our good deeds with answered prayers and a pain-free life.

I grew up thinking that way.

L

For the most part, I was a good kid. I went to a good church and we had a good family. My mother even taught Bible study for women in our community. Then I went to Bible college, served on mission trips, and played in a Christian band. Martin was the campus director of a college ministry. A Young Life leader. We were both involved in leading college Bible studies.

I wouldn't want to say it out loud, but inside, I felt like I was a pretty good person. I had been taught that God was a good God. So somewhere deep inside I believed that if I did all the right things *for God*, then he would do the right thing *by me*. When he didn't, I felt as if God hadn't kept up his end of the bargain. I was disappointed in him. I even felt betrayed.

After my time in Mongolia, I began to question everything I thought I'd believed. I decided I needed more proof about God's promises. So every time I felt God had betrayed me, I would go back to the Bible to search for the promise or commitment that God had broken. The problem was, I couldn't find any verse that said he owed me anything. Or a verse that said if I was good enough, I deserved something.

I began to realize that my disappointment with God wasn't something he'd done to me; it was something I'd done to him. I had put conditions on our relationship that were never meant to exist. I had a sense of entitlement. I thought I deserved better.

But I don't.

Nowhere in Scripture does God say that if we're good, then he'll be good to us. In fact, the Bible says the opposite. It says we're not good, yet he is good to us. The more I studied Scripture, the more I learned that I was not as good as I thought I was. On my very best days, I was maybe 66 percent good.

Is 66 percent good enough? Or did I have to be 77 percent or 88 percent good?

When I compared myself to the Bible, I could see I *always* fell short of God's standards. And more often than not, I fell short of my own standards. I couldn't even keep my end of our supposed bargain.

The righteousness scale in the Bible says that no one but Jesus makes it to the top. But despite our lack of goodness, God is always good and is always good to us.

When you look at the biblical narrative, from the beginning of creation to the end of time, the narrative breaks down into four parts: Creation, Fall, Redemption, and Restoration. Christians believe the world was created by an all-knowing, all-powerful, and all-loving God who was there before time began and will be there when time ends. The pinnacle of God's creation was a man named Adam and a woman named Eve. They were created by God, for God. He created them to worship, love, and serve him. That's the first part of the narrative.

But when Adam and Eve disobeyed him we entered the second part of the narrative, the fall. The sin that entered the world that fateful day has consequences that continue to our day. War, poverty, greed, gossip, jealousy, gluttony, cancer, and brain tumors are just a few of the ways sin manifests itself. Everything is distorted and broken. The biggest break is our relationship with God. It's called the "fall" because we've fallen away from God, and we can't get up by ourselves.

Even though God hates our sin, he loves us so much that he is determined to restore his relationship with us. He doesn't want us to spend an eternity suffering without him. Ever since Adam and Eve messed up, God had a plan to restore us.

So in part three of the narrative, Jesus Christ, the Son of God, came as our Rescuer, Savior, and Redeemer. This God-man spent his life helping those around him understand his loving Father. He showed them the Father's power. And though Jesus lived a blameless life, as part of his Father's plan he agreed to take the punishment for our sins—past, present, and future—when he was tortured on the cross, died, and then was resurrected.

Outside of Jesus, we can't stop sin or the consequences of sin. But with our faith in God's plan and in Jesus, we can now turn from our rebellious ways and have victory over sin. And all the glory goes to God. This is the part of the story where we are currently living.

But the story doesn't end there. God promises to renew the whole world. Father God promises that one day, Christ will return to judge sin and to escort in righteousness and peace. Sin and evil will be gone forever.

The world will be perfect, the way God intended it to be. All the good things we desire will be present, and at the center will be Jesus, to whom all praise, glory, and honor belong. We will worship him. We will serve him. And we will be in perfect relationship with him for eternity.

So what does that mean when we beg, plead, and pray on our knees for God to restore what has been broken now?

Let's go back to those sick travelers waiting outside of Capernaum. They wanted physical healing without spiritual healing. Restoration without redemption. But Jesus wanted them to understand that he was the Savior who had come to restore their relationship to his Father.

Yes, Jesus could have healed all the broken legs, ear infections, strep throat, breast cancers, and indigestion that was coughed up before him. But that would only have been a temporal healing. It wouldn't have healed their relationship with God. Jesus wanted more for them. He wanted to rescue them from their sin, not just from sickness. He wanted to restore their souls and put them back in relationship with his Father. Jesus had a much bigger mission than torn ligaments and athlete's foot. He was God's representative on earth, and he only had a short time to reach as many people as he could and to train his disciples to carry his message of redemption after he left.

Jesus didn't slink out of the city. He avoided the crowds because he knew what they needed more than they did. He went to be with his Father, so he could be reminded that despite his love for and his desire to heal all those hurting people, he had a bigger mission.

And so, as much as I want healing for Martin's physical body, I want healing for our souls even more.

I don't know what the broken thing in your life is. That thing that you want God to fix. The thing that he hasn't done, or that thing that has disappointed you so much. Maybe, one day, he will fix it. Maybe he won't. But don't be surprised that your life turned out the way it did.

Pain, sickness, and betrayal are brutal consequences of the fall. We still feel the results of sin, and things won't be made right until Jesus comes back.

Our hope comes in Jesus, even when he doesn't do what we want him to do. Even when he doesn't fix what's broken in our life. Maybe until now, you didn't even know you had a broken relationship with God. But Jesus has created a path of forgiveness back to his Father.

If you haven't put your faith in Jesus as your rescuer, it's not too late. Tell him you're sorry for your rebelliousness. Tell him you realize he's your Redeemer who can save you from what you deserve and the only one who can restore what's been broken. Give him the reins to your life, because you can't do it on your own.

When Jesus is with us, he's our anchor in the rough waters of a troubled life. If we want to survive the storm we need to cling to him like the salvation he is.

C

The doctor asked us to leave Martin's room. They didn't have time to move him to the surgical floor, so to relieve the pressure that was building in his head they were going to drill the hole in his head right then and there! I left his room shaky and weak, but a thought from the last day we'd spent together before his first surgery comforted me.

I'd gotten out the video camera we'd bought to record our time in Atlanta. I turned it on Martin and said, "It's the day before the big surgery. Anything you want to say?"

"Yeah, I'm about to have my brain cut into!"

"Are you scared?"

"Nope!" He smiled big. "Of course I'm a little anxious, but at the end of the day, I'm not afraid of anything because as a believer, even if the worst happens and I die, that means I'll be with Jesus."

He wasn't just being brave; he was expressing what he truly believed. In Philippians 1:21, Paul wrote, "For to me, to live is Christ and to die is gain."

We both believed that.

And that thought was what held me together while I waited.

MYTH: SALVATION IS GAINED BY THE THINGS I DO.

TRUTH: SALVATION IS GAINED BY
WHAT JESUS DID FOR ME.

FIVE

COMPLICATIONS

EVER SINCE HE HAD STOPPED BREATHING EARLY SUNDAY morning, Martin had been in a medically induced coma. The infection causing his brain to swell had forced doctors to drill a hole in his skull and put in a shunt to redirect the fluid that had been building up in his brain. Naively, I assumed once they put in the shunt and relieved the pressure, Martin would be awake and things would be better.

But that's not what happened.

After the procedure, the surgeon came out to talk to me. "The shunt appears to have worked. The CT scan shows decreased swelling, but it's not enough to stop the pressure from building up inside his brain. We're going to have to drill a second hole on the opposite side. We'll keep him in a coma until we get this figured out, but it's still touch and go. You need to know he may not survive."

It was late Sunday afternoon. I had been at the hospital since four that morning. I was tired, I hadn't eaten anything, and my energy was running low. And I didn't understand what the doctor was doing. I wanted to say, "The reason we're here is because you created a hole through his nose and he got an infection. Then you drilled another hole and he's still 'touch and go'!" But I stopped myself. I didn't want to be disagreeable; I just wanted to understand the process. Everything we were doing was uncharted territory.

"There really is no other choice," the surgeon said. "If we want to stop the swelling, this is the only way to do it. If we don't stop the swelling he will die. But you need to know, even if he survives, we're still not sure if we will be able to bring him up from the sedation."

I trembled as chills ran through my body and I had to remind myself to breathe. It was one of those moments when the seriousness of Martin's situation couldn't be denied. Martin wasn't safe, and he wouldn't be for a long time, if ever. From now on, it looked like he would make it through one milestone only to have another daunting hill rise up before him. I had to let go of my expectations for a quick and complete healing. There was no final hurdle in the distance. Martin would be jumping through medical hoops for the next several weeks.

Or he wouldn't be.

I stumbled back to the waiting room and tried to take it all in. It was hard to know what to do, and even harder to pray.

All I could do was wait.

Family and friends had been dropping by the hospital to see Martin and offer their support. It was like a reunion. We saw not only many of our new friends from Atlanta but also dozens of people from out of town who dropped everything and drove to Atlanta. I appreciated their presence more than anything they said. Several well-meaning people tried to offer me words of comfort. "I know this is a hard time for you," they'd say, but then they seemed to forget it was a hard time for me. I remember staring at the moving mouth of one person thinking, *You're really telling me about your meeting at work when I don't know if my husband is going to live or die?*

One man came in with his Bible, and he wanted to share something with me he'd read as part of his devotional that morning. After reading several long passages, he started to expound on everything he'd just read. What started out as a conversation ended up being a sermon. I closed my eyes as if I was taking it all in but thought, *Not listening to you at all. Let me know when you're done.*

Several well-meaning people came and asked the same question: "How are you doing?"

"I'm okay," I answered.

Then they'd lower their voices and say, "No, really, how are *you* doing?"

"I'm o-kay," I'd repeat firmly. It didn't matter how I was doing; it didn't change Martin's circumstances. And I didn't know how I really felt; I was just doing what I had to do. Most days I was tired and scared, but I couldn't find the words to talk about it.

Once, when I'd closed my eyes to be alone with my thoughts, I felt a soft hand touch my shoulder. I opened my eyes to find a middle-aged woman with weepy eyes and peppermint breath staring me in the face. "Laura, this is when the rubber meets the road with our faith. This is when we have to believe that if Martin doesn't make it through, we know he is going to be in a better place. God needs more angels in heaven to sing with the choir."

If that were the case, he'd take Josh Groban! I thought. Martin was tone deaf; he'd be the last person God would want in a heavenly choir.

Some days, I felt like the hostess at a party, introducing everyone and finding seats for those who'd just arrived. It was a party I didn't even want to attend, let alone throw. Didn't they understand that, while I appreciated them coming by and all of their prayers, I couldn't entertain them?

So many didn't know what to do or say in a situation like ours.

I didn't know either.

More than flowers or cartons of greasy Chinese food, the greatest thing people brought me was their presence. During the wait, which eventually stretched over two days and nights, my favorite visitors were the ones who said the three magic words: not "I love you," or even, "I am praying," but, "Here's your latte." Those words made me smile each time I heard them because the people who brought me lattes weren't trying to give me answers. They were just trying to give me coffee. They sat with me and wept with me and never said a word. They were the ones who refilled my empty cup.

I was able to relax a bit when the doctor told me Martin had made it through the second drilling, and the CT scan showed that the second hole had done its job—the swelling had stopped. But the doctor reminded me that we still faced a major hurdle. We still weren't sure if Martin would be able to come out of the sedation and breathe on his own when they removed the breathing tube the next morning.

ℒ

I didn't sleep much that night and while I tried to pray, words failed me. Martin's parents had spent the night at the hospital. We all wanted to be by his side when they removed the machines. But no one seemed to know exactly when the doctor planned to do it.

"He usually comes in around seven thirty," the night nurse said.

At eight o'clock, the day nurse said, "I'd expect him anytime between 10 a.m. and 2 p.m."

It was like waiting for the cable guy or the Maytag repairman. Nothing could be done until he showed up, but the timing they offered was so elusive we were never sure when we could expect him.

Martin's parents left to get something to eat, and a few minutes later a nurse announced, "They're bringing him up now."

"Now? Like, right now?"

The nurse nodded and turned back toward the nurse's station.

This was the moment we'd been waiting on. There was no time to call Martin's parents and get them back, so my mom came with me as I race-walked to Martin's room. I wanted to be at his bedside no matter what happened.

Several weeks earlier, after Martin's first surgery, I had befriended a girl in the ICU. Her husband made it through his surgery, but he was never well enough to come off the breathing tube, so I completely understood what this moment meant.

Because Martin was sedated and essentially kept alive by machines, the big question was whether he would be able to breathe on his own. The doctor acknowledged there were additional concerns about how much damage the surgeries and the meningitis had done to Martin's brain functioning, and he made no guarantees about whether Martin would live or die.

During the time we'd been in the ICU, I'd seen a lot of people die. It would start with a commotion in one of the ICU rooms as medical professionals rushed in with equipment. That would be followed by wails of grief from the deceased's loved ones. Eventually, the crowd in the room would leave—first, the medical professionals, followed by the sniffling friends and family holding on to one another as they left. The nurses would then come by to check on the patients in the adjoining rooms, and when they did, they would close the blinds and shut the door. Once each patient's view was blocked, the medical techs would wheel out a gurney with a body covered by a sheet. A few minutes later, the nurses would come around again, this time reopening the doors and blinds.

I'd watched this scene play out every two or three days while I'd been in the ICU with Martin. Between both stays in the hospital, I'd spent nearly three and a half weeks in the ICU. I'd seen a lot of death, and now I feared I would see Martin's. I blinked back the tears forming in my eyes. It had been more than forty-eight hours since Martin had coded, and what was about to happen next would decide everything.

Please, God, let him live.

"I want you to know, this is going to be a scary thing to watch," the doctor said. "He may not come out of the sedation or be able to breathe on his own. Right now, the machines are doing all the work for him. What we're going to do is back off the machines, one by one, to bring him out. Either he'll wake up or he won't."

I nodded.

"If he does wake up, he's going to be frightened and not understand what is happening."

I nodded again. I was as prepared as I could be for whatever was about to happen. I glanced across Martin's bed at my mom. She gripped the metal rails and steadied herself. The room got quiet except for the beeping and clicking of the machines.

As the doctor maneuvered the controls, the machine rhythm changed. I reached for Martin's hand and held it in mine. After a few minutes, the doctor slid the tube from Martin's throat. Martin began coughing. He was awake! He opened his eyes and looked around. He looked terrified.

"Hey, I'm here with you," I said.

But Martin couldn't see who was talking. "Who? Whoth there?" he mumbled.

"It's me, Laura," I said, squeezing his hand.

"Laura? What ith going on?" he asked. "What's flying at me?"

I smiled. It was as if he had regressed to being a kid. His speech sounded garbled, he was hard to understand, and he was crying. He kept saying meteors were raining down on him.

"It's okay, baby. I'm right here with you," I said, stroking his cheek. My heart felt as if it was about to burst. All of the emotions I'd kept bottled up came spilling out. I was grateful to God and relieved that Martin was going to be okay. I couldn't imagine loving him more than I did at that moment.

"Why can't I thee?" he cried.

The doctor explained his eyes were getting used to the light. "He might also have some vision problems from the trauma to his optic nerve, but we won't know the severity of them for a while," the doctor said.

The whole thing was frightening yet wonderful.

On the other side of the bed, I could see my own joy reflected in my mom's eyes. Martin and I had known each other's parents nearly as long as we'd known each other. Mom was as relieved as I was. She leaned over the bed rail, but instead of referring to herself as "Miss Story," the way Martin typically referred to her, she said, "Martin, this is *Carol*."

"Car—? Oh. Oh. Oh, okay. You're both here."

Mom could tell something was wrong. I started laughing. "Mom, you need to say, 'Miss Story.'"

"What?"

"He always calls you 'Miss Story,' and when you say 'Carol,' he thinks you're talking about a girl he dated back in college!"

"Martin, it's *Miss Story*, Laura's mom."

When he understood, his face relaxed. Poor Martin. He woke up not knowing what was going on or where he was. He couldn't see. And the first thing he understood was that he had two old girlfriends fighting over him while he lay in bed.

The doctor tried to set my expectations for what was yet to come. "He'll be in ICU for at least three to four weeks. We need to make sure he can eat solid food and swallow. We won't even get him out of bed to walk for three weeks. From the EEGs we've done, there are indications he may have had a stroke, so we'll have to wait and see what develops."

Martin was breathing without the ventilator. But he was by no means out of the woods. He would have to relearn everything he once knew.

But to me, it didn't matter. For now, we were celebrating the victory that he was alive.

C

Over the next few days, and then weeks, I began to see it would take a long time—perhaps years—to resolve some of Martin's health issues. For example, we knew he had vision problems, but only Martin knew how bad they were. Unfortunately he couldn't tell us because he didn't remember how he used to process seeing. So when the doctor asked, "Can you see me?" and Martin slowly answered, "Yesss," we weren't sure whether that meant Martin could see all of the doctor, part of the doctor, or maybe two or three of the doctor. In addition, his speech was noticeably affected; Martin spoke much slower and struggled to get out each word. This hadn't happened after his first surgery.

Martin lay in the ICU bed for weeks, unable to walk, understand where he was, or realize why he was there. Each morning, he'd wake up and ask the same question, "Where am I?"

"You're in the hospital."

"Why am I here?"

"You had a brain tumor."

"I did?"

"Yes."

"Where am I?" he'd ask again, and the same conversation would start all over. This would play out dozens of times throughout the day. At first the doctors weren't sure if the confusion was from the surgery, the brain infection, a possible stroke, or a side effect of his medicine. If Martin had a little fogginess after the initial surgery, it was as if the latest events had totally stripped his hard drive. He had to relearn everything. So I began trying to teach him rather than just answering his questions.

"Where am I?"

"Look around you. What does it look like?"

"Am I in the library?"

"No, you're not at the library. Look harder. Do you see the oxygen and the nurses?"

"Yes?"

"You're at the hospital."

"Oh. Why am I here?"

Since Martin couldn't always express what he needed, sometimes the medical staff would overmedicate him, resulting in an additional layer of confusion. For example, a nurse would come in and ask Martin if he had any pain.

"I have a headache," he'd say.

"Where are you from one to ten on the pain scale?"

Martin had no idea what she was referring to. He had no memory of what things felt like before his surgery. It just felt like pain so, to appease her, he'd say, "Seven."

Then they'd give him morphine, which would make him sleepy or loopy, or both, for the rest of the day. When that happened, he failed to make any progress. Finally I asked the nurses, "When he says he has pain, can we start with an aspirin and then work up to something stronger if he needs it?" They agreed, and most of the time, aspirin did the trick.

The days in the hospital were a bit like the movie *Groundhog Day*. Everything seemed to repeat. Each day the doctor would stop by in the morning, the therapists would come by in the afternoon, and every four hours the lab techs would draw blood. In addition, several times an hour, Martin asked, "Where am I?"

My mom often stayed with me at the hospital and the two of us would try to plan things for Martin to do each day. We'd asked friends to send cards and pictures, and we would read those to Martin to help him remember people and how he knew them. Since he couldn't remember getting the cards, we could reread them every day, and he would be just as excited as the day he first got them.

I had a lot of downtime in the hospital. I'd love to say I used that time to study my Bible, pray, and write in my journal. But honestly I only did these things a handful of times. Rather than long prayer times in the chapel like you see in the movies, the most I could manage was a quick, "Help me, God" or, "Please give me patience." It was as if I was in a stupor. As an artist, I am supposed to be in touch with my emotions, but I had no idea how I felt during that time. I spent very little time self-reflecting. My concentration was on Martin and helping him get better.

For a long time, Martin had trouble deciphering what was real from what was happening in his head. One day, we were watching television, and the news anchors were talking about the upcoming Peachtree Road Race—an annual Fourth of July tradition in Atlanta. Martin thought he was going to take part in it. While eating dinner, he mentioned that he had to carb-load to get ready for the big race. Later, when the nurse came in to take his blood pressure, he said to me, "Don't worry. She's just making sure I'm not doping for the race."

Each day I'd try to get Martin out to do something, whether it was a walk to the nurse's station or a ride in a wheelchair I borrowed from the emergency room. Martin was pretty unsteady when he first started walking. Even though he used a walker, the therapists were often reluctant to take him out because they were concerned about this nearly six-foot-five guy with a brain injury falling down in their hospital. So occasionally, when visitors came, I'd ask them to help and I'd take Martin myself.

One day, our friend John was there, and I asked him for help. Before John started working at Perimeter Church, he had been Martin's Bible study leader when Martin was in college in South Carolina. After he told me about the job at Perimeter, we moved to Atlanta and bought the condo next to him. So not only was John one of our closest friends, but Martin respected him immensely. He thought of John as a mentor.

John and I got Martin out of bed slowly, and we started walking with him down the hall. John walked behind so he could catch Martin if he fell. After Martin had taken a few steps, he realized the backside of his hospital gown was open. He reached back to close it.

"Do you need help?" I asked.

"John's looking at my butt," Martin whispered.

John could obviously hear what was said, and he chuckled.

"John's not looking at your butt," I said.

"Help me close it!" Martin got louder and more insistent. "John is looking at my butt!"

"I'm not looking at your butt," John said, laughing.

I couldn't help myself. I burst out laughing so hard that soon I was crying. But Martin would have none of it. "He's still looking at my butt!"

So the walk ended almost as quickly as it started. We turned around and went back into the room. We couldn't convince Martin that no one was looking at his butt, and the harder we tried the more we laughed. Martin was uncharacteristically upset by the whole incident. Finally I said, "John, it may be time for you to go."

As the days stretched on, I grew weary from answering, "Where am I?" for the twentieth time in an hour. When that happened, I would turn on the TV to distract Martin. One day, I found a program about former child stars. It was called something like *Where Are They Now?* The show featured backstories on Macaulay Culkin and the Olsen twins, among others. About halfway through the show, a visitor stood in the doorway. It was my boss, Randy Schlichting. Embarrassed, I quickly reached for the remote, turned off the TV, and threw Martin under the bus.

"Martin, I can't believe you were watching that show!" I said. Then I glanced at the doorway and acted surprised, "Oh, Randy, come in! I didn't see you standing there!"

Randy pulled up a chair and started talking, asking Martin how he was feeling and how things were going. About fifteen minutes into the conversation Randy said, "Martin, I don't think I've ever asked you, how did you and Laura first meet?"

"Well, we met on the set," Martin said.

The set? What on earth is he talking about?

"Pastor Randy, I don't know if you know this about me, but I used to star in a television show called *The Fresh Prince of Bel-Air.*"

"Really?" Randy asked.

"Yes, and that's where I met Laura."

"Martin!" I said, trying not to laugh. "That was Will Smith! Not you."

"Oh, okay," he said. It didn't bother Martin that he didn't know what he was talking about, but I had some explaining to do to Randy.

Most days, Martin was in a good mood and his confusion made for some hilarious moments, but there were days when I could see that he wasn't getting better and I felt sad for him. I didn't cry much and on the rare occasions I did, I tried not to cry in front of him.

One especially hard day, after we'd been in the hospital for about a month and a half, I was exhausted and dejected. Martin was sleeping and I was sitting in the chair. The tears began flowing, and I couldn't help it. Martin woke up and saw me.

"Uh, Laura, what? Why are you crying? Are you sad?"

"No, I'm not sad," I lied. "I'm just tired," which was also true.

"It's okay," Martin said. "Let's just go to the second service." He thought it was Sunday morning and I was too tired to go to the early service at church.

I chuckled at the thought. If he only knew . . .

"Okay, Martin. You go back to sleep, and we'll go to the second service."

Despite everything he was going through and the fact that he was so confused, he could still make me smile.

One day, his dad told me that a new nurse walked in with his chart. Though Martin's first name is Joseph, he'd always used his middle name. "Joseph Martin Elvington," the nurse read off the chart. "What would you like for me to call you?"

Martin paused for a moment and said, "The great stallion."

"Martin, I think they mean . . ." His dad laughed so hard, he didn't know what to say. "Just call him Martin," he told the nurse. It was the first time I'd seen his dad laugh in weeks. It was almost as if Martin knew how desperately we needed some levity in that situation.

It was days like that when I didn't know if Martin was back to his old self and playing tricks on all of us. He was so funny and childlike. Though it was sweet, he was still confused. During the weeks Martin spent in the ICU, I'd occasionally step away to get something to eat or use the restroom. Once when I came back to the room, I found a visitor from church and she said, "Congratulations!"

"For what?"

"You know," she said, smiling.

"No, I don't know."

"You're expecting!"

At first, I thought she meant test results, but then I realized she meant a *baby*.

"Martin! What did you tell her?"

That happened on several occasions. People would come into the room and when there was a pause in the conversation, Martin would say, "Did you hear the news? Laura's expecting!"

They would be gushing and trying to congratulate me, and I'd have to tell them it wasn't true. One lady winked at me and said, "I promise I'll keep it a secret!"

Over and over again, I'd have to remind Martin why we were there. "Martin, we're not here because I am having a baby. We're here because you had brain surgery."

"Did we know that I needed brain surgery before I got here?"

"Yes, I told you."

In Martin's mind, we'd come to the hospital for me to give birth, but on the way to the maternity ward, we stopped for an optional procedure they were offering husbands and he happened to choose brain surgery. It was a ridiculous thought, but it persisted for weeks, and he would bring it up in the most unexpected ways—like the day he thought a nurse was flirting with him. I could tell he was watching her carefully every time she came into the room, but I had no idea what he was thinking. At the time, he was still talking very slowly. When she left he slowly whispered to me, "I . . . think . . . that . . . she . . . thinks . . . I . . . like . . . her."

"I don't think that's true," I said.

We were talking the next time she came in, and Martin suddenly got quiet.

"Do you need anything today, Mr. Elvington?" she asked, noticing the change of tone in the room.

"No."

As soon as she left he said, "Laura . . . I . . . need . . . to . . . tell . . . her."

"Martin, you don't need to tell her anything. I promise. Everything is fine."

For the rest of the day, each time she came in he was anxious and concerned. Late in the afternoon, after she had changed one of his IV bags and prepared to leave, he grabbed her hand, and then with his other hand he grabbed mine. Slowly articulating each syllable he said, "I . . . think . . . we . . . need . . . to . . . get . . . this . . . out . . . in . . . the . . . open."

Oh, no, please don't.

"I . . . am . . . tired . . . and . . . a . . . little . . . confused."

And the nurse and I nodded in agreement, "Yes, yes you are."

"I . . . think . . . I . . . need . . . more . . . time . . . to . . . decide."

"Decide what?" I asked.

"Which . . . one . . . of . . . your . . . babies . . . I'm . . . going . . . to . . . have."

What?

"That's fine," the nurse said.

"That's totally fine with me too," I said, trying not to laugh. "How about you rest now, and we can figure that out later?" *How could I sit around crying about what was happening when Martin was so fun to be around?*

One day, toward the end of our stay at the hospital, my friends Eric and Shea came for a visit. Shea was wearing a large puffy blouse and Martin blurted out, "Shea, are you expecting?"

"Oh, Martin!" I said. While I was happy he wasn't telling her *I* was expecting, I was mortified that he would say that to another woman.

"Nope, not expecting," Shea answered with an awkward laugh.

"I'm so sorry," I gushed. "He doesn't know what he's saying. He's just not well."

Then Martin proceeded to ask her an intelligent question about current events, making a complete idiot out of me. When they finished that part of the conversation Martin said, "Did you just come back from a trip?"

She smiled. "Yes, Martin. We just got back from the beach yesterday. What a good memory you have!" She looked at me like I was the one who was confused. I started to think I was until Martin spoke again.

"Yeah, you came back in a rocket," he said.

"See!" I said to Shea, thankful that Martin had proved my point.

The doctors told me Martin would be loopy for about a month. We did see some progress during that first month, but by the time we were in our sixth week of ICU, the doctors began to suspect another problem—short-term memory loss. When they told me, I wasn't prepared to hear it. At various times, I was aware he could die. I also remembered the doctor mentioning a small chance that he could have some kinds of fits. Other complications were discussed. But I didn't remember short-term memory loss being one them. I had no grid for understanding it.

I thought back to six months or a year earlier when we didn't know what was going on with Martin. My biggest fear then was that he would have some kind of mental illness and that his brain wouldn't work right. Now, after all we had been through, doctors began to suspect my worst fear. I thought of how many times each day Martin wanted to know where he was and how I had to tell him over and over again.

Was this what the rest of our life would look like?

That was the first time I began to consider what it might mean to have a husband with a short-term memory loss.

It would be years before I fully found out what it meant.

ℒ

When Martin was in the hospital, I slept for months in an uncomfortable chair. I didn't have much of an appetite, and when I did eat, I didn't eat healthy. I neglected a lot of things, but probably the easiest thing for me to neglect while we were in crisis mode was my spiritual life. I was a professional Christian who worked at a church, but for months I didn't know how to pray, what to say, or what to ask for. I didn't spend any time in God's Word, and I didn't listen for his still, small voice. It wasn't that I was rebelling; it was that I was so busy and tired while going through our trial that I never got around to spending time with God.

In a way, I was like Martin. After being fed mush he needed to relearn how to eat solid food. I needed to relearn how to eat spiritually. For weeks, I had been fed spiritually through the tubes of others' prayers. Eventually I graduated to soft spiritual foods. A card would arrive with a Scripture verse, and I'd let it slide down the back of my throat like Jell-O. But just as Martin had to relearn how to chew and swallow to eat solid food, I also had to learn how to digest harder-to-swallow biblical truths. One of those spiritual steak-and-crab-legs meals was found in James 1.

> Consider it pure joy, my brothers and sisters, whenever you face trials of many kinds, because you know that the testing of your faith produces perseverance. Let perseverance finish its work so that you may be mature and complete, not lacking anything. (vv. 2–4)

I was familiar with the first phrase of this passage—"Count it all joy." It was the first solo I ever sang in church. I was ten or eleven years old, and my friend Erin and I were chosen to sing for our church's sesquicentennial celebration. We dressed up like the cast of *Little House on the Prairie* with bonnets, pinafores, and aprons for the 150th anniversary of First Baptist Church Spartanburg. Cliff Barrows was our special guest for the celebration. He had a song called "Count It All Joy," and Erin and I had made up a little arrangement of it. So the adults in the church thought it would be a good idea if we got up and sang it for him.

We giggled and waved more than we sang, and I can only wince when I think of what that arrangement must have sounded like. It was cute, but we had no idea what we were doing.

And we had no idea what the rest of that verse meant.

How do you count the trials of your life as joy?

We all want to persevere in our faith. We want our faith to be "perfect and complete." But who wants to go through trials to make it happen? The problem is, perseverance doesn't come from listening to a sermon. There is no inspirational bestseller we can read that will help us plumb the depths of our faith. We don't become perfect and complete by sitting in church. We learn who he really is during the most desperate part of our trials. It's about meeting God where and when we need him most. Sure, our faith grows through reading Scripture and praying, but just as we don't know the strength of our body until we test it in a physical challenge, our faith isn't perfected until it's been tested in a spiritual challenge.

Let's not misunderstand what James is saying. He isn't saying we should do cartwheels when bad things happen.

"Another hole in Martin's head? Praise Jesus!"

"A lifetime of short-term memory loss? Thank you, Father!"

That's not it at all.

James is saying that when the trials of life happen, we need to hold on to God. It's an opportunity for us to look in the dark for the less obvious blessings and mercies of God that we might overlook in the light. When we do, God shows us things that we otherwise might miss. God's light is brightest in the dark.

ℐ

Staring into the future of Martin's brain damage was frightening, but I could find true joy in seeing glimpses of Martin's personality shining through his fog. Seconds of sanity that came wrapped in hours of confusion were the times I saw God's healing. When a nurse offered a pillow, a test result came back negative, or a visitor brought a steaming hot latte, it was as if God was saying, "I'm here with you. I'll take care of you. I'll refresh you."

These are the hidden acts of grace and mercy we so often miss. When I was in the depths of despair, these small acts helped me see God was very present, he didn't abandon me, and he loved me even when I wasn't doing a very good job of loving him back.

During our trials we can feel like a garden overrun with weeds—as if life is being choked out of us. Finding time to study, pray, and worship may be impossible. But even in the overgrown weeds, we can study the seeds of mercy, grace, and hope; toss up a quick, "Help me"; and praise God that he's in the mud and muck with us. These things are like water and fertilizer helping our spirits bloom and grow. That's the kind of perseverance that matures and completes our faith.

One of my favorite verses is Psalm 43:3: "Send me your light and your faithful care, *let them lead me*; let them bring me to your holy mountain, to the place where you dwell."

The psalmist is saying that God's presence isn't something we have to work for. We don't have to seek it, search for it, or earn it. Instead, God sends his light to us and all we have to do is follow it back to him. When I am limp and lifeless and can barely speak, my simple prayer is, "Lead me." And when I ask, God is faithful to usher me into his presence. In my weakest moments, he brings his truth to my mind, his light to my dark and weary soul, and care and refreshment to my worn-out body.

Even during the darkest days of our trials, my joy came when I took tentative steps in God's direction. There, I was rewarded by seeing him and his love for me in never-before-experienced ways.

Even during your darkest trials God is waiting with outstretched arms for you to come into his presence. Take a step in his direction and let his light lead you to the joy that can only be found in him.

MYTH: WHEN THINGS LOOK DARK, GOD IS GONE.

TRUTH: WHEN THINGS LOOK DARK, GOD'S
LIGHT SHINES THE BRIGHTEST.

SIX

THE BEST-MADE PLANS

WE HAD A LOT OF UPS AND DOWNS WHILE MARTIN WAS in the hospital. There were times I thought he was going to live and times I was afraid he might die. When things were good, I dreamed of our life returning to normal. When things weren't so good—he was confused or having difficulty relearning to eat or walk—I assumed we might need help from a home health-care worker once we were back in our condo. I always planned for Martin to come home. I never considered any other alternative. No matter how difficult the struggles in the hospital seemed, he was still progressing so I just assumed that as soon as he'd made enough progress, we'd go home.

One Saturday morning, Martin woke up on the wrong side of the hospital bed. His usual sweet, childlike self was gone and replaced with a grouchy old man. Whatever I did to help only frustrated him. When I opened the blinds, he wanted them closed. When I filled his water pitcher, there wasn't enough ice in it. When I put more ice in it and set it on the tray table, he picked it up and moved it to the nightstand.

At first I was excited to see a little bit of fight in him. But as the morning wore on, all he did was fight. Nothing in our situation had changed; all of the routines remained the same. But for whatever reason, Martin was just out of sorts.

I tried to ignore his foul mood, but it seemed all he wanted to do was argue.

While Martin was in the bathroom, I called my dad. He happened to be in Atlanta for the weekend.

"Martin thinks I'm trying to hurt him."

"What do you mean?" Dad asked.

"I don't know. For some reason, he just thinks I am trying to hurt him. He's been acting really strange."

"I'll be right there."

While I waited for Dad to get to the hospital, the doctor came in on his morning rounds. I told him that Martin seemed unusually agitated and almost paranoid. "This kind of behavior isn't unusual for brain surgery patients," he said.

"Yeah, but it's unusual for Martin."

"We'll run some tests," he promised.

Of all the delusions Martin had, paranoia was the hardest to deal with because I couldn't prove his concerns weren't real. In addition, the paranoia made him lash out in unusual ways. So I was relieved when my dad arrived. He and Martin had always gotten along well.

"How are you doing, Martin?" Dad asked.

"Not good," said Martin.

"Is there something I can do for you?"

"No."

Dad could tell something was wrong. This wasn't the man we all knew and loved. He looked up at me and I shrugged. I didn't know what to make of it either. While we exchanged looks, Martin picked up the corded controller and pushed the button for the nurse.

An older nurse with squeaky shoes appeared in the doorway. "Do you need something, Mr. Elvington?"

Martin nodded. As she approached him, he whispered loud enough for us to hear, "My father-in-law is trying to sabotage my care."

Though this wasn't Martin's regular nurse, I'd seen her around. She glanced at Dad and me. I could tell she was thinking.

Martin grew more agitated. His eyes darted around the room as if he were in fear of someone or something. His fingers fidgeted among the folds in his sheet. He said it again, this time out loud, "He's trying to sabotage my care."

I'd never seen him like this toward my father. I was simultaneously worried and annoyed.

"Martin, stop," I said.

But Martin wasn't done yet. He pointed at me. "*She's* compromising my care!"

I'm compromising his care?

For nearly two months, I hadn't left his room. I'd slept on a pleather recliner that creaked every time I moved to get comfortable—which was all night long. I barely had a blanket and a pillow because laundry kept taking them, and it was hard to sleep with nurses and lab technicians coming in every four hours to check Martin's vitals and draw blood. Even when they weren't coming in, I lay awake making sure Martin didn't get out of bed and hurt himself. While I admit I wasn't exactly well rested and in my best mental state, I still couldn't understand why he said I was compromising his care.

Seeing Martin's heightened anxiety, the nurse pulled the blood pressure cuff down from the wall. "Ma'am, I'm going to have to ask you to leave," the nurse said.

Are you kidding me?

"C'mon, Laura," Dad said, taking my arm and pulling me toward the door. "I'll take you to lunch."

"This is unbelievable!" I said. But I knew Dad was right. I needed to get out of there and cool off.

Dad suggested several places we could go for lunch, but I was lost in my thoughts. This was not what I had planned. *I don't get it, God. Why this? Why now? I'm not sure how much more of this I can take!* This was an unexpected hurdle in a race I never wanted to run. But there was nothing I could do about it. I was hurt and frustrated by the time we arrived at the restaurant.

"Can you believe Martin? That was so weird!" I said after the waitress took our drink order.

Dad had been such a big help to me throughout all of Martin's struggles, always offering advice and suggestions both as a doctor and as a parent, but now he was quiet. Glancing up from my menu, I could tell something was on his mind. After the waitress took our lunch order, Dad folded his hands on the table, leaned in, and got really serious.

"You know, Laura, when it comes to Martin, I don't think you're as far out of the woods as you think you are." He paused while he considered his words.

"Okay," I said, sensing this conversation wouldn't be pleasant.

"It's not just about Martin living through this; it's more than that. Martin needs to be stable enough for you to be able to take care of him at home. It's not just about him being able to walk and feed himself. It's much more than that."

"What do you mean?"

"Martin might not be able to go home at all."

The rest of our lunch was pretty quiet.

When I got back to the hospital, I wasn't sure what kind of mood Martin was in, and I was afraid of running into the nurse with the squeaky shoes, so I decided to wait for the afternoon shift change before I went back. I headed to the ICU waiting room, where I could be alone with my thoughts. I plopped into a chair and folded my arms across my chest like a middle-schooler who'd been sent to the principal's office for something she didn't do.

Looking around at the half-drunk coffee cups, loosely folded newspapers, and torn magazines, I thought about how many hours I'd spent in that waiting room. Most of those hours had been spent wondering whether Martin was going to live or die. At every stage of his recovery, there had been new concerns about whether he'd make it. But when I had dared to imagine our future together, I'd always planned for us to be *together* in our condo.

I thought back to when the doctor brought Martin up from sedation. I remembered him telling me that Martin would go through a lot of goofy stuff. But until now, I hadn't paid much attention to what he said after that: "And we don't know whether he'll snap out of it or not."

Was he talking about this?

While it was becoming obvious that Martin wouldn't completely return to his old self, it was hard to think that he might become someone else.

Before the surgery, Martin never had a mean bone in his body. Even when we argued, he wouldn't get mad at me. I would try to bait him into a fight about something that upset me and he'd apologize: "I'm really sorry!" Or, "Oh, I did that? I'm so sorry, I won't do it again." At times it would frustrate me because he was so quick to take the blame and apologize.

But the Martin I left in the hospital room that morning was nothing like the Martin I remembered.

How will I be able to take care of him if he stays like this?

For the first time in weeks, I began to pray as I desperately sought God. *What if this is my life from now on? How can I continue to love someone who thinks I'm out to get him? How am I supposed to serve him when he doesn't believe I have his best interests at heart?*

While I was crying out to God, I felt a warm and loving voice envelop me. God was speaking so clearly to my heart that it could have been an audible voice, though it wasn't.

Laura, I do that for you every day, he said. *I love you and I care for you. I have been faithful to you, yet you doubt me every step of the way. Even now you think I'm trying to harm you, not do something good for you.*

It was as if God took a spotlight and shined it on my dirty heart and dingy soul. How could I complain about Martin thinking I was trying to harm him when every day I thought the same thing about the God I dearly loved?

I began to weep. *You're right. Just like Martin this morning, I've doubted your goodness when all you've ever done is care for me, love me, and forgive me.*

In my doubt and distrust of God, I had failed to see the good things he had done for me. When his plans superseded mine, rather than trust him, I argued why my plans were better than his and doubted his goodness.

But even when I doubted God's goodness, he was good to me.

I could do at least that much for Martin.

$\mathscr{L}$

Martin and I had planned a perfect life, but God had interrupted our plans with what seemed like a much worse plan of his own. Have you ever felt that way? If God had just listened to you, things would have been okay. But now you are held captive by situations you never wanted to be in and can't seem to get out of by yourself.

If you've ever felt that way, you're not alone.

The ancient Judeans had perfect plans for their lives too. Living in Jerusalem, the capital city of Israel, they had simple, ordinary dreams. They wanted to get married and start a family. They'd probably live with extended family members and maybe have a little garden out back. Most of all, they planned to grow old together in the community where they were born and watch their kids and grandkids do the same.

But in 589 BC, their plans were interrupted by political and military actions they couldn't control. King Nebuchadnezzar, the brutal ruler of Babylon, began his final siege against Jerusalem. When the city fell, he took the Jews to Babylon, where he held them against their will.

What a dramatic change in their life plans! Imagine how shocked they must have been to go from freedom to slavery in such a short period of time. While held in captivity, they weren't sure what to do. How could they make sense of the twists and turns their life plans had now taken? How long would they be held in slavery? And where was God in all of this?

Through the prophet Jeremiah, God revealed that he was the one who had allowed his people to be taken into exile in Babylon. And worse, he sucked the air right out of their tents when he said they would be there for *seventy years* (Jer. 29:10). That was not what they had planned. How could a loving God allow this?

Fortunately, God backed up that bad news with some good news:

"For I know the plans I have for you," declares the LORD, "plans to prosper you and not to harm you, plans to give you hope and a future. Then you will call on me and come and pray to me, and I will listen to you. You will seek me and find me when you seek me with all your heart. I will be found by you," declares the LORD, "and will bring you back from captivity. I will gather you from all the nations and places where I have banished you," declares the LORD, "and will bring you back to the place from which I carried you into exile." (vv. 11–14)

God reminded them that he had a plan. His plan would help them prosper and give them a future even better than the one they dreamed about while they were living in Jerusalem. So they had to decide whether to throw up their hands in despair—or to trust that God is who he says he is and that he had a better plan for them.

If I were one of the captives, I think I'd be tempted to say, "God, that's a dumb plan. Why do I have to go into exile and suffer captivity for seventy years, only to be brought back to where I started?"

That would be a fair question.

I asked similar ones while I was in the hospital with Martin. When Martin and I started on this journey, we thought we'd only be in the hospital for five days. At this point in time, we'd been held captive by Martin's medical issues for more than two months—with no end in sight!

But that day in the waiting room, I began to see that God was using our hospital captivity to teach me about his character and to draw me closer to him. When I was alone pouting about how my plans hadn't worked out, God was able to break through my stubbornness and reveal another plan for me, a better plan—one that would draw me into a closer relationship with him.

It had been easy for me to see how Martin had turned against me that day, but until that moment in the waiting room I hadn't thought about how I had turned against God. If I had lived out my perfect plan, the one I thought was better than God's, there are things about his Word and character I never would have experienced.

Fortunately, God is faithful to us even when we are disobedient to him.

ℐ

When I got back to Martin's room that afternoon, the nurse on the next shift told me they'd discovered Martin's sodium levels were low, and that was what was causing his paranoia. They adjusted his medications and, in twenty-four hours, Martin was back to his jovial self. By the grace of God, he was no longer paranoid, angry, and distrustful of me.

We each have plans and dreams for our lives. We think we know what's best and if God just followed our plan, everything would be great. But God's plans are much bigger than ours. Part of what God revealed to me that day in the waiting room was that just because God's plan differed from mine didn't mean that God's plan wasn't good, or that *he* wasn't good. And it didn't mean that he had abandoned us.

Though we like to think our plans are better than God's, in fact, it's quite the opposite: God's intentions are so much grander than ours, we can't even fathom what he has planned for us.

I don't know what your original plan was, or how it may have gotten off track. Certainly your circumstance is not what you anticipated. It's hard to think about starting your life over. But God has something better planned for you.

If you find yourself struggling in a situation you didn't see coming, consider it an opportunity to trust God. When we trust that God is for us and not against us, we can see our future as he sees it. It is a future filled with plans to prosper you and not to harm you. Plans to give you hope and a future.

And plans that will ultimately draw you closer to him.

MYTH: THE PLAN I HAVE FOR MY LIFE IS MUCH BETTER THAN THE PLACE WHERE GOD HAS ME RIGHT NOW.

TRUTH: WHERE GOD HAS ME RIGHT NOW IS THE BEST PLACE FOR ME.

SEVEN

THE CHURCH CAME TO US

IT WAS A DAY WE NEVER THOUGHT WOULD COME. Standing outside the hospital while Mom went to get the car, I could hear the sounds of traffic and the chatter of busy people with places to go. Looking at the crisp blue sky and lazy white clouds, I felt as if a weight of worry had been lessened. I looked down at Martin in the wheelchair. He blinked several times before covering his eyes from the bright July sun. I'd been outside once or twice in the past few weeks, but Martin hadn't been outside since the day he arrived for rehab and was admitted due to the leaking skin graft in his nose.

In total, we'd been in the hospital for more than two months. In addition to the two and a half weeks we'd spent there for the original surgery, we'd spent another four weeks in ICU for the repair of the graft and the resulting meningitis, and then two more weeks in a regular room.

Those past weeks hadn't been easy. Several times we thought Martin was going to die, but by God's grace he pulled through. Since his last surgery, Martin had graduated from receiving nutrients through an IV, to eating mush, to being fed solid food, to mostly eating on his own with a knife and fork. While he had a ways to go in relearning how to walk, he was now using the walker to take ten or twenty steps. It was slow, but it was progress. Leaving the hospital felt to us like an accomplishment that, until now, we'd only hoped and prayed for.

Martin wasn't going home, though. The doctors released him to a step-down unit, an inpatient rehabilitation facility where he could get the kind of concentrated therapy and life skills he'd need to return home. He couldn't bathe himself (they'd been giving him sponge baths in the hospital), and his balance wasn't good enough for him to walk on his own. The therapy promised to help not only his physical movement but also his speech and cognitive abilities.

The rehab facility was located just a couple of miles from our condo. The rooms were clean and bright, and the facility had a dining room with a courtyard. It was like a cross between an extended stay hotel and a senior center, except the patients were much younger. We saw people, like Martin, with brain trauma, but there were also people with no mental impairments, like the forty-year-old man who'd broken his leg from his hip to his ankle. It was easy to gauge that some people were in better shape than Martin, but some were in worse shape.

We got Martin settled in and my mom left. At dinnertime, I wheeled Martin down to the dining room. There were large community tables and smaller two-person tables. I chose a two-person table, pushed Martin up to it, and then sat down across from him. We'd only been married for a couple of years, and we hadn't sat across a table from each other in more than two months! It was wonderful to be able to look into his eyes while we talked. His speech was still slow and he had trouble recalling some words, but I didn't care. I was sitting at a table eating dinner with my husband. It was the first normal thing we'd done in months.

Martin was doing a decent job of using his fork and knife to eat the spaghetti, though I occasionally had to assist. At one point, Martin looked up and noticed a man sitting at the table across the aisle from us. The man was opening a packet of Parmesan cheese and sprinkling it on his spaghetti.

"Cheese. Cheese," Martin said to the server. "Want some cheese!"

The server handed him a packet, and I watched as Martin slowly ripped off the top, holding it carefully so he didn't waste any of the cheese. But instead of sprinkling it over his spaghetti, he poured it into his *milk*. Then he picked up his spoon and gingerly stirred the mixture until the powdered cheese dissolved in the milk.

Then he drank it.

Huh. Cheese-milk. Maybe we're not as close to normal as I thought.

In some ways, the cheese-milk was a good sign. Martin had remembered what cheese was, what it was called, and that he liked it. He also showed great motor skills in opening the packet and stirring the Parmesan. I was confident the rest of it would come soon enough; it was only his first day in rehab.

At bedtime, the facility's staff told me I had to leave. It was the hardest thing I'd had to do since Martin entered the hospital. I'd spent every night (except the night he coded) in a chair next to him. I always wanted to be there in case he needed anything.

If I leave, who will help him in the middle of the night? What if he tries to use the restroom by himself?

In the hospital, following the new skin graft, we'd used arm restraints to keep him from tearing out the packing in his nose. When that was no longer a concern, we continued to use the restraints at night so he couldn't get out of bed unless someone was there to help him. But as I prepared to leave the rehab facility for the night, I didn't see the restraints. So I spoke to the nurse.

"I'm fine with not spending the night with him," I said, even though I wasn't. "But Martin can't walk. And he doesn't know that he can't walk. Some nights he attempts to get out of bed to use the bathroom, and if someone is not there, he'll take a step or two and then fall. So he needs restraints to make sure he stays safe."

The nurse looked confused. Maybe she didn't know what I was asking.

"At the hospital, we used this belt thingy to tie him in the bed—"

"We are not that kind of hospital," she said, as if I had just suggested they killed puppies at midnight. "We do not tie up our patients!"

"I don't think you understand. He really needs it so he doesn't hurt himself."

"We're not going to do that here," she said emphatically. Then she waved her hand as if dismissing me.

"Well, someone needs to keep an eye on him," I said.

"He'll be fine. We *keep an eye* on all our patients."

I was already nervous about leaving him, and she didn't make it easier.

Even though I was in my own bed for the first time in months, I didn't sleep well that night.

L

The next morning the facility opened at seven; I was there at 6:45 a.m. waiting. As soon as they opened, I headed straight for Martin's room, but a nurse I'd never met stopped me.

"Mrs. Elvington? I need to talk to you."

"Yes?"

"Apparently Martin tried to get up during the night, and we found him sitting on the floor. It doesn't look like he has any bruises, so I think he's fine."

"What do you mean he was *sitting on the floor*?"

"We think he got up to go to the bathroom and when he tried to walk he just dropped. He was on the floor next to the bed waiting for us when we came in."

I took a deep breath. *Be nice. These people are caring for Martin when you're not here.* "How long was he on the floor?"

"We're not sure. We *told* him to push the nurse call button if he needed to go to the bathroom."

Did these people know why he was here? Martin couldn't remember that he *doesn't walk*, so how was he supposed to remember to call a nurse in the middle of the night when he needed to use the bathroom?

"From now on, I really feel like we should use the restraints," she said, as if it were her idea.

"I'm fine with that," I said calmly. What I really wanted to say was, *You think?*

Before I left that night, and every night thereafter, I made sure *I* was the one who put the restraints on Martin because I didn't trust that they would. It was hard to do, but I knew it was for his own good. Despite the fact that I was tying him to the bed, Martin was always sweet and tender about it. Most nights we'd be watching TV when it was time for me to go and I'd remind him of what I was doing.

"It's time for me to leave, but before I do, I need to put a belt on you so you don't get hurt."

Every night, as I wrapped it around him and attached it to each side of the bed, we would have the same conversation.

"Are you tying me up?"

"Yes, I need to tie you to the bed for your own safety."

"I promise I won't run away," he'd plead. "I promise I won't run away!"

"Martin, you won't even know it's there. You'll be fine."

He never cried, but there were nights I almost did. It was heartbreaking to think of him waking up in the middle of the night all alone and tied to his bed. I was always the last visitor to leave each night at eleven and the first inside the next morning at seven.

When I arrived each morning, the well-intentioned nurses would tell me how he called for me in the middle of the night. They'd hear his confused and frightened voice calling, "Laura? Laura?"

I think they thought it would make me feel good to know he missed me, but each time they told me, it tore me up from the inside out as I thought about how alone he must have felt.

ℒ

As much as I wanted him home, I knew he was in the right place. Unlike the hospital, where he spent the whole day in bed, in rehab he had a schedule. From nine to ten, he labored through physical therapy. From ten to eleven, he had speech lessons. Then he took a break and napped because he was exhausted from the morning activities. In the afternoon, Martin had occupational therapy. And, once a week, the staff brought in animals for pet therapy.

The goal of pet therapy was to give brain injury patients an opportunity to improve their motor skills by petting or brushing the dog. One day when Martin was taking a long time getting dressed, I told him he needed to keep moving.

"Remember, you have pet therapy today," I said.

"Is that where I tell my problems to a dog?" Martin joked.

I laughed at the thought of a dog wearing glasses and telling Martin, "Lay down on the couch." Moments of levity like this, where I could see Martin's goofy personality coming out, gave me great hope for the future.

In the evenings we would try to do something fun. Simple things felt like such a treat after so many weeks in the hospital. Understandably, not being hooked up to an IV and being able to leave his room gave Martin a greater sense of freedom. We liked taking our ice cream from the dining room and eating it on the patio where we could see the trees swaying in a light breeze and listen to the birds chirping in the evenings. Sometimes we would play cards, or Martin would practice shooting an inflatable ball into a basketball goal. Martin was a favorite of the orderlies, and sometimes they would take a break to shoot hoops with him.

To me, one of the sweetest sights was when two or three of Martin's Bible study friends came to play cards. I would walk into the dining room and find them all hunched around a table, cards fanned out in their hands.

"Do you have any twos?" Scott asked.

"No twos," Martin said.

"Go fish," Robby said.

These men worked full time and had families and other obligations. But instead of just studying the love of Christ, these men lived it out by loving Martin.

$\mathcal{L}$

Four days after we arrived, the facility held a Fourth of July party. Everyone was supposed to decorate his or her wheelchair and then parade down the main hall of the center. John and his fiancé, Whitney, bought supplies and helped us decorate Martin's wheelchair, Martin won the prize for the most spirited wheelchair. We found a level of normalcy at the rehab facility that we had not experienced in a long time, and it was refreshing.

As a result of his surgeries, Martin's equilibrium was off, so he spent most of his time in the wheelchair. The orderlies helped him bathe and get dressed, allowing him to do as much as he could on his own. Martin was working hard to improve in every area.

In speech class, they played a game called Think Fast. They would take plastic fruit and vegetables (like in a child's kitchen play set) and toss them one at a time to Martin. He'd have to catch one and then identify what it was.

Broccoli.

Banana.

Carrots.

In his occupational therapy class, they would ask him questions like, "What do you do if your house is on fire?"

The correct answer was to leave the house and call 911. But Martin offered a much more detailed account. "Well, if my wife was there, I would make sure she got out. Then if I saw smoke, I would crawl on the ground. I would feel the door and the doorknob to see if they were hot, and if they were, I would turn around and go to the other door—"

But when the therapist asked, "What did you have for breakfast this morning?" Martin would have no idea if he'd even eaten.

When the therapist asked Martin how we met, Martin would tell her every detail about the FCA barbecue in my friend's backyard and the moose overalls I wore while eating my hot dog. But when she asked, "Is your wife here with you now?"

Martin would respond, "I thought she was . . ."

Martin had always been intelligent, so some of his answers were much more thorough than they expected for someone in his condition. On the other hand, some of his answers were much worse than they expected. It was like a child who gets As in all of his classes, except for the one class where he receives an F. Martin was getting an F in short-term memory.

Over the next two weeks, it became clear that Martin wasn't making progress with his short-term memory. Since he was improving in other areas, I assumed more time in therapy would help that get better too. I assumed the same thing about his ability to walk. He was making some progress, but after nearly three weeks of physical therapy, he still couldn't walk on his own. The best he could do was lean against a wall. I was hopeful that the intensive therapy would help him regain enough function to come home in a few months.

That's why I was shocked at what happened next.

ℒ

On July 20, we were one day short of being at the facility a full three weeks. And just like every other day, the doctor came by to do his rounds before Martin started therapy.

"I have some good news!" he said.

I wasn't surprised by his excitement. I assumed he was going to tell me how well Martin was doing. I'd seen the progress Martin had been making, and I figured that if he kept it up at the same rate, Martin would be able to come home in six months or so.

But that wasn't the good news.

"Martin is healthy, so I am going to discharge him tomorrow," he said, scribbling a note in Martin's chart.

What?

"What do you mean he's healthy?" I asked.

"His body is stable. He's no longer at risk for postoperative complications, and we've done everything possible to improve the areas that we can."

I was stunned.

Martin couldn't walk, he couldn't remember basic things, and the orderlies were still bathing and dressing him. As tired as we were of being in hospitals, and as much as I wanted Martin to come home with me, I never expected it to happen this soon.

The doctor continued, "We believe he can live a very functional life."

"What do you mean by that?" I asked.

"We think he will eventually be able to walk by himself, as well as feed and bathe himself."

But he's twenty-eight years old! Those are things people say about seventy-year-old stroke victims, not a young man who is just starting his career.

Apparently *functional* did not mean Martin would be *fixed.*

"Can I talk to you in the hall?" I asked.

This wasn't at all what I was expecting, and I didn't want to upset Martin by discussing it in front of him. We stepped outside the room. Once I was sure Martin was out of earshot, I asked, "Why are you discharging him if he's not better?"

"Well, we'll continue to see him for outpatient care a couple of times a week for the next month or two."

What good is that going to do? How will I even get Martin home and out of the car? What about the stairs at our condo? How in the world can I bathe a six-foot-five, two-hundred-thirty-pound grown man or pick him up if he falls? What about his short-term memory problems? How can you let him go without that getting any better?

A million other questions ran through my mind, but I took a deep breath and tried to focus on the most important ones. "I've seen the progress he's made with the walker. His speech has improved and his cognitive abilities, problem-solving skills, and long-term memory have all made progress. But his short-term memory isn't getting any better. Why would you discharge him now? Don't you want to make sure he's better before you discharge him?"

The doctor flipped to another page in Martin's chart. "Due to the nature of Martin's brain injury, that's the one area that may not get any better. On all of the short-term memory tests we've done on him, there has been almost no improvement." He explained it to me that it was kind of like a phantom limb. "We can exercise it all we want, but if there's nothing there, the exercises can't help it perform better."

"So to clarify, when you say Martin can live a *functional* life, you're describing very basic things, like walking and eating?"

"Yes."

When I think functional, I'm thinking he's twenty-eight. *Functional* is Martin finishing school and becoming a graphic designer. We want to have kids, so *functional* is his being a dad and the breadwinner. When I think of *functional*, I'm envisioning Martin functioning as he did before.

"Martin is doing well for all he's been through. He's only three months out, and you may see a few more improvements in the next six to nine months."

"So what's next?"

"We'll release him tomorrow and then starting Monday you can bring him back in for outpatient services."

"But . . . but . . . what about his blood tests?" Martin had blood tests every four hours to make sure the medication was doing what it was supposed to do. If one of his medications was off, they'd told me he could die in as few as three days.

"We'll test it on Monday when he comes in."

Monday? They were releasing him on Friday. That was three whole days before he'd be tested. How would I know whether his medications were doing what they were supposed to be doing?

"Is there anything else?" the doctor asked.

I wanted to say, "Yeah, how do I make sure I keep him alive all weekend?" But I was so stunned I didn't say anything. I just shook my head.

Oh, God, how are we going to do this?

I composed myself and returned to Martin's room to help him get ready for his therapy session. Sometimes I attended his therapy sessions and sometimes I didn't. Today, I couldn't stomach the thought of watching him work so hard to remember things that I now knew he would likely never remember.

"Martin, I'm going to grab lunch, and I'll be back to eat with you when you're done with your therapy."

"Okay," he said happily.

The weight that had lifted off my shoulders the morning we checked out of the hospital had returned.

And brought a friend.

My weary shoulders sagged under the heaviness of sorrow and thoughts of permanence. *This might be as good as it gets.*

ℒ

I walked to the parking lot, unlocked my car, and sat dazed as the reality set in.

Martin had teams of medical professionals taking care of him in the hospital and in the rehab center. Now all of that would be up to *me*. I thought of all the things they did for him, from the blood tests to his morning bath. There was no way I could help him in and out of the shower; I was too small. And medically? I'd failed chemistry *twice!* I didn't even know how to use a blood pressure cuff. And there were other more practical things that would be difficult too.

How would I even get him up the stairs?

I thought about the steep flight of stairs that led to our condo. Even if I found someone to help me get Martin up the stairs, what would prevent him from trying to go down them by himself?

I felt like a first-time mother leaving the hospital with her newborn baby, but mine was too big to carry in my arms. Our condo was not prepared for him to come home to. The steep stairs and the gas fireplace were among the many things that would make our home unsafe for Martin.

It didn't make sense to me that they were releasing him now. My dad was a cardiologist, and when he operated on someone they left the hospital in better shape than when they came in. He *fixed* their hearts! It never occurred to me that the doctors would release Martin without fixing him.

There were other worries, too, like how would we pay for all of this?

I'd been working at Perimeter for a little more than ten months, but I'd taken a month off before the surgeries and nearly three more afterward. I'd already missed four months of work out of the ten I'd been there! The last weekend I'd actually gone to work was the Saturday night Martin coded and I left early.

What am I going to do? How will I earn a living for both of us?

Martin and I were in our late twenties; we still had another forty years or more to pay for. Not only did I need a plan for what to do with Martin for the weekend, but I also needed a long-term financial plan in case Martin couldn't return to work.

When I finally gathered my senses, I thought of the two worship conferences I'd attended before Martin was diagnosed. At the first one, a professor from Covenant Seminary gave me his card and said,

"If you ever feel the Lord calling you to full-time vocational ministry, give me a call. We'd love to have you as a student."

I pulled the card out of my wallet. If this wasn't a call to full-time vocational ministry, then I didn't know what was. I called the number and left a message.

I glanced at the clock and realized I needed to get my lunch now so I would be back in time to eat with Martin. As I started the car and pulled out of the parking lot, my thoughts raced.

I'll have to go back to work soon, and then who will watch Martin? Maybe I can take him with me. But how will I get him up and down the stairs? People at church offered to help, but how can I ask them to help me when I don't even know how to help him myself?

"Welcome to Chick-fil-A. How can I serve you?"

"Can I get a chicken sandwich and a water to go, please?"

I got my food and headed toward the door. As I was leaving, Carol Pope walked in. Carol was the wife of Randy Pope, the senior pastor at Perimeter Church.

"Laura! How are you?" Carol asked.

"Um, I don't know. They're discharging Martin tomorrow."

"What do you need? What can I help you with?"

Everything I had been thinking about spilled out. "We don't have anywhere to go. Our condo is on the second floor, and he can't walk well enough to get up the stairs—"

Without hesitating, Carol interrupted, "You're going to come to our house. We just finished building a suite for Randy's mother when she comes to visit. It will be perfect for Martin until you get things figured out."

"Are you sure? That seems like a lot of trouble."

"It's no trouble at all. It's brand-new and handicap accessible. We put ramps into the room for a wheelchair and bars along the walls so he won't fall. It has a kitchenette and a handicapped bathroom—everything you need. Y'all can stay there until Martin can walk and we figure out what happens next."

"Oh! Thank you so much. We'd love to stay there. I promise we won't be a problem. You and Randy won't even know we're there!"

"It's our pleasure. Just come to our house tomorrow after he's been discharged, and we'll have everything ready for you."

As I got into the car and headed back to the rehab facility, I was reminded how God knows our need even before we do. Running into Carol at Chick-fil-A was an answer to a prayer I hadn't even yet prayed. And it was a tangible reminder that God would continue to meet all of our needs.

C

The next day as we prepared to leave the facility, the staff gave me a list of Martin's medications and the schedule for his next dose. They made sure I understood it was critical he took them three times a day. They also gave me a blood pressure cuff and a pile of prescriptions. But they didn't give me what I wanted most—a button I could push to call a nurse if I needed one. There were no after-hours phone numbers to call, and there would be no one in the hall to grab if I needed help.

As we said our good-byes, I hugged the staff members. They had championed and encouraged Martin the whole time he was there. When I teared up, I wasn't sure if I was sad to be leaving them or if I was scared to go home without them.

"We'll see you again in three days when you come back for therapy," the nurse said, peeling my arms back from around her neck.

As they helped Martin into the car, I felt overwhelmed. *What am I supposed to do with him for the next three days?* At times I couldn't even understand what Martin was saying.

For months I'd dreamed about Martin coming home, and there had been a lot of dark days when I thought it might not happen, so I was extremely thankful we could go home. But I'd never pictured it like this. I had always pictured it with Martin returning to our condo the way he'd always been—strong, funny, organized, and capable. Instead we were heading to a temporary home at my boss's house, and Martin and I would have to learn what he could and couldn't do.

Randy and Carol were waiting when we arrived. "Thank you both so much. I don't know what we'd do without you," I told them. It wasn't a cliché. I truly didn't know what we would have done without them. "We won't be any trouble. You won't even know we're here!" I promised again after they got us settled in our room.

The suite was perfect. Martin and I felt very much at home. We were both exhausted, so we went to bed early that night. It was the first time in months I'd been able to sleep in the same bed with my husband and it felt great. I fell into a deep sleep and didn't wake until the morning sun warmed my face. I yawned and turned over to see if Martin was still asleep.

All I saw was a pile of twisted sheets.

He's not here!

I jumped out of bed. "Martin? Martin?"

His wheelchair and walker were right where we left them the night before.

"Martin!" I checked the bathroom and he wasn't there.

I nervously checked the floor on his side of the bed in case he'd fallen and I hadn't heard him. He wasn't there either.

Where else could he go?

I was terrified. A man who couldn't walk on his own had disappeared in the middle of the night. I was the one who was supposed to protect him, and I didn't even wake up.

I decided to get help. I opened the door that led out of our suite and into the main house. As soon as I did, I could see Martin sitting at the bar in the Popes' kitchen.

"Martin! What are you doing?"

Martin was seated on one side of the counter eating, while Randy stood on the other side of the counter with a spatula in his hand. An empty frying pan still crackled on the burner.

I stopped, suddenly embarrassed that I was in my boss's kitchen in my pajamas. "What's going on?" I asked Randy, trying to play it cool.

"When I came out to the kitchen this morning, Martin was already here. I asked if I could get him anything and he said, 'Eggs.' I asked how many he wanted, and he said 'Two,' so I made him two eggs."

I was mortified.

I'd promised Randy and Carol we'd be no trouble and on our first morning in their house Martin had already treated my boss, *the senior pastor*, as if he were a short-order cook at a diner.

"Oh, Randy, I am so sorry. This is not your responsibility!"

Randy laughed and was gracious about the whole thing. But all I could think of was how I'd promised them, "You won't even know we're here."

Until Martin demands that you make him breakfast.

Apparently Martin had used the bars along the wall in our suite to guide himself into the Popes' kitchen. Once we figured out what happened and had a good laugh, I was surprised that Martin hadn't requested toast and bacon while he was at it.

I had always been self-reliant. I told myself I didn't need to depend on anyone; I could take care of myself. But from the day Martin started sleeping through the sermons at church to the day I showed up in the pastor's kitchen in my sleepwear, I learned that I'd never had the control I'd thought I had.

Until Martin's illness, I never realized how much I needed the help of people from my church. There had been so many opportunities to serve us and they availed themselves of each one. As a staff member, I felt as if I should have been the one serving them. It was both humbling and humiliating to me.

Until I learned, *it wasn't about me.*

ℒ

When I was young, I thought church was all about a building on Sundays. That was the day we got dressed in our good clothes and drove to a brick building with red-carpeted aisles. But while Martin was in the hospital and especially when he got out, the two of us experienced church in fresh, new ways—ways that had ancient beginnings.

The first-century church wasn't something experienced in a building on Sunday mornings. In fact, there wasn't even a building. Church happened when people naturally gathered together to learn more about the man named Jesus from his friends, the apostles, and others who'd seen the miracles he'd performed.

During these gatherings, there was such a sense of interconnectedness that if one person in the community was hurting, then the others in the group would sell their possessions so they could help (Acts 2:44). Whatever individual identity they processed had been swallowed up by this new corporate identity. They were the first Christ followers.

Or as we call them today, Christians.

And they didn't meet *in* the church. They *were* the church.

That's the kind of church Martin and I experienced when we were hurting. Our church building looked like the inside of the Popes' house. Services weren't at nine and eleven; they were Randy making Martin eggs, a group of women who scrubbed our condo clean, and all the people who covered for me at work. Offerings looked like gift cards. Incense smelled like chicken casseroles and lasagna that church members dropped off so I wouldn't have to shop and cook.

Just like the church in Acts, no matter how many times the people of Perimeter Church served us, they did it with glad and sincere hearts. The beauty of the modern church isn't found in architectural columns or stained-glass windows, as beautiful as those things are to me. It's found in the lines on the faces and the joy in the eyes of those who drop what they are doing so they can be the church and serve those who need it most.

What we witnessed was a beautiful picture of Christ's love for us. It was also very humbling.

Some days it was hard for me not to view our neediness as an imposition on so many others. I've always been the one who helped others, and it was against everything inside me to accept so much charity from the church around us. But through his Word, God revealed to me that the church wasn't serving us because we were so pathetic that they felt sorry for us.

It wasn't about us at all.

These precious people served us, not because we were worthy but because they wanted to serve Jesus. When the gospel takes hold of you, you can't help but respond by giving yourself away. It wasn't our worthiness or even our need that compelled them to help. It was the manifestation of God's grace and his redeeming work, powered by the Holy Spirit in their lives, that motivated them to play Go Fish, decorate a wheelchair, invite us into their home, cook a meal, and clean our condo. As Christ followers, when we see the depth of sacrifice Jesus made for us, bringing a few meals or sweeping some floors for someone in need is nothing. It's an opportunity for us to learn how to be more like Jesus.

We become servants because he was.

While we were going through this season of brokenness, the church wasn't a place we went on Sundays—most Sundays we couldn't even manage a shower. Church was the people who came to us, every day of the week. Sometimes two or three times a day. In our brokenness, the staff and volunteers at Perimeter served us like Christ had first served all of us. We didn't have to do anything to earn it. We never got dressed up to receive it. But when they came bearing gift cards, flowers, and casseroles, we always knew who sent them.

They were our brothers and sisters in Christ, a family who wrapped their arms around us, sent by the Father above who loves us. It was never about us and always about him.

MYTH: THE CHURCH IS A BUILDING WITH SERVICES.

TRUTH: THE CHURCH IS THE PEOPLE OF
GOD AS THEY SERVE ONE ANOTHER.

EIGHT

NEW LIFE

WE'D BEEN STAYING IN THE POPES' SUITE FOR TWO weeks, and Martin was going to outpatient rehab several times a week. Since we'd spent the summer in the hospital, Mom asked if we wanted to join them for a few days at the beach. Though he was still unsteady, Martin had made progress walking, and I thought he might enjoy a weekend away. I felt comfortable going because my dad would be there. If anything went wrong, he would know what to do.

Being at the ocean with Martin was an amazing experience. I'd never thought we'd go to the beach together again. While we were there, we enjoyed the little things—smelling the saltwater, squishing sand between our toes, and lying out in the sun by the pool. The trip refreshed both our bodies and our souls. But it was obvious that Martin's body was still adjusting to life after the tumor. His hair wasn't growing in evenly, so we'd shaved his head, revealing both of his scars. He'd gained weight from being sedentary in the hospital, and he was still a little bloated from the surgeries. He wore a sort of permanently dazed expression on his face and wobbled a bit when he walked. I'm sure I didn't look much better. For certain, no one would have mistaken us for swimsuit models as we lounged by the pool.

One day, Martin and I were relaxing at the pool with my sister and her kids. I had just finished applying sunscreen to Martin's face and body, and I leaned back in my chair to read a magazine.

"I want to go swimming," Martin said, standing up.

"Okay, I'll take you in the pool." I stood up, took his arm, and led him to the steps. He gingerly walked down them, until he stood waist-deep in the water, then he moved toward the middle of the pool where it was a little deeper. I watched him do a couple of knee bends, so he could cool off. Seeing him enjoy something so simple and normal made the whole trip worthwhile.

My sister asked a question, and I turned to answer her. Then one of my nieces interrupted us to show us a new trick she'd learned in the water. As we applauded her efforts, my sister suddenly screamed, "Martin!"

I turned around to see Martin facedown in the water, his arms extended from his sides.

"Martin!" I yelled as I raced toward him. He didn't move; his body just bobbed in the water. I grabbed him by the leg and pulled him back to where we could both stand. He was coughing and spitting out water as he struggled to stand.

"Are you okay?" I asked, terrified that something horrible had happened.

"I was swimming," Martin said, a grin spreading across his face.

"No, you weren't! You were drowning!" I yelled.

Martin looked at me like I was crazy. "What is your problem? I was just swimming."

Looking back, it was kind of funny—Martin thinking he could swim. At the time, he couldn't understand why I was so concerned. He lacked the self-awareness to understand the danger he'd put himself in or why it scared me so much.

I wasn't the only one he frightened. His silliness combined with his lack of self-awareness occasionally alarmed others too.

On our last night at the Popes' house, Randy and Carol asked if we would like to join them for dinner. "Our kids have been praying for you guys and tonight they're all coming over for dinner. We'd love for y'all to join us."

Martin and I were friends with all four of the Popes' adult children and their families. We felt honored to join them for dinner and to hear what was taking place in their lives.

During the dinner conversation, I felt the love the entire Pope family had for us, and it was touching to hear how they had been praying. Out of sincere concern, one of the sons asked Martin a question. "I know you're still healing, but are you out of the woods, or are you still worried about having a stroke or anything?"

For some reason, Martin thought it would be funny to have a stroke—right there at the dinner table! It wasn't even a compelling stroke. He just started staring off in the distance and then let his head drop to one side. I'd been around him long enough that I knew exactly what he was doing, but no one else at the table had any idea. Everyone froze and their eyes grew wide, but before anyone could react, Martin lifted his head and said, "Ha . . . ha . . . ha." Then he picked up his fork and started eating again.

Confused and a bit terrified at what had just transpired, they looked at me for an explanation.

"Martin was playing a joke," I said.

Later, I had to explain to Martin how he'd scared them and after all we'd been through while he was in the hospital, a fake stroke probably wasn't the best idea.

$\mathcal{L}$

We had been at the Popes' for three weeks when we were finally able to return to our condo. I beamed all the way from their house to ours, making up silly songs in my head about bringing my husband back home. It was another milestone for us, another one I wasn't sure would ever happen. But now that it had, I felt ready for it.

My mom met us there to help me get him settled in. Martin was walking well, but the outside condo steps proved to be a challenge. They were steep, and he was still unsteady. With his balance issues, it took two of us to guide him upstairs. It was clear that living in the condo would not be a long-term solution for Martin—he'd never be able to come or go by himself.

There were other adjustments we had to make after being away for months. As a musician and an artist, I fit the stereotype. I could be flighty and spontaneous, living in the moment and not thinking about the future. Martin had always been the responsible and organized one. That's why he had handled all our financial issues and paid all the bills.

The day before his surgery, I walked into his office and saw that he was busy.

"What are you doing?" I asked.

"I'm making a list of all our bills, the account numbers, and the passwords for all the accounts."

"Why are you doing that?"

"Well, if something happens to me, I don't want you to be clueless about all of this."

"That's ridiculous!" I said. "Let's go get ice cream."

At the time, ice cream seemed like a really fun idea, more fun than making lists of bills and account numbers. But now that we were back home in the condo, I realized I had a serious problem on my hands. We hadn't paid the bills in *three months*, and when I went to the office to pull up his spreadsheet, it was blank. Because we'd gone to get ice cream, Martin never had a chance to start the list. He was right; I was clueless. I didn't know where we banked, who provided our utilities, what bills were due, or the passwords to any of our online accounts. I had to ask my friends, "Hey, do you know how to find out who provides electricity to our condo?" I didn't even know the right words to ask the right questions.

A few days after we moved back in, a Georgia Power truck pulled up and I recognized the logo. I ran to the door and said, "I need to talk to you. I think we might owe you—"

"Ma'am, you'll have to call the company. The only thing I am authorized to do is cut off your power."

"No, wait! I'll write you a check right now."

"Sorry, ma'am, I can't take your check. You'll have to work it out with customer service."

I called customer service, and they would give me a reprieve if I went to their downtown office that day and gave them a certified check by 5 p.m. That meant I had to go to the bank first.

I could tell from the mail we'd received that I'd already made a mess of our accounts at the bank. I put Martin in the car and drove to the local Wachovia. While Martin sat in the lobby, one of the managers took me into his glass-walled office. I explained everything that had gone on in our lives and told him I needed help in getting things resolved.

"What's your PIN?" he asked.

"I don't know our PIN."

"What's your password?"

"I don't know our password."

"Well, then, I need to speak to your husband because I can't change this without the proper authorization. I need your PIN or your password."

"Okay, that's him sleeping there in the lobby," I said, pointing. "You can talk to him if you want; but he doesn't even remember the name of your bank."

Somehow we figured out the banking mess, got a certified check, and met the power deadline. When we got home there was so much I had to learn about running the house. There was also a lot I had to learn about Martin. When the doctor told me that Martin had short-term memory loss, I thought I knew what that meant. But once we were home, I learned more about it every day—sometimes in the most surprising ways.

$\mathscr{L}$

Martin had no concept of time and how long it took to complete a process. His perception was completely out of whack. He would take forty-five-minute showers, until I realized I had to let him know it was time to get out. Or I'd ask him to follow me, and he'd say, "I'll be there in a minute." An hour later, he would come in, believing only minutes had passed. He couldn't remember if he ate dinner the night before, which wasn't a big deal because we ate together. But it mattered when I told him it was time to take his medications, and he couldn't remember whether he'd already taken them. The medications were what kept him alive, and if he didn't take them, there could be immediate repercussions. The doctor said if he didn't take his medications three days in a row he could be sick enough to die.

His visual perception was also off. When he poured creamer into his coffee, at first, he'd completely miss the cup. But because he was so intelligent, he realized what was happening, even if he didn't know why. He would adjust so that most of the creamer landed in the cup.

When those things occurred, I wasn't sure if it was his memory loss or his impaired vision. And he didn't know either. To know what was wrong in a specific situation, he had to remember what was right. He didn't always understand that he had problems, so he couldn't communicate to me why something was happening. As humans, so much of what we do is based on a cumulative evaluation of ourselves, but for Martin nothing cumulative existed. I had to spend a lot of time watching him and guessing at clues to figure out what was going on with him.

With so much for me to manage, at times I felt overwhelmed. I was thankful my mom was there with me during many of those early days. She was such a big help physically and emotionally. Fortunately a lot of people were praying for us in those early days.

One group was the college ministry Martin had worked for when we lived in South Carolina. They had been faithfully praying for Martin since the day they heard about his diagnosis. A few weeks after we returned to the condo, they asked us to come to their training in Atlanta. They wanted Martin to visit with them, so they could see how he was doing. I knew it would do Martin good to see them, so we planned an afternoon trip to the house where they were staying.

We arrived during their lunch break, and they invited us inside. Twenty of Martin's former coworkers were there, and they were glad to see him because they knew he almost didn't make it. But I could also see they were uncomfortable and nervous around him.

Martin was still having difficulty walking. He was still bloated and had that now-familiar dazed look. But he broke into a smile as he looked into all the faces that greeted him. He was not uncomfortable at all. He walked up to his old friends and asked how they were doing, which warmed them up and made them feel more comfortable. We had a really nice visit. Before we left, the director (who happened to be Martin's former boss) stopped us. "We would love to pray for you and have you pray for us, if that's okay."

Martin immediately said yes.

The director sat Martin in a chair, and I sat next to him. The director placed his hands on Martin's shoulders and began to pray. As he prayed, I could hear people weeping. It was one of the most beautiful things I'd ever been a part of, and I was thankful Martin had such godly men who were faithful to pray for him.

But Martin had no idea what was going on. As soon as the first person started crying, Martin peeked at me. Then as a few tears turned to bursts of sobbing, Martin opened his eyes and stared at me. He had no idea why they were weeping. He was completely confused. "What's going on?" he mouthed to me.

Just then, the director finished and asked Martin to pray.

I started chuckling because I knew what Martin was thinking. He was wondering what had happened to this group since he left because it sounded to him like they were all falling apart.

I could hardly sit still, imagining what he was going to pray.

"Well, Lord," he paused. "Um, you know what is truly going on in the hearts of these people. And I, uh, I just pray for whatever is going on with this group." I watched him peek at me. He gave me a helpless shrug and closed his eyes again and kept praying. "I just pray for some of the hard things that they are dealing with right now. In Jesus' name. Amen."

I thanked the director and quickly guided Martin to the car.

"What was going on in there?" he asked. "There were grown men crying!"

"I know," I said, trying to stifle my giggles. "I know."

$\mathscr{L}$

Life continued to move forward and God continued to answer more of our prayers. A few weeks later, when someone unexpectedly offered to buy our condo, we sold it and bought a house in a nearby residential suburb. The house had three bedrooms and a small backyard. Since there were no stairs, Martin found some freedom of movement.

Though his walking had improved, Martin's equilibrium was still an issue, and it affected his balance. Because his center of gravity was off, if he lost his footing, he couldn't prevent himself from falling over. Little things could trip him up, like the threshold between a carpeted floor and a tiled floor, a rug, or steps. A young child learning to walk trips over it the first time and then remembers to slow down and carefully step over it the next time. But with Martin's short-term memory loss, he would forget that he had tripped over something, and he'd fall over it again the next time he passed that same way. So it wasn't Martin's lack of balance that worried me when Martin tried to go up or down stairs; it was that *Martin wasn't concerned* about going up or down stairs.

I couldn't always anticipate what would trip Martin up physically, or for that matter, mentally. So I was constantly learning new ways to prevent him from hurting himself. I was also in denial as to how bad his disability was. But a couple of events brought me back to reality.

We had booked a cruise a year earlier, but because of Martin's health, we had to postpone it several times. We had one last opportunity to take advantage of it, or we would lose our money. I asked my parents if they would travel with us, and they agreed. So we drove to Florida and then set sail for even warmer waters. During dinner the first night of the cruise, Martin needed to use the restroom, which was only about fifty yards away. I didn't think much of it as he excused himself to go. Mom, Dad, and I enjoyed the view and had great conversation while he was gone. But someone noticed Martin seemed to be taking an unusually long time.

Dad got up to check the restroom.

He came back with a worried look on his face. "He's not there."

I got up to check the women's restroom, thinking perhaps he'd gone in the wrong door. "He's not in there either!"

We divided up and headed in three directions to look for Martin, yelling his name when and where it didn't disturb other passengers. After ninety minutes of searching, I was afraid something terrible had happened. When my dad went to notify security, Martin had just arrived there. He'd been wandering around on a different deck. The security team had seen him earlier but had just assumed he was drunk like so many other passengers on the ship. When I finally got to him and asked what happened, he didn't know. He'd taken a wrong turn out of the bathroom and couldn't find his way back to the table.

That was one of the events that changed the way we did things. From then on, we made sure that when we were in a restaurant, we were seated within direct sight of the restrooms, or that someone accompanied Martin and waited outside the door.

Things like this concerned me when Martin's friends from church asked if they could take him on the fall men's retreat. At first I wasn't sure, but his friends were so committed and so convincing that against my better judgment, I finally relented. When they came by the house to pick him up, I reminded them, "It's critical that Martin take his medicine three times a day at the same time every day."

They understood and immediately synchronized their watches and phones by setting the alarms, so that whoever was with Martin would remember that he needed to take his medicine. They promised to take great care of him.

When they brought him home from the weekend, the men were so proud of themselves and how they had taken such great care of Martin. Each time their alarms went off, they would remind Martin to get up from whatever he was doing and go to the bathroom where he could take his meds. But after they left our house, Martin seemed really disoriented. When I checked his pill case, I was appalled to see that half of his meds were still there. Apparently, when the men sent him to the bathroom, he'd gotten distracted and left without taking his medication. I immediately called his doctor, and he helped me figure out what to do.

It was a wake-up call for me. I knew these men. These were three of our closest friends who were keeping an eye on him. They had no idea he wasn't taking his medicine. They just assumed that if he went into the bathroom, that's what he'd do. When they asked him he said yes, because he couldn't remember that he hadn't taken his meds. In the meantime, when he was in the bathroom, he was clipping his nails or washing his hands.

That event helped me understand that I couldn't take my eyes off Martin for a minute, and none of us could trust him to do what we asked of him—he either didn't remember or just said yes to please us. The weekend taught me what I should have already known: I needed to watch him at all times.

It was my *job* to keep Martin alive.

𝒞

It was a terrifying responsibility to make sure Martin didn't hurt himself, that he took his medications on time, and that I anticipated any problems he might have navigating the world with his mental disability. I wanted nothing more than to do it well, to help him get better, but it was hard to manage when it wasn't my only responsibility. I was still a newbie at my worship leader job and I really wanted to do well, especially since it was our main source of income.

Because there wasn't another option, I had to bring Martin to work with me. Since he was now undergoing radiation, he was exhausted all the time. John had a futon in his office, and he brought it into mine so Martin would have a place to sleep. For the first six months, that's mostly what Martin did—sleep.

While he napped, I'd do my work and go to meetings. I always told him when I expected to be back, but sometimes with his memory problems, he'd forget that I'd gone to a meeting. He would wake up and look around.

"Laura? Laura? Where are you?"

When I didn't answer, he would start wandering around the church because he was worried. He stopped other staffers to ask, "Have you seen Laura? I haven't seen her in hours," even if it had only been a few minutes. He couldn't keep track of the passage of time.

Everyone at church knew who he was and what was going on, but the church was so big, he could end up wandering around for a good while before he found me or someone else found him and guided him back to my office.

At times, I left to go to the restroom and I'd be gone less than five minutes, but when I came back, Martin would be gone. Then I would have to go look for him. Other days, I could be in a long meeting and when I got back to the office, he'd say, "Aren't you supposed to go to a meeting?" He didn't realize I'd been gone for a couple of hours.

More than once, Martin would be wandering a hallway and someone would stop him.

"Hey, Martin, do you need something?" they'd ask.

"I can't find Laura, and I'm really worried about her!"

"Let me walk with you down to her office. I bet she's in her office."

If this had happened in any other workplace, it would have been extremely bizarre, but everyone at Perimeter knew us and had prayed for us, and it just was what it was.

After two months of rehab, the doctor called me in for a consultation.

"In some areas Martin is far more advanced than any other brain-injured person we see. His speech has improved dramatically, his balance has stabilized, and his cognitive skills seem to be almost completely back to normal. There is only one area where we don't see improvement—his short-term memory. So we're going to teach him skills for a life without his short-term memory."

The next few months were spent teaching Martin how to use tools to compensate for the things he couldn't remember. When that ended, Martin began radiation five days a week to shrink any residual tumor that was left.

It was clear that Martin wouldn't be able to drive or return to work as he had known it before. He could not remember to take his medications without assistance. Much of Martin was still the same, but so much about him had also changed. Martin and I had to face the reality of the new life that was ahead of us. At this point, neither of us knew what to expect.

$$\mathscr{L}$$

Like many in the church, I grew up believing my faith was only as strong as the number of quiet times I had each week, the number of verses I memorized in a year, and the number of Sundays I attended church. I often heard people talk about how their faith had grown stronger on a mission trip; mine had certainly grown while I was in Mongolia. And in my mind, praying while lying on the couch wasn't as effective as prayer on my knees on a wooden floor at five o'clock in the morning.

But I hadn't done *any* of those things in months. While we were in the hospital, I could add up all the quiet times, verses memorized, and hours spent in prayer or church, and they wouldn't have amounted to much. I was too busy keeping Martin alive to attend a Bible study. My prayers were often nothing more than, *Help me, Lord.* And frankly, *I was the mission trip other people went on.*

But now more than ever, I needed to have strong faith.

How could I find it in my current circumstances?

While meeting God in my brokenness, I'd already discovered that church wasn't what I grew up thinking it was—a building on Sunday mornings. *Was it possible that growing my faith involved something other than the list of to-dos?*

Isaiah 55:11 says that God's Word always does the work he sends it to do: "So is my word that goes out from my mouth: It will not return to me empty, but will accomplish what I desire and achieve the purpose for which I sent it." This can be hard for us to understand because we usually think about doing the work ourselves. But God's light and truth are like twin homing pigeons. When we're down, he sends them out to lead us back to him. Even when we are in a really dark place, God doesn't wait for us to muster up enough belief. To grow our faith, he sends his light and truth to hog-tie us and drag us back into his presence. Strong faith doesn't come from how hard I work.

It's not what I do.

It's what he does.

It is not how strong my *faith* is.

It's how strong my *God* is.

Think of a mother who is crossing a busy street with a toddler. She takes the child's hand and, at first, the child holds on. But somewhere in the middle of the intersection, the energetic toddler lets go and tries to wriggle free. At that moment, the child's safety and security aren't based on how hard the child can hold on—he's already let go. They're based on the strength of the mother's grip and how hard she hangs on to him.

After being in the hospital for so long and then coming home to so many new challenges, it was a relief to know that God's hold on my life wasn't contingent on my hold on him. In those seasons of life when I've been distracted, God has held me that much tighter.

It's never been about how hard I work; it's always been about how hard God hangs on to me.

The strength of our faith rests on the person of our faith. I have a big God, so I have a big faith, even if what I bring to the table is faith the size of a mustard seed. And big faith, strong faith, sure faith, and sustaining faith isn't mustered up. It is a gift from God.

A big, strong, sure, and sustaining God.

Understanding this redefined how I thought about my faith and how God could increase it. I began to approach Scripture with a completely different view.

I didn't have time for an intensive curriculum study or even a consistent quiet time. I was too busy keeping my husband alive. But even in three short minutes, I could open up his Word and read a psalm and pray something as simple as, "God, may your Word take root in my heart. I need you to hold me tight today, to let your Word feed my soul, and sustain me when I am weary."

I didn't have to make it hard or complicated. God's Word was a love letter to me, filled with his promises. In his Word, his light and truth led me into his presence, whether I had three minutes or thirty minutes.

Understanding that faith wasn't about what I did but rather all about what God does meant I could open my Bible and allow him to lead me into his presence. Once I started doing this, I found that occasional reading wasn't enough; I began to crave more of God's presence, even if it was only a few minutes at a time. Soon I was reading Scripture every night before I went to sleep, covering myself with its promises like a warm blanket.

The Bible isn't just a book of clever greeting card slogans and memorable stories. If you're reading your Bible merely for "inspiration" to get you through the day, you are missing the meat of it. There is so much more to be discovered.

Psalm 19 says that God's Word refreshes the soul, makes the simple wise, gives joy to the heart, and gives light to the eyes. It says that God's commands are more precious than gold and sweeter than honey from a honeycomb.

Something supernatural happens when we read God's Word— our faith grows, our doubts fade, and our strength increases to endure our circumstances.

In those early days at home, I believed I had to work to keep Martin alive. And though I once believed I had to work hard to have strong faith, I learned that wasn't true. It was God's gift to me. When I was too busy or too tired to do the spiritual disciplines I'd once pursued, my new response was to stop trying and allow his light and truth to lead me into his presence.

MYTH: THE STRENGTH OF MY FAITH IS BASED ON HOW STRONGLY I BELIEVE.

TRUTH: THE STRENGTH OF MY FAITH IS BASED ON THE STRENGTH OF MY GOD.

NINE

NEW GRIEF

WE HAD A NEW LIFE, BUT WE SOON REALIZED A NEW grief accompanied it. Martin's short-term memory deficit meant he wasn't aware of how long it took to accomplish a task. He would brush his teeth for five minutes and then spend ten minutes deciding on a shirt to wear. It wasn't just that he was moving slower; it was that *he had no concept* of how slow he moved.

We fell into a routine where I did everything for Martin. Because his body temperature failed to work properly, I laid out his clothes every day. If I didn't, he might wear a sweatshirt in the summer or short sleeves in the winter. I reminded him when to take his medicines, and I cooked all his meals. If he had a doctor appointment, I was the one who made it, drove him there, called in the prescriptions when we got home, and picked them up when they were ready.

When Martin's friend Ty wanted to take him to lunch, he would call me to set up the date and time. And on the scheduled day, whether I was at home or at work, I would remind Martin, "Ty's picking you up in an hour." I'd remind him again a half hour later. And then again, fifteen minutes before Ty arrived. When Martin left the house, I was the one who reminded him he needed to wear his watch and take his wallet, and I'd pack any medications he needed to take with him.

I was constantly trying to hold Martin to a schedule he couldn't comprehend. I was exhausted from doing everything for him, while at the same time my professional life that paid the bills was requiring more from me.

The success of "Indescribable" brought invitations to travel and perform concerts, lead worship at other churches, and go on mission trips. About six months after Martin got out of the hospital, I started accepting many of those invitations. I enjoyed leading worship, and it was an opportunity for me to step into my calling. I'd grab a few musicians from Perimeter, and we'd rent a van and drive to a destination, or the church would fly us in. Martin would come along, and while we set up and did sound checks, he would curl up on the back pew and go to sleep. His stamina still wasn't what it used to be.

For the most part, Martin's personality was the same, though he experienced periods when his self-confidence wavered. With his memory deficits, it was hard for him to reconnect with old friends. They would start a conversation and tell Martin what they'd been up to, but the next time Martin saw them, he drew a total blank; he couldn't remember anything they'd said. At parties, when the conversation turned to current events, Martin didn't have anything to add. He may have watched a story about something on the news, but he couldn't remember it long enough to add anything of value. And when he met someone for the second time, he would have forgotten that he'd already been introduced.

It was challenging for him socially.

Martin had always been the life of the party, but now he felt awkward in social situations. Because he was self-conscious, he wanted me to stay near him. I tried to help him join the conversation by saying, "Martin, why don't you tell them about . . ." I would then mention subjects I knew he was comfortable speaking on, but it wasn't the same. Friends have a shared history, and they talk about that history when they get together.

"How did that job interview go?"

"Did you have fun at Myrtle Beach?"

"Remember that time we did that crazy thing?"

But Martin couldn't recall the recent history he'd shared with anyone.

For example, if Martin had lunch with a close friend who'd just lost his job, Martin could really be supportive in that moment. Martin is a good comforter, and he gives great advice. But the next time Martin saw that same friend, he wouldn't remember to ask how the job search was going; or worse, he might ask a really insensitive question because he'd have forgotten that the guy lost his job. Not being able to have those give-and-take conversations hurt Martin's ability to relate to his friends.

When Martin felt loved and accepted, he could still be his old out-going self, but even he recognized that people treated him differently than before he had the brain tumor. I saw it too. It was heartbreaking to watch.

C

One day, we were in the grocery store and Martin was searching for the pickles. Because he doesn't have peripheral vision any longer, it's like he's wearing side blinders. He can only see what's directly in front of him. He also has some double vision and his eyes don't work well together. As a result, he only has 50 percent of the vision that everyone else has.

On that day at the grocery store, he locked in on the pickles and then turned to walk down the aisle. But he didn't see a toddler who was walking with her mother, and he tripped over the little girl.

The mom rolled her eyes and shook her head. "Watch where you're going," she mumbled under her breath.

The store was only a mile away from our church, so I knew there were people in the store who might attend Perimeter. That was the only thing that saved me. I was ready to go from music minister mode to "You want a piece of me, woman?"

Instead of screaming at her in the store, I screamed at her in my head. *How dare you roll your eyes at my husband! Do you have any idea what he's gone through? Do you know what he faces every morning when he wakes up? Try going through what he goes through every day. You wouldn't make it a minute!*

Unfortunately, this wasn't the only time things like this happened. We would be in a fast-food restaurant, and Martin would ask if it cost extra for cheese. Ninety seconds later, he'd ask the same question. The snot-nosed high school kid working the register would say, "I *just* told you, 'It's seventy-five cents extra, if you want cheese.'"

These kinds of public interactions with my husband made me angry. He wasn't stupid; he was brave. Martin woke up each morning not knowing what day it was. And he had to depend on someone else to help him get somewhere because he couldn't drive. By the time he had public interaction, he'd already experienced eight to ten things that had made him feel stupid that day. He didn't need one more. It was heartbreaking to see people treat my husband the way they did. I tried to protect Martin by not putting him in situations where these things could happen.

When Martin first got out of the hospital, he wasn't aware that his new limitations would prevent him from having the same kind of job he used to have. I could have let him go to an interview and fail, but I felt that wasn't the loving thing to do. So we had to have a number of hard conversations. They were hard on him, but they were also hard on me.

Before we got married, our premarital counselor told me, "The whole world could be against your husband, but as long as you are for him, you give him wings. And if the whole world is for him, but you're against him, it's like pouring concrete in his shoes."

I'd always believed it was my job to tell Martin, "You can do anything you want." But now, by telling him he could do anything he wanted, I would set him up with unrealistic expectations. I felt as if I had to protect him by being the one to pour a little concrete in his shoes.

I hoped that would prevent someone else from pouring it into his heart.

$\mathscr{L}$

Martin's life is a series of snapshots. He holds a picture of a moment in his hand, but he doesn't know what came before it or what happens after it. The rest of us live in a movie, rich with context of the scene we're in as well as the scenes that came before and after. Based on what happened in the immediate past, we can easily predict what happens next.

But Martin doesn't have that context. He senses that other people seem to have all this information about life that he doesn't have. So when someone makes him feel that he doesn't get it, it only confirms what he already believes.

That couldn't be further from the truth. Martin's intelligence was still there, even if his memory wasn't. I've talked to a lot of people who've dealt with brain injuries in their families. Though they don't have the exact same disability, Martin is more functional and positive than anyone else I've ever encountered. Many of them describe brain-injured family members who developed addictions to deal with their disability or who suffer from clinical depression. While Martin has experienced moments of depression, he's been spared from long seasons of hopelessness.

But I know it's hard for him. He's lost a lot of things he used to enjoy.

For example, he used to love watching movies, but now he doesn't enjoy them because he has to continually ask me questions. He can't recall what happened earlier in a film, so when the movie ends and everyone talks about the great ending, Martin doesn't have a clue as to *why* it was so great. Before the tumor, he loved to read books. But now he only reads devotional-length materials, and it takes him a long time to get through each one.

We used to enjoy going out to eat, but Martin had trouble deciphering all the choices on the menu. He'd ask dozens of questions, until I'd finally just place the order myself. Over time, I realized that his confusion was the worst at dinnertime—his lowest point of energy for the day. Going out for breakfast became our preferred choice because he was more alert and functioned better in the morning.

ℒ

As a result of his disability, Martin and I were inseparable. Not only was I his wife, but I also functioned as his mom, his life coach, his nurse, his tutor, and the only person who helped him process the reality he faced daily. After months of spending that much time together, Martin and I started to get on each other's nerves. It was more than just the time we spent together—it was because we didn't get any time apart. I hadn't had dinner with a friend since before Martin went to the hospital. Now I was afraid to leave him alone.

On the other hand, Martin felt I was treating him like a child.

And it was true. I *was* treating him like a child.

It wasn't because I didn't love him as a spouse; it was because I felt it was the most pragmatic way to get things done. But I realized it wasn't what was best for Martin.

Martin already felt emasculated, and those feelings were worsened by the fact that he couldn't drive or go anywhere on his own. Therefore, he was completely dependent on me. Add to that little things like having to time his showers and laying out his clothes, as any good mom would do. No wonder he was frustrated with me! I had everything he wanted—I was the breadwinner, I had a career I loved, and I had the freedom to drive anywhere I pleased.

But I was frustrated with him too. He had everything I wanted—

someone else to be the provider and worry about the finances, and the ability to stay home. I was tired of driving everywhere!

We each longed for something we couldn't have. But instead of dealing with it in a healthy way, we blamed each other and our marriage began to suffer. Resentment began to grow. I had no idea how to be supportive without enabling him. But what things were realistic to expect him to do on his own? And what things should I be doing for him? I was exhausted from doing everything for Martin, plus working full-time in ministry. At the same time, I didn't want to offer him false encouragement that would set him up for a big fall.

But I wasn't always doing the best for him. In fact, I was doing a terrible job of equipping Martin to be independent.

We were in a big mess.

The biggest problem was that I couldn't tell anyone we were a mess. My music career was doing so well that it felt as though I was always being put on a pedestal—and not one of my own making. When someone brought me in for an event, I was there to help them. I couldn't tell them how much I needed help. Personally, I felt like a tree whose branches were growing and expanding faster than my roots. I could tell that at any minute the whole thing could topple over.

Fortunately, we had good friends who weren't afraid to jump into the mess we'd made and help us clean it up. Two couples from our church, Bill and Debby Wood, and Carl and Sherri Wilhelm, came highly recommended for mentoring younger couples. Sherri and I became fast friends. Likewise, Bill invited Martin to attend his Friday morning Bible study and was kind enough to pick Martin up at six fifteen every Friday morning. If Martin was running late, Bill would call or honk his horn to help Martin get moving. Sherri and I often met for lunch, and when we got together she'd ask me hard questions like, "Are you spending more time worshipping from the stage or in private?"

Some people thought we were fragile. They treated us as though we had cancer. They would tiptoe around us and murmur under their breath, "Poor Martin and Laura." They'd bring us occasional casseroles or tell us they were praying for us. While we appreciated their prayers and their baked ziti, we didn't need their pity.

Bill and Sherri weren't like that. They were the kind of friends who were brave enough to be honest with us. They weren't afraid to call us out when they saw something they didn't agree with—and the more they got to see of our marriage, the more they had to call us out.

As soon as Sherri saw how I was treating Martin, she told me I needed to stop.

"Martin needs to have more independence," she said. "You're treating him like a child."

"I'm so afraid he will fail, though, and I don't want that to happen."

"So what?" she said. "If he fails, he fails."

"Yeah, but I don't want him to get hurt."

"Maybe *you* don't want to get hurt," she challenged me. "Maybe it's hard for you to see him get hurt. But that's life. We're all going to get hurt, and without pain he won't grow. He needs to be independent. *You* need him to be more independent. Could it be that God is writing his story in Martin's life and that *you're* standing in the way?"

We needed a change. We wouldn't stay married if we continued doing things the same way. So with Martin in agreement, we began the difficult process of breaking the destructive patterns we'd formed in our marriage.

Instead of trying to hold Martin to a schedule he had trouble following, I started making lists and taping them to his bathroom mirror. That way, Martin could check off each task as he accomplished it. Together, the lists combined into a routine he could use to judge how far he had to go rather than how much time he'd taken. He could then use those routines to move from the shower, to brushing his teeth, to picking out his clothes. Whenever he left the house, we put together a list of things he needed to take with him and put it on his dresser so he'd remember his wallet and watch. But perhaps the hardest part for me was letting him take responsibility for his own schedule.

The next time Ty called to set up lunch, I handed the phone to Martin. When they hung up, I reminded Martin to put it on his calendar, but I didn't double-check to make sure he'd done it. At 11:50 on Wednesday morning, I looked up from my computer. Martin was still in his pajamas. It felt heartless not to remind him, but we'd already agreed he needed to learn how to take responsibility for his own calendar. So I kept quiet.

When Ty showed up, Martin wasn't ready to go.

"Why didn't you remind me?" he asked.

"Because you need to learn how to do this yourself."

It was hard to say to my brain-injured husband that I wasn't going to help him remember things anymore. It was like letting your child leave home before you think they are ready. I wanted to do everything I could for him to make sure he was as successful as he could be. But as I would soon learn, I was the one holding him back.

Fortunately, we had friends like Bill whose wisdom showed me how wrong I was. When I didn't think Martin could manage getting ready for his Friday morning Bible study on his own, Bill believed he could. And though it was hard for me to watch because I was afraid Martin would fail, Bill was willing to patiently walk him through the process. He started by telling Martin he would be in the driveway at six fifteen on Friday morning. If Martin wasn't there, he was no longer going to call or text him. Instead, he would wait three minutes and then he would leave.

The first Friday that Bill drove off without Martin was hard on everyone. Martin woke up late to see that he had missed Bible study. Since Bible study was the only thing he was doing at the time, it would now be another week before he had an opportunity to socialize with his friends. I could see how down in the dumps he was and I hurt for him. I so badly wanted to set my alarm for the following Friday to make sure he got up, but Bill encouraged us both not to let that happen.

Missing Bible study the week before was all the motivation Martin needed. When I woke up the following Friday morning, Martin's side of the bed was empty. He had made it to Bible study on his own!

Bill had been right. Martin was capable of doing it on his own, though it took a lot of work on Martin's part. Starting the day before, he had to think about setting his alarm and making sure he had everything ready for the next day. But Martin could do it.

More importantly, Bill helped me to see that when I tried to keep Martin from failing, I was also preventing him from growing. To really love Martin, I had to let him make mistakes and learn from them. When I was weak, Bill helped me to stick to the plan, and Martin eventually got better at mastering his own schedule. Though it was hard work for everyone involved—especially Martin—I have to admit, I never would have attempted it without Bill's encouragement. Though there are still dark mornings when Martin has to chase Bill's taillights down the street, Martin has been able to gain another level of independence.

Bill became a blessing to both of us. He took over having some of the hard conversations with Martin that I'd been having and had some hard ones with me that I needed to hear. Sometimes it's easier to hear something from a brother who loves you than it is to hear the same thing from your spouse. Bill tried to help us keep our marriage sacred and set apart from the other things we were adjusting to in our daily lives.

We were surviving, but barely.

C

After the initial flurry of activity in the first year, the second and third years seemed to crawl by. The exhaustion became a chronic weariness. Each day was a painful reminder of how much our lives had changed, and I began to mourn the deaths of all we'd lost.

When Martin and I said, "I do," we set out on a boulevard of marital bliss. Then came a bumpy detour called "Brain Tumor." We took the detour and followed its winding ways. But I kept thinking the detour would take us back to the main road. It took me several years to realize that it wasn't a detour; it was the *road*. It was taking us farther away from anything familiar and would never lead us back to the boulevard of dreams where we started.

Martin and I had only planned to stay in Atlanta for two years. In fact, we were so sure we'd be back in Spartanburg that we'd almost rented our house instead of selling it. Now those two years had passed without any of the gains we'd expected. Martin didn't have a graphic design degree or the job he'd planned to get in South Carolina after graduation. Instead, I had a job in Atlanta and Martin had doctors he couldn't leave. There was no way we could move back to Spartanburg now. I had to let that dream go.

I had to reconsider other dreams. Our parents had always been our role models—both our dads worked outside the home while our moms took care of their homes and children. That was our dream too. I'd always wanted to be a stay-at-home mom. Now my only option was to be a working mom. I didn't know what that would look like, or even if I could do it.

How disabled was too disabled to start a family?

And when I said disabled, I didn't mean Martin; I meant *our marriage*.

Martin and I both wanted kids, but we weren't great at being a couple. Martin's brain had a disability, but our marriage was the thing that was truly disabled. How could we bring kids into such an environment? Even if we were going to have kids, it would take a miracle. My clock was ticking, and I knew the chances of us having biological kids were slim. I also thought we might be terrible candidates for adoption because of Martin's tumor.

Everyone around us was having kids. I envied them—they had the life I wanted. But there wasn't anything I could do about it. I began praying about whether God wanted us to have kids. When he finally answered, his answer seemed clear.

℃

Two years out from Martin's surgery and my gut-wrenching prayers for God to spare my husband's life, we went on a cruise with friends. Late one night, standing on the deck alone, I prayed to God to allow us someday to have children.

His reply was a question: *If I called you to a life without children, would a loving marriage be enough?*

The question was a good one, and I answered it as honestly as I could.

It would. And if it's not now, I think it could be.

If I called you to stay how you are right now, will you be content, or will there always be something else you want?

The Lord wanted me to look honestly at my discontent, and he was telling me I could spend a thousand years learning how to love Martin, and I still wouldn't do it well. For the rest of our lives, the two of us would experience new ways of honoring, respecting, and loving each other like God loves us. God reminded me that Martin *was* my family. We were also blessed with other family, like our friends whose kids called me Aunt Laura.

Despite the fact that Martin and I had to let go of our dreams and let them die, I knew we were where God wanted us. It's always hard to let go of a dream. But what did I have to complain about? I'd prayed for Martin to live and he had, when a lot of husbands didn't survive similar medical situations.

I accepted God's plan for us and chose to move forward. I didn't want to talk about it further, even when Martin tried several times to get me to open up. I was proud, and I wanted people to think I had it all under control. The people at church had spent months helping us, and now my job was to help others. I just wanted to move on.

Though we tried our best, you don't move on from a brain tumor.

Not long after we returned from the cruise, our car broke down and we had to replace it. By this time, we'd let go of the idea of having a minivan full of kids. So Martin and I agreed to get the most non-child-friendly car we could find—a MINI Cooper. It didn't replace the children we wanted, but it was a start in welcoming whatever God had in store for the two of us.

Despite every dream we let go, we still believed that God was good. And that he was *for* us.

And eventually, that's what would change us.

℃

We often think about worship as the songs we sing in church, but the truth is that worshipping God is about surrender. Surrendering to God's will when it doesn't match ours or when we're too impatient to wait for him. Surrendering that which is most important to us. And surrendering our personal story to live out our part in God's greater story. Worship is surrendering everything for God, valuing God so much that we're willing to let everything else go.

If you want to see a life full of lessons on surrender, look no further than Abraham. He was selected to lead a nation of chosen people who were beloved by God. But for Abraham to be that leader, God asked him to leave his country, his people, and his family. He trusted God in that moment and did as God asked. But not long afterward, while Abraham and his wife, Sarah, were traveling, he was asked if Sarah was his wife. "No, she's my sister," he said. While it was technically true that they shared a father, Abraham was lying to protect himself. He had stopped letting go.

Despite Abraham's sins, God still promised to protect Abraham and even reward him for his faith. But Abraham was consumed by the fact that he and Sarah didn't have children. He knew Sarah was too old to give birth, so when she suggested that he visit her maidservant to have a child through her, Abraham agreed to help God by helping himself. Once again, despite Abraham's sin, God was faithful to his promise. Sarah gave birth to Isaac. So when God asked Abraham to sacrifice the gift of his son, Isaac (Gen. 22:2), it was Abraham's chance to show us what he'd learned.

In Genesis 22:3, we see that *Abraham got up early*. He went to the mountain and prepared to sacrifice the child he loved dearly. After a lifetime of learning who God is, Abraham finally surrendered himself in obedience. He stopped insisting that he write his own life story and instead sacrificed his desires to God. He was willing to obey, because he understood that worshipping the Giver was greater than worshipping the gift he'd been given. His most faith-filled moment involved letting something go.

What have you had to let go?

Maybe it was something tangible, like your dream car or that house in the ideal subdivision where all the happy people hold entertaining parties. Maybe, like me, you longed to have children and you couldn't. Or you envisioned staying home with your children but ended up having to work. Maybe you gave up your career for someone else. Perhaps someone has disappointed you—a husband who cheated, a wife who strayed, a child who rebelled—and you fear you will never have the life you desired. Maybe your marriage isn't what you expected and you've had to sacrifice the dreams you had on your wedding day. Maybe it's your opinion of yourself—you're so afraid of failure that you fail to live.

What is your Isaac that God is calling you to sacrifice?

For me, it was Martin's healing. For a long time, I wanted him to have his memory and vision restored; I wanted him to be able to drive, for us to have two or three kids and a house with a picket fence. I wanted to be one of those moms who saw new recipes on Pinterest, tried them, and then blogged about it. I wanted assurance that Martin's tumor would never come back. I didn't want to wait for the results of another MRI ever again. I didn't want to face the thought of doing everything we'd already done a second time and ending up in a worse place.

It took me a long time to let go of all that, and as I write these words, I can't promise you I am all the way there—yet.

There is something we're all struggling to let go of. God is stirring something in our hearts and encouraging us to trust him. Maybe he wants us to surrender it, to loosen our grip, and allow him to take it.

As Martin and I live out God's plan for our lives, we've had to let go of many of our dreams. But we believe that God's plan is better, that his timing is perfect, and with that trust and confidence, we want to sacrifice our dreams when he asks—even the most painful ones.

We don't gain God's blessings by hanging on.

We gain them by letting go.

And when we gain them, that's when we can use them to bless others.

No matter what God asks, I pray that my hands are open and my grip is loose. *Take what you will. And what you bless me with, I will use to bless others.*

I pray that prayer for you too.

MYTH: I GAIN BY HOLDING ON.

TRUTH: I GAIN BY LETTING GO.

······················ **TEN** ······················

WHY?

QUESTIONS AND DOUBTS PLAGUE MY MIND MORE THAN I care to admit. The single word *why* haunts me the most. Like a stuck needle on a vinyl record, there are days when it replays over and over again. In those dark moments when I am obsessed with finding out why, I'm sure that if I just had an answer to my question, I'd feel better. Even on those occasions when I do get an answer, it rarely leads to satisfaction and always leads to more questions.

I'm not the only one who feels this way. Everyone wants to know why bad things happen. When I lead worship at a church or perform in a concert, hurting people come up afterward and share their stories with me. And each person's story comes with its own list of unanswered whys. Here are some I've heard dozens, and in some cases hundreds, of times:

"Why did my husband commit suicide?"

"Why did my daughter die so young?"

"Why did he start using drugs?"

"Why can't I have children?"

"Why was he born disabled?"

"Why did she get sick?"

"Why did I lose my job?"

"Why did she betray me?"

"Why did he molest my child?"

In the midst of broken circumstances, we ask why. We're not the first to ask, and we won't be the last. Ever since God gave us the ability to ask questions, we've been asking that question of him.

"Why, God, why?"

For many, the only thing they hear when they ask God why is silence. They feel alone and abandoned. Sometimes they grow angry and bitter at what seems to be his lack of response. When I meet those people, I think how wonderful it would be if we could meet God at Starbucks and, over a muffin and latte, ask him all our questions and clearly hear his answers.

While there were no lattes in the ancient world, there was a group of men who broke bread with God in the flesh. These men could ask Jesus any question they wanted. *Why* was a question that came up often. One of my favorite question-and-answer sessions is found in the Gospel of John. It took place as Jesus was leaving the temple, running from Pharisees who planned to stone him. While on the run:

> As he passed by, he saw a man blind from birth. And his disciples asked him, "Rabbi, who sinned, this man or his parents, that he was born blind?" (John 9:1–2 ESV)

Blindness was common at that time and still is in some areas of the Near East where they don't have access to modern medicine. Unsanitary living conditions and poor hygiene can be contributing causes to blindness at birth, which is why we give babies antiseptic eye drops to prevent the spread of gonorrhea of the eyes from mother to baby. But in those days, blindness was considered punishment for a sin that the blind person or his parents had committed. Blind men were considered defective and could not be priests, and blind animals couldn't be offered as sacrifices.

There were no cures for blindness and no social programs to help the vision impaired with basic life or job skills. Blind people were sentenced to a life of begging—hence, the term "blind beggars." It's likely that ever since he was old enough to beg, the blind man had been sitting outside of the temple waiting for people to drop coins in his tin cup.

But there was also another form of blindness that was much more prevalent—spiritual blindness. Though the Pharisees were well educated in religion, they were blind to the fact that Jesus was the Son of God—the long-awaited Messiah. Since they were the ones charged with enlightening the people on religious matters, their lack of spiritual insight affected the entire region. This is why Jesus referred to the Pharisees as the "blind guides" of the blind (Matt. 15:14; 23:16).

So it's ironic that while Jesus is running from a group of spiritually blind men, he takes interest in a physically blind man. When the disciples notice Jesus regarding the blind man, they take the opportunity to ask Jesus a why question.

"Why was this man born blind?"

Their curiosity wasn't about the man's physical state or why bad things happen. The disciples were decidedly less compassionate. They wanted to know where to place the blame. Was it this man or his parents who sinned? Who was at fault for this man's life sentence?

Put yourself in the sandals of the blind man. He was sitting outside the temple, and he knew their question was directed at him. He'd heard it before. It always sounded like an accusation targeted directly at his heart. Maybe he was angry with the templegoers who had theological debates about him rather than opening their hearts (and wallets) and showing compassion. Maybe the blind man didn't even care about answers anymore. Maybe he was convinced he would never understand why he'd been born blind.

What would you have done if you were the blind man and you heard the disciples ask that question about you? Would you be ashamed of your unknown sin? Humiliated? Would you have felt frustrated—or angry? Would you crouch a little lower or maybe raise your tin cup a little higher, hoping that since the disciples took notice, they'd also help out?

Perhaps you know exactly what you would do in the blind man's situation because you're in it now. You have a debilitating medical condition, a child with a disability, a breakup, or a home without children, and you've been asking *why*. Worse, you've had to explain your broken situation to friends, family members, and even strangers who want to know how you got that way. For years, you've tried to assign blame or place fault on someone or something else while secretly fearing that maybe your sin caused your brokenness. In those difficult moments, public questions leave you with a deeper sense of shame, humiliation, and anger.

This passage grips my heart. I know what it feels like to have religious people ask those kinds of questions about Martin. Whether they mean to or not, they essentially blame him for his brokenness. Even when their questions are covered in Christian language, the implications are hurtful.

"Have you guys *really* prayed about this?"

"Have you prayed *in faith* for him to be healed?"

They imply that we haven't prayed long or hard enough, used the right words, or sufficiently trusted God, and that's why Martin wasn't healed. In those moments, I want to respond, "Oh, faith! That's a great idea! We should try that. Until now, we've haven't been praying *in faith*, we've been praying in the sandbox!"

More times than I can count, we've been at a church, and I've shared a bit about what Martin and I have gone through. Afterward, someone will come up and say, "Before you leave, we'd love to pray for you and your husband."

Martin is such a man of faith that he always says, "That would be great."

But I know what's coming.

They encircle us and start praying, and then someone says, "Lord, if there is any unconfessed sin in Martin's life that might have caused this to happen . . ."

Martin is then forced to wrack his injured brain for sins he might have committed and hadn't confessed. It seems so cruel to make him go through that.

It's also poor theology.

I've read this passage in John 9 many times, but the first time I read this passage after Martin's surgeries, I read it with fresh anticipation.

> "Neither this man nor his parents sinned," said Jesus, "but this happened so that the works of God might be displayed in him. As long as it is day, we must do the works of him who sent me. Night is coming, when no one can work. While I am in the world, I am the light of the world." (vv. 3–5)

Jesus was clear. Neither the man's nor his parents' sin caused the blindness. Not only was this theologically groundbreaking, but it was also personally liberating! Imagine the deep sense of relief the blind man must have had to hear that neither he nor his parents caused his blindness. Jesus wanted the disciples, the blind man, and the religious leaders listening to his conversation to know that it wasn't one person's specific sin that caused this man's hopeless situation.

Now hang with me here. The next part of the passage can be confusing, so it's important to understand the nuances of the translation.

If you read the sentence as "Neither this man nor his parents sinned, but this happened so that the works of God might be displayed in him," you might come up with the wrong impression. Jesus was not saying the man was born blind so God's glory could be displayed in him. In the original language the phrase, "so that the works of God . . ." precedes the next verse. There are eleven uses of this kind of phrase in the Gospel of John, and at least four of them precede the main sentence rather than follow it. Scholars believe this sentence should follow that pattern, so it should be read as: "'Neither this man nor his parents sinned,' said Jesus. 'But so that the work of God might be displayed in his life, we must do the work of him who sent me while it is still day.'"

As *The NIV Application Commentary* explains, "The purpose clause now explains that Jesus must work *so that* God's work may be displayed in this man's life. God had not made the man blind in order to show his glory; rather, God has sent Jesus to do works of healing in order to show his glory. The theological nuance of the two translations cannot be more different."

Jesus was clear that neither this man's nor his parents' sin caused his blindness.

But neither did God cause it.

Two thousand years later, we now know the man's blindness was likely caused by unsanitary conditions and could have been prevented if antiseptic drops were available when he was born. Sickness and disease are consequences of the fall—a result of humanity's sin. There weren't unsanitary conditions in the garden. It was only after Adam and Eve sinned and were forced out of the garden that the earth began to decay and sickness and disease entered the world.

Romans 5:12 tells us, "Sin entered the world through one man, and death through sin, and in this way death came to all people, because all sinned." When man sinned, everything changed. Creation, though still made in the image of God, became marred, and we now see God's image in a dim reflection of what it used to look like. But this is why Jesus came back and will come back again—for the redemption of all things. There will be no more cancer, no more blindness, no more pain, tears, or unemployment. Addictions will be gone, depression won't last, breakups won't happen, and children will all be born healthy. God sent Jesus not only to redeem people but to redeem all things. So just as Jesus came to heal our broken relationship with God, he also came to heal the consequences of the broken world we live in.

That's why Jesus had such a sense of urgency to heal the hurting. Life was hopeless and dark for those who couldn't physically see. Life was even more hopeless and dark for those who couldn't see God.

Jesus had not only the power but also the compassion to bring his healing light into the darkness of both impairments. His primary

role was to heal our broken relationship with God—to bring us out
of spiritual darkness. But as we saw earlier, the spiritually blind
Pharisees refused to believe in his divinity. To prove he was there to
do his Father's work, Jesus demonstrated God's power by healing the
physically blind.

> After saying this, he spit on the ground, made some mud with
> the saliva, and put it on the man's eyes. "Go," he told him, "wash
> in the Pool of Siloam" (this word means "Sent"). So the man
> went and washed, and came home seeing. (John 9:6–7)

Healing the physically blind without modern medicine (perhaps
even with modern medicine) was something that only God could do
(Ex. 4:11; Ps. 146:8). Ancient prophecies revealed that the Messiah
would heal the blind (Luke 4:18), and this miracle was evidence that
Jesus was who he said he was. Jesus also offered his physical healings
as proof to John the Baptist that he was the Messiah (Matt. 11:2–6).
He was living out the prophecies.

You should read the rest of John 9 and the beginning of chapter
10. It's grand theater! After Jesus' powerful manifestation of God's
power, the once-blind man, who now could see, tried to describe
Jesus, the man who healed him, though he'd never physically laid
eyes on Jesus. With the realization that the blind beggar had vision,
the spiritually blind Pharisees interrogated him to find out how this
miracle could have happened, though they themselves were blind to
recognize Jesus' power. It was like an ancient version of the old com-
edy routine, "Who's on first?"

I don't want to laugh at the Pharisees' blindness. I want to learn
from it. At times, we also can be the ones who are blind to God's
presence and power.

For those of us with *why* questions, we can stop the story here
with the comfort of knowing that Jesus wasn't accusing anyone of the
blind man's physical defect. Instead, he was all about healing it. Jesus

came to restore both physically and relationally what had been lost in the fall. This gives me great peace about Martin's condition, and it should give you peace about your situation too.

The answer to our whys may be obvious now, or they may never be answered in our lifetime. But even if we knew why, it's likely we wouldn't be satisfied with the answers anyway.

We ask God why, believing the answer will provide us with some kind of deep soul satisfaction. But too often, we don't get the answer we want. I don't think that means we should give up asking questions; we just need to understand their role in our brokenness.

Questions can be a great help in mourning our loss, communicating our frustration, and expressing our feelings. We belong to an almighty, transcendent, yet approachable God who loves hearing our questions. Our questions are important to him, and the Scriptures are full of hurting people asking questions. Look at the Psalms. David wrote many of them when he was broken; and, in them, he poured out some painful and intimate questions. Sometimes David got answers. Sometimes he got silence. But even when David's questions weren't answered, his faith in God was stronger than his need to know.

Just like David, my why questions allow me to go before my heavenly Father and pour out my heart to him. They help me process what I am going through.

What are some of your why questions?

Have you ever talked to God about them?

I want you to take a minute, set this book down, and get a pen and piece of paper. Then I want you to write down all your why questions. Start with "Why did this happen?" or "Why me?" Then get more specific. Try to remember each of those why questions that kept you awake at night. For some of you, it may be a single why question that has plagued you for years. For others, it may be a long list of whys that have changed as often as your circumstances. Don't try to answer them until you have exhausted your list of questions.

But stop and do it now.

I'll wait right here until you get back.

Did you make a list?

How did it feel to write down your why questions?

Was it a relief, or did it make you angry to put your whys on paper?

Were your why questions answered? Or did most of your questions go unanswered?

Yeah, me too.

It's important to know that nowhere does the Bible promise that all our questions will be answered this side of heaven. God doesn't promise our stories will make sense in and of themselves. But he does promise they will find their greater purpose in light of his greater story of redemption.

If I am honest, I find that as I look at my list, there is a sense of peace that comes from owning my own why questions. But at the same time, I've discovered that the longer I focus on why, the less progress I make. When I continue to ask why, somewhere deep inside me the repeated questioning and lack of answers feeds a sense of entitlement. When that sense of entitlement grows, it usually leads to bitterness.

But there is an alternative.

The disciples asked, "Why was this man born blind?" In this question, they were asking *why* for all of us. But in his answer, Jesus didn't respond directly to the why. Instead, he changed the *why* question to *how*. "Neither this man nor his parents sinned," said Jesus, "but this happened so that the works of God might be displayed in him" (John 9:3). How might this man's blindness be used to reveal the work of God?

Just as surely as he turned water into wine, Jesus turned the disciples' blame-seeking *why* question into a God-seeking *how* question.

Man asks why.

Jesus asks how.

Man asks, "Why did this happen?"

Jesus asks, "How might my Father's glory be displayed through this situation?"

The answer to why doesn't help us heal. But knowing that God's glory can be displayed, even in the brokenness of our lives, gives us hope despite our circumstances. I promise you will find more purpose and joy in your life if you set aside the why and begin to ask how.

How does my story fit into God's greater story of redemption?

Even when we can't immediately see how our story fits into God's story of redemption, Scripture promises that it always does.

In the Bible, I see a picture of all things working together for good—a good that, frankly, I sometimes don't understand. Somehow God mourns the death of a three-year-old, yet he also uses that sweet baby's death to bring glory to himself. If you don't understand how he can do both, well, join the club. I don't know either. But that's because I am looking at it from my perspective. Without seeing from God's perspective, I can't answer how that story or any other story, including mine, fits into his overall story.

But the Bible does reveal to us that sometimes God uses things he hates—things like cancer, divorce, suicide, addiction, death, and more—to accomplish the things he loves. He does this regularly and faithfully. It's only when we bring our pain to him that we can find our dwelling in him.

However, when we play the blame game, we're focusing on everyone but him.

Let me give you an example from my own life. My friend Shea is the kind of healthy person who eats only free-range, vegan, grass-fed, organic food. About a year ago, she was diagnosed with cancer. She's thirty-six. She has four kids. And her husband works at a church. When she was diagnosed, my first reaction was, *Why her?*

I can give you two reasons.

One is because sin entered the world, and it looks like cancer.

The second is that even though God hates cancer, it can be used to reveal his glory.

Those whys aren't easy to accept, but it is in the hows of her story that I find hope.

Every time my friend goes through one of her chemotherapy treatments, she depends on God's strength to help her get through. That is when I see his power to overcome cancer. When she smiles and laughs, even though I know she's in pain, I see God's peace and love shining through her eyes. When I watch her faith grow despite her trials, I marvel at how God never leaves us alone and is always drawing us closer. A month after she was diagnosed, she came to the hotel where I was staying and sat by the pool. She told me that her marriage was better than it had been in years—the trials had brought them closer. God uses even cancer to strengthen marriages and to remind us how precious our families are.

If I were stuck asking *why* this happened to her, I'd never see *how* God was working through her. The same is true for you. If you made a list of why questions before, I want you to turn that page over and make a new list. A list of how questions. Maybe you've never thought of how God could use what you're going through for his glory. Maybe this is new to you. If so, let me help get you started by giving you a few questions:

How might God use your current trial to glorify himself?

How might God use your weakness, infirmity, or disability to display his power?

How might God use your hard circumstances to show you something about himself?

How might God use your hard circumstances to show you something about yourself?

How might God use your pain for a purpose?

How might God make this mess into a message?

How might God use your current chaos to make you into a man or woman who walks by faith, not by sight?

How might God use your situation to show you that true peace is found only in him?

How might God use an untimely death to stir the hearts of others and show them the importance of eternal security in the life to come?

Take a moment and ask God for wisdom in writing your own how list. Refer back to your why questions for inspiration if necessary, but know that your questions and answers may be incomplete or even unsatisfying. I'll be right here when you finish.

Now look over your why list and your how list. Which questions have more answers? Which answers do you have more control over? Does one side of the sheet bring more meaning and purpose to your broken story?

Some of you can't even think about how yet, and that's okay. Stay in why as long as you need to. But when you get to a place or time when you feel that your why questions are unproductive, try coming back to this chapter and listing your how questions.

I'm not saying you're more spiritual if you get to how, but I am saying that the why questions will eventually suck you dry, slowly draining the life out of you. I know this from talking to and observing those who are stuck in the past. They can't understand why a good, holy God has allowed something bad to happen to them.

What I want to gently tell them is that God doesn't owe us an explanation this side of heaven. There's nothing in Scripture that tells us we're entitled to an answer. It's not that God is secretive and doesn't want us to know; it's that we're incapable of seeing the big picture.

You can sit around and ask, *Why me?* for the rest of your life, and no one can do much about it. In fact, after hearing some of the stories I've heard, I want to say, "I get it. If your story happened to me, I might want to go sit in a closet and be bitter at God, too, because that one's a doozy!"

But I also know that staying stuck in the why, or worse, running away from God, only brings more pain and sorrow. You have to run *to him*. You have to believe his promises in the midst of your hard situation because not only is that the only thing that will bring you hope, it's the only thing that will save your life. When people go through the kind of heartache you or someone you know is going through, the only other response is to slip away into isolation and wait until the evil one eats you alive.

We have to come to a point where we say, "I don't know why my life looks this way. But I don't have to understand why. It's enough for me to believe that God has a plan and that he has promised he will never leave or forsake me, and he will be by my side through every trial I face." I know this counters everything we think we want, but there is freedom in not having all of the answers—especially the answer to why.

I met a woman once who was married for twenty years to an unfaithful husband before they divorced. She spent the next two decades asking why and being bitter toward God. Twenty years after her divorce, she still had no answers—only bitterness. But now, she has lost forty years of her life to the jerk she married. How would her life have been different after her divorce if she'd moved from why to how?

Our faithful and compassionate God allows us to ask any question we want no matter how difficult. Don't lose another day of your life asking unproductive why questions. When the time is right, move forward by asking how.

I'll confess there are lots of why questions that I am still holding on to. I'm not perfect in this area. But the one question I've never asked is, *Why me?* Or, *Why did Martin get a brain tumor?*

My thought has always been, *Why not me? Why not Martin?*

The reason I've never asked that particular why question is not because I'm superspiritual. It's because I've heard too many stories about things other people are going through, and many of them sound much worse than our difficulties. My mentor Sherri often says, "If everyone got together and put their problems in a bowl, I'd rather leave with my own problems instead of taking on someone else's." In fact, if you and I were trading problems, I'd ask for mine back. Maybe that's because despite the sin and brokenness in this world, God is good. He knows what, with his help, we can handle and where we most need to see his work.

It's easy to sign up for a short-term mission project or donate money to a building campaign at church. And it's true; we can see God working in those places. But would you be willing to sign up for the brokenness in your life, if you knew your brokenness would bring glory to God and enable you to learn to trust him in everything?

We're tempted to measure our circumstances on the world's scale, but God's economy uses God-sized scales. His story is so much bigger than ours, and one day when we see it in totality, we'll have all the answers we desire.

MYTH: CONTENTMENT BEGINS WITH UNDERSTANDING WHY.

TRUTH: CONTENTMENT BEGINS WITH ASKING HOW GOD MIGHT USE THIS FOR HIS GLORY.

ELEVEN

RECORD EMOTIONS

MY FIRST SUNDAY BACK AT PERIMETER WAS HARD. Worship was something my soul desperately needed, yet I felt less adequate than ever to lead it. As I began my preparations, I looked at all the songs I'd loved singing so much before Martin's surgery. They were all upbeat and fun songs celebrating God's goodness. My heart sank. I didn't feel like singing any of them.

How am I supposed to lead worship when my own life is such a mess? How do I stand in front of the congregation and sing about how great God is when I don't feel like he's been great to me? Can I sing songs that I'm not sure I believe?

Alone in my office, I struggled to get the lyrics out of my mouth. On some level, I did believe that God was great and deserving of all our praise. But I just didn't *feel* it. It was hard to praise God when Martin and I felt so broken.

While I understood there had to be a way to reconcile God's goodness and sovereignty with our broken dreams, at the time, I didn't know how to lead the church in singing a song I didn't feel. So I did the only thing I could. I scratched it off the set list and put "Mighty to Save" in its place.

Fortunately, I worked with a staff of caring people who saw my struggles and met me there. "It's okay," said one wise friend and co-worker. "You don't have to sing that song in every season of your life. Put it away for now, and one day you'll feel like pulling it back out." I was thankful for her understanding, but I wasn't as confident as she was. I didn't know if I would ever be able to sing about God's greatness again.

"Mighty to Save" was a popular song at the time, and it was something I truly believed—that God was mighty to save. He'd saved me from my sins, and he'd saved Martin's life more than once. As I led worship that Sunday, I closed my eyes and let the music wash over me like a prayer. With my back to the choir and my face to the congregation, I soaked up the sounds of the worshippers on the stage and in the pews, and I begged God to fill my life with hope, peace, and a sense of purpose. On that Sunday, and so many Sundays afterward, the words of that song became my prayer.

A worship leader's job is to stand in front of the church and lead the congregation in a time of praise and worship. To do that well, a worship leader must be the *lead worshipper*, praising God with all that he or she is. That was my problem.

I found it difficult to worship God when things were hard at home. It felt disingenuous to lead the congregation to a place where I had trouble going myself. If I didn't genuinely feel a particular phrase in a selected song, I left that song off the rotation list. I wanted to be authentic in leading the congregation in what I believed. If I didn't feel it, I didn't sing it.

$\mathscr{L}$

My lack of desire to worship God and my job as a worship leader collided on a whole new level when I received an unexpected phone call from a music executive at a record label. It was the same executive who'd contacted me around the time of Martin's diagnosis. He had wanted to sign me to a record deal then but, for obvious reasons, I'd turned them down.

"I'm going to be in Atlanta next week," he said, "and I want to talk with you about a project."

Martin and I were now entangled in the messiest and most confusing time of our married life. I didn't have time for a project. I was too busy trying to do my job and take care of Martin. But for reasons I still don't understand, I agreed. A week later, Martin and I sat across the table from James Rueger, head of the A&R department from Fair Trade Services (formerly known as INO Records), at Macaroni Grill.

"I see your gifting, and I think that what's happening in your life is an extraordinary story that the Lord is using," James said. "I'd like for you to do an album of worship songs."

I choked on my rigatoni.

"You've got to be kidding," I said, wiping off the marinara sauce that dripped from my chin.

"No, I'm not," James said emphatically. "I think now is the time for you to take things to the next level and start a national ministry—and it all begins with an album."

"Look, I'm not sure what you see in me, but my life is complete chaos. Even if you thought I was a good candidate for this before, I'm not now. Ever since my husband's surgery, my faith is dust. I don't even know what I believe anymore."

James leaned in and said, "At the end of the day, you need to do what is best for your family. But let me ask you this: What if God is calling you to write worship songs in the midst of your trials?"

"That's a great idea!" Martin chimed in. All of a sudden it was two against one.

What if the album I did was about how to worship in the midst of brokenness?

"It's not like I have the time, even if I wanted to do that," I said, knowing I *didn't* want to do that.

"I'm just asking you to pray about it. Maybe try writing some lyrics or music," James said.

When I didn't feel like praising God personally, it was a hundred times harder to lead a congregation. The thought of writing and singing worship songs on an album, which would have to be promoted by doing concerts, was even more daunting. It seemed ludicrous that the worse things got in our personal lives, the more I was pursued to launch a national ministry.

While I appreciated the offer, emotionally I was spent. The thought of mustering up the emotions needed to write and sing an album full of worship songs seemed beyond my capabilities. As the meeting ended, I promised I would pray about it.

Driving home after the meeting, I thought about all the reasons that doing an album was a bad idea. The timing for a project like this was wrong, not only because I was busy trying to keep things together at home, but also because our story wasn't finished. We didn't have a happy ending. I'd been in church long enough to know that no one gives their testimony in the *middle* of their trials. They always wait until their trials are over and things turn out well before they speak or sing about it in public. If they hadn't overcome their own trials and brokenness, then how could they encourage or inspire others to do the same?

If Martin had been miraculously healed, I would have loved to do a worship album and sing praises from stage about how great our God is. But the doctor had just informed us there was no end in sight. We'd always be in the middle of our struggle—Martin would have to endure the side effects of his brain surgery forever. While we had faith that God could heal him, that healing hadn't come yet. There was no *after* in our story. We didn't have a resolution, and there was no happy ending.

Our happy boat had sailed.

Personally, I wasn't even sure I believed the songs I sang while leading worship at Perimeter. The thought of increasing my audience by doing an album seemed like a terrible idea when I wasn't comfortable worshipping privately or leading certain songs publicly.

God, I want to worship you, but how do I do that on days I don't feel like it?

But I did as I promised James.

Over the next few weeks, I prayed about doing a worship album, and I prayed about my ambivalence toward the worship songs I chose not to sing in church. As I prayed, I began to remember the role worship songs had played in my life. As a child, when I attended church with my family, I often fell asleep in my mother's lap while the preacher delivered his sermon. But whenever the organist struck the opening notes of one of the old hymns and the choir began to sing, I was fully upright and awake. I remembered how each verse built and swelled until the final climactic chorus, when the robed singers unleashed their last notes and the organ thundered the last chord. The hairs on my arms tingled, and I could feel the music pulsating in my heart. When the hundred-voice choir sang about the glory of God and the sopranos let loose their last high note, I could feel his glory in my soul.

The words of the anthems we sang are as familiar to me now as they were then. Reflecting back on those memories, I realized I learned not only my love of music in church, but also my theology through those hymns. It was through the lyrics we sang that I learned who God was and the attributes of his character.

Was it possible I might somehow be able to play a part in doing that for the next generation? It was humbling to think how God had blessed the song "Indescribable." People were singing it in church or in their cars and gaining a new perspective on how big our God is. *Might God use my songs to reveal himself to others?*

$\mathscr{IC}$

As I was struggling to process this opportunity in light of everything else that was happening in my life, I did what any other Christian would do. I ran to the Scriptures. What did the Bible have to say about this elusive thing called worship?

The book of Psalms proved an appropriate place to start because it was the church's first hymnal. Not only did it contain songs of praise, but there were also laments and hymns of grief—many of them written by David. What I loved about David was that he wasn't afraid to show his emotions or to admit what he was feeling—even when it seemed almost disrespectful to God. When David felt that God wasn't listening, he flat-out told God to listen (Ps. 5; 17) and answer him (Ps. 4). When David feared his enemies, he told God to fight them on his behalf (Ps. 36). If he was mad at God or frustrated when he felt alone, he did the same thing as when he felt gratitude or praise—he wrote songs about his feelings toward God. Regardless of whether his feelings were positive or negative, David boldly expressed them.

David was a musician and songwriter, so it was easy for me to identify with him. I also knew he'd endured the pain of betrayal and experienced deep grief. In Psalms, I read how, despite his deep pain, David continued to praise God—even when he didn't feel like it. Even in his trials, David always seemed to authentically praise and worship God. As I struggled to do the same, I looked to him for answers. One day as I was reading, I came across Psalm 40 where David spilled his secret—David wasn't doing it at all.

> I waited patiently for the LORD; he turned to me and heard my cry. He lifted me out of the slimy pit, out of the mud and mire; he set my feet on a rock and gave me a firm place to stand. (Ps. 40:1–2)

When David stood at his lowest point emotionally, he was still authentic to his emotions. He didn't stand in front of the temple choir with a fake smile and sing, "I've got the joy, joy, joy, joy down in my heart," and hoped, down in his heart, that no one noticed. No, he did what we all do in that situation—he wept, prayed, and cried out for God's help. Despite his pain, David said he waited patiently and God heard his cry. God rescued him from his brokenness and gave him a sure and sturdy place to stand.

But that wasn't all God did. David said, *"He put a new song in my mouth*, a hymn of praise to our God" (v. 3). He said it was *God* who put a new song in his mouth. It didn't matter whether David felt like worshipping or not. David was able to praise God regardless, because God put a new song in David's mouth and God's song was a hymn of praise. Through the Word, David was telling me I didn't have to manufacture false enthusiasm; I didn't even have to feel like praising God to authentically lead worship. All I had to do was be willing to let God lead the church through me. It wasn't about *my* mustering up some good feelings; it was about *God*, who was singing this new song in me. He was the one who put the praises on my tongue and worship in my mouth.

In Psalm 30:5, David wrote, "Weeping may stay for the night, but rejoicing comes in the morning." In some cases, weeping is only for a night, though often it remains for a season. But David said it won't remain forever. Joy will come. David knew this from experience; after mourning the death of his child, he eventually stopped grieving and experienced hope. David knew his emotions were valid; he didn't stuff them or ignore them. He took time to grieve. But when that grieving season was over, he moved on to rejoicing. His psalms are testaments not only to the authentic grief he experienced but also to his authentic joy after God put a new song in his mouth.

This wasn't an instant thing for David; it happened over time. The first and second verses of Psalm 40 say he had to wait patiently for this to happen. When it finally did, David said it wasn't because of anything he did, but because of everything God did.

David might be the most authentic worship leader the church has ever seen. He worshipped God regardless of his emotional state. He recognized that he didn't have to work himself into a rapturous frenzy to worship God because he knew it wasn't his feelings that mattered. Rather he could wait on God to put the joy in his heart, the song in his mouth, and eventually the desire to sing despite his circumstances.

Psalm 40 taught me it was okay for me to come and worship

God *just as I was*. I didn't need to psych myself up to have a better attitude or wait for a day when I was all Pollyannaish about that morning's set list. All of those times when I had been paralyzed by grief and felt as if I couldn't muster up enough strength to sing certain songs, David was telling me I didn't have to. God would help me sing a new song.

In fact, the Psalms revealed to me that worship had very little to do with emotion and everything to do with God's faithfulness. In Psalm 103, David had to command his soul to praise God, "Praise the LORD, my soul" (v. 1). In Psalm 34, David wrote, "I *will* extol the LORD at all times; his praise will always be on my lips" (v. 1). Worshipping God was an act of David's will, not his emotions.

$\mathscr{L}$

When I started trusting that God would put the song in my mouth, I became a better worship leader. No longer was I trying to lead the church in worship, I was now a conduit, allowing *God* to lead them. I felt more comfortable in my worship-leader shoes, knowing I didn't put on a fake smile trying to prove that things were okay.

Worship was like exercise. Some days I went into it kicking and screaming, but I did it anyway, and I always felt better afterward. Even when things weren't okay, I found that when I assumed the posture of worship, my emotions usually followed. Whether it was singing praises to God or humbly asking for his help to lead others closer to him, the simple act of worship birthed the desire to worship.

As I continued to study Psalm 40, verses began to jump out at me, and I started thinking about the worship album more. "Blessed is the one who trusts in the LORD, who does not look to the proud, to those who turn aside to false gods" (Ps. 40:4).

Am I trusting in the Lord? If he put a new song in my mouth to help me worship during my trials, could he also help me birth new songs out of my trials that would benefit the church?

Many, Lord my God, are the wonders you have done, the things you planned for us. None can compare with you; were I to speak and tell of your deeds, they would be too many to declare. (v. 5)

God had been faithful to Martin and me even during our worst times. Was it time for me to declare his goodness to those outside of the church?

"I desire to do your will, my God; your law is within my heart." I proclaim your saving acts in the great assembly; I do not seal my lips, Lord, as you know. I do not hide your righteousness in my heart; I speak of your faithfulness and your saving help. I do not conceal your love and your faithfulness from the great assembly. (vv. 8–10)

I want to do your will. But are you asking me to do more than I'm doing now? Are you asking me to do an album so I don't conceal your love and faithfulness from a larger audience?

As questions like these stepped, glided, and dipped among my prayers, it became clear to me that God was calling me to do this album. Once again, it wasn't about me. It was about God the Father, who was worthy of worship even during my brokenness.

Throughout Martin's ordeal, I'd learned to trust God in new ways. While writing songs, I went to that same intimate place of trust, depending on him for the outcome. When I finished a couple of songs, I sent them to James and my good friend and producer Ed Cash to see what they thought. The songs were simple. I wrote about how the promises of God were meeting me in my daily brokenness.

A few days later, I heard from both of them unanimously. "This is exactly what you need to be singing about because this is where so many people are living." They encouraged me to keep going. Because of all I'd been through, and the many ways my faith had been tested, I had something to say through each of my songs.

Though it was humbling to think God waited to give me a national platform until my faith was shakier than it ever had been, no matter what happened next, I knew I could trust him.

God had put a new song in my mouth.

MYTH: I WORSHIP BECAUSE I FEEL GOOD.

TRUTH: I WORSHIP BECAUSE HE IS GOOD.

TWELVE

EXPOSING MY
VULNERABILITIES

ONE OF THE INGREDIENTS OF WRITING A SONG WAS TO have time alone to dream, think, and process. But I hadn't been alone in three years. Neither had Martin. We both missed being alone occasionally. So much of our time was spent figuring out how to do life in light of our new normal that we never considered how drastically the disability had changed our marriage. It was as if we woke up one morning and realized we were both disappointed on some level. I'm sure every couple feels this at some point.

When I see a tabloid headline about a movie star getting divorced because of "irreconcilable differences," I can't help but reflect on my own marriage, *That sounds just like Martin and me.* We can't reconcile our differences either. He thinks he's more important than I am, and I think I am more important than he is. I wish that weren't the case, but it's likely never going to change. We were all born selfish and instinctively think of our own needs above others.

I think there comes a time in every marriage when the fairy-tale wedding and honeymoon are over. Now two selfish and sinful people are living together in a home—and disappointment can set in. On those days, marriage felt like an uphill climb out of an emotional hole. But regardless of whether I looked ahead or behind, it seemed as though we weren't making much progress out. Those days reminded me of another climb out of another deep hole that Martin and I made together.

Martin and I love to hike, and we took our first postsurgical hike when he'd only been home from the hospital a few months. In the years since then, we continued hiking, carefully working ourselves up to longer trails. Eventually we even tried camping, taking a backpack full of supplies and spending a night or two outdoors.

One weekend, we decided to take a camping trip to a waterfall friends told us about. Our plan was to do the three-and-a-half-mile hike, camp for the night, and return by the same route the following day. For experienced hikers, a three-and-a-half-mile trek isn't that far; we'd recently done much longer ones. This hike, though, would be more strenuous because we would be carrying camping equipment and supplies on our backs. But it was still quite doable for the two of us, and I wasn't worried.

When we set out, the path had a slight incline with a few hilly ups and downs. For the most part, it was an unremarkable, flat hike. About a mile and a half in, we took a left turn, and I could see that the path went down into a gorge—*two miles nearly straight down* into the gorge!

We started off carefully, shifting our packs so they wouldn't pitch us forward. As we walked, there were moments we had to step gingerly to keep from losing our footing. It was slow going, and exhausting, but by late afternoon we finally reached the bottom. We found a flat space, set up our camp, and built a fire. I watched as Martin relaxed and took in the sights and smells.

I wanted to do the same.

I'd been busy at Perimeter, so I looked forward to spending the weekend with my husband. I wanted to enjoy all that setting offered—the refreshing spray from the glistening waterfall, the soft colors of the sky above the rim of the gorge as the orange sun waved good-bye, and the glimmering stars on a velvet canopy covering us through the night.

But I didn't enjoy *any* of those things.

For the rest of the afternoon and evening, I was completely distracted by the thought of the climb we would have to make the next morning. I scanned the horizon for other paths. *There's got to be another way out!* I wondered if carrying all the equipment on our backs would be too much for us. As we got ready for bed that night, I knew we would need an early start the next morning. *It will be a slow hike to the top—will we make it out while it's still light?*

The next morning as we loaded everything into our packs and hoisted them onto our backs, they seemed twice as heavy as they did the day before. On the way down, the backpacks seemed to push us along, but as we struggled up the incline they felt like restraints slowly pulling us backward.

But what else could we do?

It's not like we could call a helicopter, or even a cab to come get us. We had to walk out of there regardless of whether we thought we could. Our only other choice was to stay stuck in the gorge, whining about how bad the climb would be. What good would that do? Two days of sitting at the bottom of the gorge wouldn't change anything except our food supplies—they'd be gone—and we'd still be stuck.

So we did the only thing we could do. We put one foot in front of the other, and then we did it again. And again. One step at a time. Each step an upward climb. Our only option was two miles of one foot in front of the other, resting when we needed to rest, no matter how long it took to get out of that valley. It was a grueling hike to the top, but eventually we made it out.

That hike became a metaphor for me when I thought about our trials.

When friends said, "We're so proud of how well you and Martin are doing," all I could think was, *What choice do we have?* We could stay stuck in our brokenness, but what good would that do? Instead we did the only thing in life that we could do, the same thing we did to get out of the gorge. We took one step and then another. One surgery, followed by another. Eating mush to eating with a fork. Wheelchair to walker. From reminding Martin of his schedule to teaching him to remind himself.

Pretty soon, people were congratulating us on "making it through." But that's where the metaphor broke down. After a long struggle that weekend against the elements and our own fatigue, Martin and I made it out of the gorge. But in real life, we were still wandering around in the valley of the brain tumor's secondary medical effects. I wanted to tell them, "We're not through. We'll never be through. We'll always be doing a two-mile uphill climb with baggage on our backs and none of the stamina we used to have."

What was the point? Unless someone had dealt with a disability firsthand, they really didn't understand. Our choices were to give up or keep moving. We chose to keep moving.

Now we were facing a similar climb with our marriage. Only this time, I wasn't sure how to get out of the disappointing marriage gorge. Would it be like our medical trials? Would we be destined to wander around endlessly, or was there another path out?

For us, that meant trying to understand our frustration and disappointment with each other, and I was pretty sure that had something to do with our expectations of each other. So I started by examining mine.

How much of my disappointment in Martin was rooted in my unrealistic expectations for him? Though I didn't say it out loud, one of my unspoken beliefs was that he would love me perfectly. Was it fair to think he would love me perfectly even though I was not perfect? I didn't even embrace that expectation for myself. So why did I expect it of him? I would forget to ask about the details of his day, inquire as to how he was feeling, or a thousand other things I seemed to think he should do for me.

It was all about finding a balance in our expectations of each other.

Unfortunately, I wasn't very good at it.

I had high expectations for myself and for Martin, hence me planning that stupid hike in the first place. While I could often meet my own goals, Martin had trouble with basic daily objectives. When my expectations were too high, he wasn't capable of achieving them and I'd get frustrated. Then he would be frustrated with me for setting impossible standards.

This happened frequently when he got sick.

Martin's immune system wasn't what it was before the surgery, so he could now get sick at the drop of a tissue and have to go to bed for days. And I would get annoyed. When I got sick, I still had to go to work.

Sometimes his medications and his illness meant that he was not himself. Instead of being understanding and realizing Martin's foul mood was because he didn't feel well, I'd feel put out that I had to drive to the drugstore and didn't have anyone to help unload the dishwasher.

Other days, I expected him to do things that he could never live up to because of his memory. One day, I came home from teaching a women's Bible study that was really important to me. I'd worked for a week on the lesson and was really nervous about delivering it. But it was a great success, influencing lots of women to take a step closer to Christ. I was both excited and relieved, and I couldn't wait to talk about it. But when I got home, Martin failed to ask how the study went, and I was hurt.

When something like that happened, I had three options for how to handle it. One option was to not talk about it with him. Instead of sharing the moment with my husband, I could call a friend and tell her the details. In some cases this was a fine alternative, but the risk of doing it frequently was that instead of celebrating the good moments in life with my life partner, I was sharing them with someone else. I was making Martin irrelevant. That's not what I wanted in my marriage.

Another option was to bring it up in anger. "I've been home for an hour, and you haven't even asked me how the Bible study went!" Out of frustration, I occasionally chose this option. I hated it when I did, because I knew it was unfair to Martin because of his memory issues. It also put him on the defensive, which fueled my anger, and then I didn't want to talk about what happened in the first place.

The best choice was to come home and say to Martin, "I led a great Bible study today!"

That would remind him to ask about it, and he'd say, "Oh, yeah, tell me how it went."

When I set it up this way, I was giving him an opportunity to be successful. I was lobbing the ball to him, and like the great husband he is, he would knock it out of the park. He would ask a thousand questions because he cared, and he really did want to hear about my day.

To choose that third option meant believing he is for me and wants to celebrate me. Sometimes it was just a matter of giving my spouse the benefit of the doubt. Unfortunately, I didn't choose the third option as often as I should have.

Of course, I'm not the only wife who has a problem with unrealistic expectations. Plenty of wives set their husbands up for failure rather than success. Consider the wife who fails to mention an upcoming wedding anniversary, and when her husband fails to remember to get her a gift, she becomes angry. Or if he does remember to buy something, she berates him about the cost. "What? Do you think we're made of money?"

Because it's an impossible situation, there's no way for the husband to win. And husbands aren't immune. They have their own ways of setting up impossible expectations for their wives rather than trying to help their wives be successful.

Christians believe life is about being on the road toward the crucified self. We believe it is more of God and less of me. But somehow in marriage, where we constantly have to deny ourselves in service to our spouse, we seem to forget that. It becomes less about you and all about me. We're a sinful people with selfish natures.

One of the paradoxes of marriage is that wives want their husbands to be great men. And men want their wives to be great women. But we forget that to be truly great, we have to *help* our spouses be great. It's more than *wanting* our spouses to be successful in life and in their family relationships; it's that we need to help them succeed in these areas.

For me, this meant I couldn't sit and wait for Martin to notice or acknowledge things on his own. I had to direct him. Instead of blaming him for forgetting, I needed to help my husband win by remembering. I learned to say something like, "Hey, I've been thinking about what I want you to get me for my birthday."

And he'd pick up the cue. "Yeah, I've been thinking about that too."

Then I'd give him a screenshot and a web address of the shoes I wanted. I got what I wanted, and he got a big win for getting it right.

I know some people feel that it's somehow less satisfying to have to remind their spouse of these things. I don't feel that way at all. To me, the satisfaction comes from seeing the delight on my husband's face when he knows he's pleased me. (And it's much better than an argument about why he forgot my birthday!)

To make it work, we both have to lower our expectations. I can't hold Martin to standards he can't achieve, and he can't hold me to standards that aren't fair. We have to get our expectations in sync and then find ways to help our spouse succeed.

Despite our innate selfishness, we can choose to be loving and giving in any given moment. And when our spouse is hurting, we can do it for days or weeks at a time. The key is learning how to do it for longer stretches of ordinary days. But like the uphill hike, it doesn't just happen. Martin and I never would have gotten out of the gorge on our hike unless we'd taken deliberate steps. And we wouldn't get out of our marriage struggles unless we were intentional about finding solutions.

When our differences seemed irreconcilable, one thing that

really helped us was asking for help. When we shared our marital problems with others, God was faithful to provide us wise people to help us get past those issues.

Our mentors, Bill and Sherri, offered advice and accountability when we needed it. As neutral third parties, sometimes they gave us a point of view that we hadn't considered. Other times, they affirmed that my decision was correct but that I had bowed to the idol of efficiency and hadn't properly or lovingly consulted Martin's input. I can't tell you the number of times we had one of them on the speakerphone at eleven o'clock at night to help resolve an argument so we wouldn't go to bed angry.

As much as we wanted to keep our problems private, we tried to be vulnerable and involve others when needed. We sought counseling from our church and occasionally opinions from friends who knew us well. No matter how far apart Martin and I were on any issue, the one thing we always tried to do was be together on our knees asking God for help.

I truly love Martin and want what's best for him. I don't believe I am *stuck* in this marriage to him any more than he is stuck in this marriage to me. I believe I was uniquely *chosen* by God to be the one who gets to love Martin as a wife. No one else has that role or gets to serve him in that way. Though I'm not always good at it, I have plenty of opportunities to get better. As long as we are married, there will be new challenges. The key is for both of us to adjust our expectations. We need to see marriage not as a union to make us happy but as a union to make us holy.

In my job at Perimeter, I often helped people reset their expectations about God. When someone came into my office and told me they were disappointed with God or felt that somehow he'd wronged them, I'd ask them to go deeper. "Where does that disappointment come from?" I'd ask.

Typically they'd say God didn't do what they thought he should. Sometimes it was the death of a loved one whom they prayed for but had died. At that moment, they felt as though God hadn't answered their prayers. Other times it was work related: they'd lost a job or didn't get the job they felt they should have gotten. Often their disappointment with God stemmed from a relational problem—a spouse who cheated or a falling-out they didn't see coming. They'd tell me how they bargained with God for the results to be different. They made promises to work harder, love more, attend church regularly, stop smoking, drive slower, pray more, and a host of other "good" behaviors. I sympathized with them. I'd tried all of those things too.

"The disappointment you feel seems to imply there was some sort of promise or commitment that God didn't follow through on."

"Yes! That's exactly right," they'd tell me. "He didn't!"

"Okay, let's take a look and see if we can figure out why. Can you show me where the promise you're claiming is in the Bible?"

As much as they searched, they couldn't find a promise that people wouldn't die, jobs would go to the most deserving, or spouses wouldn't leave them. In fact, sometimes they would find examples of just the opposite—innocents dying, workers being paid equally despite unequal work, and spouses who not only cheated but murdered.

As these hurting, teary-eyed people sat across from me and, for the first time, understood that God hadn't promised them any of these things, they'd say, "But he's a good God, and I'm a good person. Why wouldn't he want me to have that?"

Or, "Why would a good God let that happen?"

Or even, "That's not fair! I thought God loved everyone equally!"

The betrayal and disappointment they felt was real, but the promises they thought he'd broken were not real. In their minds, they'd made a bargain with God that they'd do something he wanted if he would do something they wanted in return. But there's a big difference between a bargain that we initiate and a promise that is found in God's Word.

As gently as I could, I would help them see that their disappointment didn't come from God breaking a promise but from their own false expectations. They expected God to do what they wanted him to do, to be obedient to *their* commands. When he wasn't, they were disappointed and unhappy with him.

But that's not how it works. Scripture says we're not good people. We can't know the mind of God. And unconditional love sometimes means unequal treatment. We were the ones who disappointed God, but he loved us anyway.

That's the kind of love Martin and I needed to demonstrate to each other.

Over the years, Martin and I worked hard to find tools that not only helped our relationship but also helped him manage his life. We set up a series of alarms on his iPhone that, together with a pill case, helped him remember to take his medications on time. We discovered that writing things down helped him organize and remember details. He made extensive use of the notes and calendar features in his phone, tracking even the most mundane pieces of information so he had a reference when he needed it.

Through trial and error, Martin learned that taking notes while he was on the phone, or during a conversation, meant he could later "recall" those pieces of information. For example, he used the notes section of each contact on his phone to record information about a friend's family, the ages of their kids, and what had recently happened in their life. I learned that if I wanted him to remember something, it was better to send him a text than it was to verbally tell him. I used calendar invites to make sure he had important events saved for the right day and time. And I made sure to include days that were important to us both, like birthdays and our anniversary. These simple things did much to decrease our frustration with each other.

C

In 2008, the album *Great God Who Saves* was released and reached number twenty-five on the Billboard Christian Album chart. The album brought more opportunities to tour and do concerts. I loved touring, especially when I was a part of someone else's tour, because I got to do ministry alongside some great artists.

I usually opened the concert with a twenty-five-minute set, during which I would sing and tell a few stories to encourage the audience. After the performance, I'd do meet-and-greets, where I'd talk to members of the audience while I signed their CDs. Then we'd all get on the bus and sleep while we traveled to the next location. When I wasn't performing, I had the rest of the day to myself, and I used that time on the bus or at the location to study and write papers for my online seminary courses.

It was great to have Martin touring with me, but I could tell he was struggling with where he fit in. Everyone on a tour has a job, and when people asked what Martin's job was, he'd say, "I'm with Laura."

He'd found several odd jobs in Atlanta, like helping the PE teachers at Perimeter's school, but they were all jobs where he could pick up and leave on tour with me whenever he had to. As a result, they weren't jobs that were meaningful to him. But we didn't have a lot of other choices. He wasn't ready to stay home for days without me. I did my best to include him in life on the road, but Martin wasn't a musician. In short, touring was not the life he would have chosen.

I knew that the attention I received while touring had the potential to hurt both of us. Martin already felt left out, and if I wasn't careful I could lose Laura Elvington—the wife, friend, daughter, sister, and music minister at Perimeter—to the Laura Story on the radio. Fortunately, my friends saw these potential risks and did their best to keep me accountable.

Sherri always asked me the hard questions. After being gone a few days on tour, she'd say, "How much time did you spend onstage singing about God versus privately reading from your Bible?"

After I had driven with Martin to a nearby state and done a weekend of solo concerts, she asked, "How much time did you spend serving strangers this weekend compared to serving your husband?"

Her questions pierced the protective shields I put up publicly. It was much easier to stand onstage and look like I had it all together than to actually have it together at home. But Sherri and my other friends cared deeply about whether Laura Elvington was thriving in her walk with the Lord, loving in her marriage, and balancing family and work. And they cared less about the Laura Story they heard on the radio.

With the success of the album, the label soon came back and asked for another one. "We want you to make it more personal, though. We feel like that is where people connect with you. Can you dig deeper into your pain and brokenness and tell your story through your songs?"

My first thought was, *Are you kidding?*

My life was still too messy to write about. Martin and I weren't done climbing out of the gorge; we were still struggling uphill. There was no neat-and-tidy bow on our life package—it was still unwrapped with half the contents missing. How could I hand a present like that to someone else, even if it was in the form of a song?

I was mostly happy with how things were going publicly; but personally, there were still days I felt as though I was barely limping along. The disconnect between who I was onstage, and who I was off of it, could be hard to reconcile. I loved leading worship, but there were times I didn't feel like I could fully be myself. From a performance standpoint, I was competent. But I never felt as though I had it all under control. I felt like I didn't belong in the limelight. There were lots of musicians who were far more talented than I was.

And I knew there were faithful Christians whose walk was more admirable than mine.

I worried that if I said out loud the things that troubled me, everyone would find out what a fraud I was. What if I admitted there were days I didn't know what I believed? Would the audience run? Would I lose my job at the church? If I said I didn't understand why we prayed so hard and yet Martin was never healed, or admitted I was disappointed in God for not answering our prayers, would churches stop inviting me to sing? How could I tell the public that my husband wasn't happy about life on the road and there were days I wasn't a good wife?

I didn't know why God had me center stage, but it was obvious to me that God wanted me there for a reason. Every night that I took the stage, I'd cry out some version of this prayer: *Oh, God, this is too much! This is too big for me. What do I possibly have to offer them?* And every night, he responded in my heart with the same one-word answer.

Me.

So I tried to do what I'd already been doing in my marriage and during our medical trials. I took one step at a time. I did what I knew to do next. I moved one foot in front of the other so that I wouldn't stay stuck. Despite my inner turmoil, my fears, my failures as a wife, my lingering doubts, and my disappointment with God, I tried to offer the audience more of him and less of me.

When you're moving so fast, you don't always take the time to reflect on where you've been and where you're going. So it wasn't until a few years later, on a road trip to Bentonville, Arkansas, that I really began to think about life from a ten-thousand-foot perspective.

It was four years after Martin's surgery, and we were on the road to another event. We were on I-20 heading through Birmingham around ten thirty at night. The touring and concerts had become consistent gigs, and I was spending a lot of time on the road in buses. But this time, I was in my own car—the blue MINI Cooper that Martin and I bought when all our friends were having babies and buying minivans.

I looked at Martin in the passenger seat and smiled. He wanted to stay awake and keep me company until we got there, but it had been a long day and he was already asleep. I didn't mind. Things had been so busy that I didn't have much time to just think and pray. I reached over and turned off the radio. Martin snuggled down into the seat. Above the gentle hum of the car, I could hear him softly snoring.

When I was busier than I should have been, it was rare for me to have a few quiet hours to reflect and pray. So as the lights of Birmingham faded in my rearview mirror, I began to think about our first five years of marriage.

My first thought was, *This life doesn't look anything like I expected it to.*

I realized I had used the e-word.

Expected.

What were my expectations for our first years of marriage?

As I mentioned earlier, I grew up thinking that if I were a good Christian, if I had my devotional times, and did everything the Bible said to do, then God would bless me with everything I thought I needed or wanted. My family would be safe. My husband wouldn't get a brain tumor; I'd have kids because, you know, everyone has kids. *All these things that I thought my life should look like, these things that even you label as good, I felt like you should have given them to me.*

Another word caught my attention.

Should.

It is also a word of expectation.

Driving through the dark countryside, I realized I had expectations of God the same way all the disappointed people in my office had expectations of him. We'd all made bargains. And we all felt as though God hadn't kept up his part of the bargain. So, just as I counseled the hurting people in my office, I asked myself where those promises were in the Bible, and I didn't have an answer.

But had God kept the promises he made in his Word?

If someone had told me on our wedding day that all of this would happen in the next five years, I don't think I would have believed him. There hadn't been any resolution to our situation. Our lives were broken in so many ways, yet somehow we were okay.

Some people receive miracle healings. I am so happy that God chose to answer their prayers and bless them in that manner. But our healing had been slower and different. God had given us miraculous grace to heal our hearts and our minds and to bless us financially.

You have blessed us, God. Even though we are going through this medical ordeal. Even though Martin still has effects from his brain tumor surgeries. Though we don't have kids. Though I'm the one behind the wheel and working a full-time job, instead of Martin. Despite all of those things, I still see that we have been blessed.

Growing up, I'd heard that God could sustain me through any trial. I'd *heard* that. It seemed nice, like something I'd read on a greeting card. And during a hard time I would have somewhat believed it, because that's the kind of thing a loving God could do.

But now, Lord, I believe that you can sustain me through any trial. I believe in that like I believe in the air that I breathe. I am as dependent on you as I am dependent on the next breath I take.

If someone had told me earlier that we'd go through three months in the hospital, another six months of rehabilitation, and a lifetime of doctor appointments, I wouldn't have believed I was capable of doing it. But I knew without a shadow of a doubt that if I hadn't gone through all of this, my relationship with God wouldn't be where it is today.

When we were in the hospital, I started writing down the names of everyone who helped us so I could write them thank-you notes as a way of telling them how much I appreciated what they'd done.

But God had sent so many of his people that I couldn't write them down fast enough. There was no way I could repay everyone who called, wrote, visited, brought meals, stayed with Martin, and comforted us. *God, they were your hands and feet for us. You allowed me to see the body of Christ at work in ways I'd never seen before. They were your blessing to us, and just like your abundant grace, they overwhelmed Martin and me with your love. I can't repay them, and I can't repay you.*

But that was his point, wasn't it?

He didn't promise that we wouldn't have trials.

He promised that he'd be there when we did and that he'd never leave our side.

We all want to say that we'll have joy in the midst of our trials, but we don't really know whether we will until we face them. And driving down that highway, with Martin asleep beside me in the MINI Cooper, I realized something.

I do have joy.

I do have a real joy that no one can take away. I wouldn't have known that it even existed before, let alone thought that I could experience it.

The joy comes because God's promises are real. They went from being theories I learned long ago, to the proof that I am alive and able to get out of bed and face each new day. Things are still hard, but even during the chaos we're okay. Martin and I have found joy in the midst of our trials.

There were so many times when I wondered whether God would catch me. Would he really sustain me? It had taken me until this moment to look back over the past four years to see that he had! *You've given me so many unexpected blessings through this trial. Like a sweet, deeper intimacy with my husband.* It has been such a blessing to me to serve my husband. Most women will never have the opportunity to serve their husbands in the ways that I've been able.

I thought about how it all began. Martin and I had prayed for blessings, healing, and protection. All of the things people usually prayed for in situations like ours. But, thankfully, God didn't give us what we asked for. Instead he'd given me something even more valuable—a deep intimacy with him and with Martin. There's nothing wrong with praying for safety for your family, for healing, and for protection or any of those kinds of things, but what if there are blessings that God offers that are greater than just a pain-free life?

What if it wasn't about my husband getting better? What if that's not the blessing? What if the blessing is about learning to do life while loving God and loving others—even in the middle of our disabilities?

And what if those blessings actually came through raindrops, not sunshine? What if the healing wasn't from a doctor patching up

Martin's brain, but instead from the tears I'd cried out to God during all of those sleepless nights in the hospital? What if the trials we've walked through were really his mercies to us?

Maybe you heard our prayers, but you didn't give us the things we asked for because they were lesser things.

I wasn't sure if any of those things were really true, but it seemed like they could be. It seemed like that was what we'd experienced. God had bestowed blessing after blessing on us and none of them were the things we'd prayed for, but the things we got were better than anything we'd hoped or prayed for!

While thinking about these things, words seemed to flow and a tune came to mind. When we neared our exit, I knew I wanted to capture my thoughts and prayers, so I took a Sharpie and a gas receipt out of the cup holder and started jotting down words.

> We pray for blessings, we pray for peace;
> Comfort for family, protection while we sleep.
> We pray for healing, for prosperity;
> We pray for your mighty hand to ease our suffering.
> And all the while, you hear each spoken need,
> Yet love us way too much to give us lesser things.
>
> 'Cause what if your blessings come through raindrops?
> What if your healing comes through tears?
> What if a thousand sleepless nights are
> what it takes to know you're near?
> What if trials of this life are your mercies in disguise?

I quickly wrote a verse and the chorus, leaving the rest to be finished at another time. It was unfinished and too personal a song to share with anyone else, so I tossed the receipt in my backpack and didn't think much about it.

For the next couple of weeks while I was busy touring, I was also thinking about the new album. The record executives weren't the only ones who were compelling me to tell more of my story. Through my personal study of Scripture and in my prayers, I felt as though God was asking the same thing. He'd been so faithful to me over the years that he wanted me to tell others how he'd sustained me through my trials.

As I prayed about it, God continued to work in my heart, challenging my assumption that I needed to have my story wrapped up nicely before I could share it so it could be helpful to anyone. One day, I remember crying out in prayer, *God, I can't do this! I can't admit in public the voices of doubt in my head. I can't explain my story when I still have more questions than answers.*

Inside my heart, I heard God clearly answer, *I've called you to this not because you have all the answers but because you've learned to run to me with your questions.*

It was easy to tell people the story of our hike out of the gorge, but it would take a whole new level of vulnerability to tell them about our wanderings in the valley of the shadows of a brain tumor. I had a choice. I could continue to keep my brokenness and doubts hidden, or I could expose them for the world to see. One would prevent God from entering into my brokenness; the second would allow him to penetrate it.

That choice was easy.

I wanted God in my brokenness.

And he wanted me to be upfront about my need for Jesus.

The more I prayed about it, the more I was convinced that God wanted me to exchange my "minister of music" title for "minister of vulnerability." God was asking me to reveal the brokenness in my life not to show how faithless I was, but how faithful he is. God wasn't going to use me in spite of my hard story; he was going to *use my hard story.*

Doing the album meant that I would have to be more vulnerable and transparent than I'd ever been, and I wasn't sure I welcomed that. But what if the worst thing I had to offer—my broken story—was really the best thing I had to offer?

MYTH: GOD CAN ONLY USE MY STORY
WHEN THERE IS A HAPPY ENDING.

TRUTH: GOD CAN USE MY STORY WHEN
I TRUST HIM IN THE JOURNEY.

THIRTEEN

CHOSEN TO TELL

WE ALL HAVE THINGS WE'D RATHER KEEP HIDDEN. FOR me, it was my doubts and fears. I didn't want people—especially the church people—to know I didn't have all the answers. When I was in the midst of my unresolvable brokenness, the last thing I wanted to do was stand on a stage and tell people my story. How could I give them hope when I didn't have a happy ending? How could I inspire them when I felt alone and without answers? How could I encourage them to come and meet Jesus when there were days I wasn't sure I wanted to meet with him myself?

It was clear God was calling me to tell my story, but why? And to whom? Wasn't there someone else who would make a better ambassador for him? Someone with a happy ending to their trials?

It was hard for me to imagine how God could use my broken life story.

Has God ever asked you to do something you knew you couldn't do? Or maybe you felt you were the wrong person to do it? Maybe he wanted you to share your story, but you felt your past was too tainted to be used by a holy God. You didn't have the knowledge, the training, or even the courage to do what he asked you to do.

Surely God made a mistake when he wanted to use you! There are so many more qualified people he could have chosen instead.

That's how I felt when God was calling me to tell my story. A story without an ending. A story, not of hope but of being held by him during my hopelessness. I wasn't the best person for the job. I didn't have all the perky, inspiring anecdotes so many Christian leaders had. Why would he want me?

In John 4 there is a story about a Samaritan woman getting water from a well. The Samaritans didn't get along with the Jews or the Gentiles, so this woman had been set up for failure since birth. Finding her at the well at midday meant something else was wrong. Respectable women came in the morning.

Then Jesus entered the scene. Through their conversation, we learn that this woman had had five husbands and was currently living with a man she was not married to. Her family was broken. Her heart was shattered. Her past was very checkered. But this was a divine appointment created by God, and Jesus told her that he was the Messiah. In fact, she was the first person he told he was the Messiah.

Why not the disciples?

Why the Samaritan woman?

To the rest of us, she looks like the wrong choice. A bad plan. A mistake. Why would Jesus choose her to be the first? Why did he choose her?

The disciples entered to see Jesus talking to the outcast, but before anyone could react, the Samaritan woman used their arrival to make her exit.

> Then, leaving her water jar, the woman went back to the town and said to the people, "Come, see a man who told me every-thing I ever did. Could this be the Messiah?" (John 4:28–29)

How did she get the courage to go? What would those townspeople do to her when she got there? Would they stone her? Would they laugh at her? Would they avoid her at all costs?

What would she say to them? "Hey, I was hanging out by the well when this strange guy . . ."

Can't you just hear the crowd erupt in laughter when she told them she was talking to yet *another* guy? And a Jewish rabbi at that. "And oh, by the way, this guy thinks he's the Messiah, and I kind of think so too."

I imagine the crowd chuckling before turning their backs on her. They knew that no Jewish rabbi in his right mind would have been caught talking to such a sinful woman. I envision the crowd getting angry and throwing things at her—chicken bones, fruit peels, maybe the pigs' food.

But something in the way she said what she said, or did what she did, got them to take notice. They listened to her. And they believed her. John tells us they first came to know Jesus because of her. "Many of the Samaritans from that town believed in him because of the woman's testimony, 'He told me everything I ever did'" (John 4:39).

She used her story to win them to Jesus? Her broken story?

Yes. That's exactly what Jesus wanted. And that's why she was the divine appointment at the well, set by the Father, kept by the Son. While we can't understand why he chose her, we can get an idea from an earlier verse. Since Jesus was a Jewish rabbi and he and his disciples were devout Jews, this eastern route would have been the expected path for them to take on their way to Galilee. Instead, Jesus chose to go directly through Samaria. In fact, John wrote that Jesus and his disciples *had to* go through Samaria (John 4:4). The Greek word for "had to" suggests a moral obligation or a constraint that arises from a divine appointment. In other words, John was telling us that Jesus was ordained to do this by the Father—it was a divine appointment set up by God.

God knew from the beginning of time that this woman was the one he wanted to use.

And she had something on me.

She was willing to be used.

Imagine the pluck it took for the Samaritan woman to go into her village and say she'd met a man who she believed was the Messiah. Not only that, but she told them the reason she believed he was the Messiah was because he knew everything about her.

If the listeners didn't know anything about her, they did now. She had to tell them the rest of the story—how Jesus knew of the five husbands in her past and the man with whom she was currently living. If the listeners already knew her story, she took an incredible risk to bring it up again. She aired the dirty laundry of her past and not only hung it out to dry, but hung it out to dry in the main square.

What nerve.

What courage.

What authenticity.

Would *you* be willing to do that?

Would *I* be willing to do that?

Jesus didn't tell the Samaritan woman that she *had* to use her story. He didn't even tell her to go back to town and spread the word. He didn't have to. Her encounter with Jesus changed everything about her! She was no longer ashamed and hiding out at the well during off-hours. She was downtown telling everyone who would listen. And you bet they were listening.

For years, this woman had lived outside of the mainstream of her religion. Yet after one conversation, she became a religious insider. Her shame lifted. Her countenance changed. Guilt was gone, and there was no reason to hide. She was free from that thing that couldn't be quenched, and she wanted to share her story with everyone— including those who had turned their backs on her. She walked in the light with her sin exposed but also forgiven.

People listened to her.

I would.

You would too.

Wouldn't you rather hear about a diet from someone who lost a hundred pounds than from someone who never weighed more than a hundred pounds?

Wouldn't you rather get help for your child's addiction from a recovering addict than from a teetotaler who has never experienced the temptation of a high?

If you wanted your sins forgiven, wouldn't you rather learn how from the one who had her very long list of sins forgiven than those who claimed they had never sinned?

God didn't use her *in spite* of her story.

He *used her story*.

And the people responded to Jesus because of it.

> So when the Samaritans came to him, they urged him to stay with them, and he stayed two days. And because of his words many more became believers. They said to the woman, "We no longer believe just because of what you said; now we have heard for ourselves, and we know that this man really is the Savior of the world." (John 4:40–42)

A divine appointment had been set from the beginning of time. Jesus crossed religious, racial, social, cultural, and gender divides to meet with the Samaritan woman. To reveal her sin and pain, to love her more deeply than any man she'd ever known, and to show the fullness of his grace.

Jesus goes out of his way to meet up with the hurting, the marginalized, and the broken.

What makes us think that he wouldn't do the same for us?

And why wouldn't he want us to tell others the story of what he's done for us, even if it's an unfinished and broken story? If we're willing to let him use our story, our whole broken story—not the sanitized, social-media-filtered version we want to share—our stories can be used to spread his unconditional love and to reveal his astounding grace to our community.

MYTH: I AM DEFINED BY MY PAST.

TRUTH: GOD REDEEMS MY PAST
AND GIVES ME A FUTURE.

FOURTEEN

YOUR STORY BRINGS
GOD GLORY

EVERYTHING I KNOW ABOUT GOD I LEARNED FROM STO-ries about his people. A child's picture Bible was my first introduction. Later, my Sunday school teacher taught the Bible with the help of a flannel board and felt cutouts. The fabric props were used to recreate some of the greatest stories in the Bible, which made the stories even more interactive and memorable than reading a book.

For example, when David took out his slingshot and hit Goliath, the teacher asked one of us to rotate Goliath ninety degrees counter-clockwise, until he was lying on his back making an angry face at the sky. We all knew that meant he was dead.

Moses was a thicker version of Abraham, and he carried a shep-herd's staff. But after years of yelling, "Let my people go!" to the pharaoh, the crook of his staff broke off, which made him look like a chubby Abraham with a walking stick. The felt cutout of Jacob had twelve felt cutout sons but only one coat. And though the lions had pink, fuzzy felt tongues dangling from their snarling mouths, when-ever the teacher stuck and unstuck Daniel in their den, he never got bitten.

The flannel board was our generation's video game except we didn't have a controller, a video, or a game. But we did leave church each Sunday with a coloring sheet and a story so ingrained in our imaginations that many of us can still recall the details today.

The moral of each story was always similar.

"Be obedient like Noah who built the ark, and God will save you like he saved Noah from the flood."

"Be persistent like Abraham who prayed for a son, and God will answer your prayers like he answered Abraham's prayers."

"Be faithful like David, because no matter how old you are, God can use you for great and mighty things."

Each week we heard a new story, and then we were told that we should *be like* the hero of that story. If we behaved as they behaved, then we would find favor with God like they did. But the more I tried, the more I came up short. As I grew, I learned that while the basic truths were still there, these heroes of the faith lived much more complicated, unpredictable, and disobedient lives than what was illustrated on the flannel board or in picture books.

Noah's story took a dark turn after the floodwaters receded.

Abraham's journey to trusting God started long before the sacrifice of Isaac.

And there was more to David's story after he successfully stood up against the giant.

Which part of their stories were we supposed to emulate?

Were we supposed to be like the Noah who had the courage to build an ark when it wasn't even raining? Or like the Noah who got drunk after dry-docking the ark and was discovered by his sons lying naked in his tent?

Were we supposed to be like the David who defended God by using his slingshot to kill Goliath? Or like the David who took a census that resulted in seventy thousand deaths by a plague and later arranged for his friend Uriah to be killed in battle?

Were we supposed to be like Abraham the faithful father, willing to sacrifice his own son at God's command? Or Abraham the faithless liar, who tried to save his own skin by misrepresenting his relationship with his wife (twice) and having an illegitimate child with her handmaiden, breaking covenants with both his wife and God?

Did you know all of that is in the Bible?

The Bible is filled with rapes, murders, betrayals, child sacrifices, and other atrocities. Reading Scripture will reveal that heroes of the Bible are broken and morally depraved people.

Just like we are.

Abraham lied more than once. We've sinned repeatedly and unrepentantly.

David coaxed Bathsheba into cheating on her husband. But look at us: we've cheated on tests, on our spouses, and on our taxes.

Noah celebrated God's provision for him and his family by getting drunk. We've promptly forgotten his provision for us because we get drunk with power, money, and success.

So many times, our actions haven't been God-honoring or Christlike. We've been faithless more than we've been faithful. The fact that our life stories can't withstand moral scrutiny any better than biblical life stories can shouldn't surprise us. That's the story we're living in. God's perfect creation has been corrupted by the fall, and our sins are the result. We're living in a broken, fallen, and morally messed-up world.

With that understanding in mind, I went back and looked at some of those heroes of the faith, and I discovered that God didn't call me to be like them. And he doesn't call you to be like them either. He never asks us to be like Noah, David, Daniel, or any other biblical example—except *Jesus*. God the Father sent us the hero he wants us to emulate, and it is his Son. He wants us to model our lives after Jesus.

Be obedient like Jesus, who was obedient to the Father.

Be prayerful like Jesus, who sought solace to talk to his Father.

Be willing to be used like Jesus, who took the punishment for our sins by his crucifixion, death, burial, and resurrection.

We're called only to be like Jesus and no one else.

So if these characters are not the heroes of the Bible, and we're not called to be like them, why are their stories included in the Good Book?

Their stories aren't in the Bible because these characters are heroes. Their stories are in the Bible because *God is the hero* of their stories. Think about it. Who was the hero: Noah or the Supreme Being who saved Noah from the floodwaters? Was Daniel the hero, or was it the Great I Am who saved him from the lions? Was Abraham the hero, or was it Abba Father who made him the father of nations?

Just as the faithfulness of the men and women whose stories are told in the Bible points us to Jesus, so can their brokenness. In their brokenness, hurts, and sorrow, we see their humanity. We see their need for a Savior. Though these people appear to be leading actors in their stories, when we look at the larger story, we see they are supporting characters in God's story. God is on every page of the Bible. He's in every one of their stories, working in them and through them.

The Bible is a book of broken stories and of sinful behaviors that cry out for redemption. That's why the entire story of the Bible points to a Redeemer. And that Redeemer isn't Noah, Abraham, Moses, David, Peter, Paul, or even Mary.

The entire Bible points to *Jesus* as the Redeemer—our Redeemer.

The story we're living in is *God's* story. In this context, broken doesn't mean disabled; it means enabled to point to Jesus instead of ourselves. Sinner doesn't mean failure; it means need for a Savior. The same is true for my story. The reason God wants me to tell my story isn't because he wants me to be embarrassed talking about my lowlights or bragging about my highlights. He wants me to tell my story because my story points to Jesus. My life is but one miniscule, very broken story in his much larger story of redemption.

And so is your story.

He is the lead character and I am the supporting actor in my life story. And he is the leading character in your story, where you are just a supporting actor pointing to his greatness.

When I look at it that way, I wonder why my story or your story should look any different from the stories of real people that we read about in the Bible. Why should our stories have any more highlights or fewer lowlights than theirs? Why shouldn't we have a broken story when some of the ancient pillars of the faith had terribly broken stories?

We're all encouraged when we read through Psalms. But what did David endure to experience the depth of love he has for God? What kind of heart-shredding pain did he go through before understanding how real and present God was and just how much God loved him regardless of his brokenness?

Understanding the whole story of the Bible, it's much easier to see that my brokenness has a purpose. When Martin and I faced a crisis and I wondered where God was during our trial, I only had to open the Bible to see that God was on every page of every biblical character's trials, so why wouldn't he be present in mine? And if God could use their story, why couldn't he use mine? Even though we're not called to *be like* those heroes of the faith, we can still learn from their life stories, because their stories sound an awful lot like ours.

In fact, I couldn't begin to tell my story without talking about the Scriptures that got Martin and me through all those trials. My story isn't just a series of things that happened to me. It is how God used the things that happened to me to draw me closer to him. And my story is part of a much bigger story of God drawing all of us closer to him. A story of his faithfulness intersecting with my faithlessness.

God is the hero of the broken story.

That's why he wants you to share your highs and lows too—it's a part of his story, and it can be used to bring others closer to him.

Maybe like me, you have objections to sharing your story. Perhaps you're afraid it isn't finished yet, or maybe you're worried it's not compelling enough. Or maybe you're worried, as I was, about others knowing your deep, dark secrets. But telling your story doesn't have to start with standing on a stage and telling your innermost secrets. It might start with telling your spouse.

One Sunday morning at Perimeter, the pastor preached about the sanctity of life. A woman in our church who had an abortion decades earlier and never told anyone—not even her husband—could no longer carry the guilt and shame she felt. She cried during the service. Later that afternoon, she said to her husband, "I need to tell you something I've never told anyone else. Long before we were married, when I was very young, I had an abortion."

His response was beautiful: "I love you unconditionally, and I am sorry that you have been carrying that pain all by yourself for so many years."

Telling her story started with telling her husband. With his help, she sought counseling to deal with the twenty years of guilt and shame with which the evil one had tormented her. After two decades, by finally releasing her deepest, darkest secret to those two people, she was finally able to heal. Over time, she felt God calling her to share her story with other women. Eventually, she started a postabortion care ministry where she helps other women heal from their past. This is literally a life-saving ministry. Many women who have gone through secretive abortions suffer from years of depression and suicidal thoughts. Her willingness to share her story has saved countless lives, and many of those women have gone on to share their stories too.

Maybe your story isn't as dramatic. It doesn't have to be. It might be as simple as sharing your daily struggles. One day I was teaching a women's Bible study at a local church, and I asked the women sitting at tables to introduce themselves to one another. I also encouraged them to share something they were struggling with at that moment.

A young woman named Renee introduced herself as a mother of four kids, ages five and under. She talked about how overwhelming her days were and how hard it was to keep up with all she had to do. "Some days, I just can't take it anymore!" she said in exasperation. The other women around the table nodded in sympathy and continued with their introductions.

Across the table from Renee was an older woman. "My name is

Elaine," she said. "I'm really struggling with mild depression. I have three grown kids and the last one moved out of the house recently. I miss them and their friends being around. The house feels so empty, and I feel so alone." She went on to encourage Renee by saying, "The days may seem long, but the years go by quickly."

Renee and Elaine didn't offer up spiritual platitudes. They didn't give their life history. They merely told the stories they were living that day and that week. After class, I overheard the two of them talking. Renee told Elaine how much her words encouraged her. "You reminded me that this season is temporary, and it won't last forever. Thank you."

When each of them shared their stories—their lowlights, not just their highlights—they found a friend who could understand. Instead of allowing their brokenness to isolate them, sharing their stories allowed God to enter into them. God entered into Renee's story, giving her a new perspective on her kids and a renewed patience for those difficult days. And he entered Elaine's story to give her hope that even though her kids were gone, God had other plans for her— like encouraging Renee and other young moms. There was nothing overtly religious or spiritual about what those two women did. They were just willing to be authentic and vulnerable about the story they were presently living. No other woman at that table could have encouraged Renee in quite the same way Elaine did.

What if your story could do the same? Would you be willing to share it?

While there are lots of life stories in the Old Testament, I think that David's stands out as an example of someone who was willing to share his highs and lows to bring God glory and praise.

David had some amazing highlights. He began as a shepherd boy who cared for sheep, and he became a king chosen by God. As a youth, he learned Goliath was blaspheming God, and no one could stop him. So David fearlessly went into battle armed with only a slingshot, five smooth stones, and a desire to defend his God.

As a grown man he was a great warrior, yet he also knew how to exercise restraint. For example, when he could have killed Saul, he chose not to because David believed him to be the Lord's anointed.

David was an accomplished musician and songwriter. In addition, he was perhaps the finest worship leader the ancient world had ever seen. With his eyes fixed on his God, he worshipped full-on, abandoning everything else to the point where even his own wife mocked him. Perhaps because of his zeal, he was the only person in Scripture called "a man after [God's] own heart" (Acts 13:22).

From his highlights, David had many admirable qualities. But when we look at his lowlights, we learn he wasn't exactly a saint.

God warned David not to take a census, but he did anyway. As a result, God sent a plague and seventy thousand people perished. David misused his power and didn't go to war when he should have. That resulted in a string of deadly decisions. First, he committed adultery with Bathsheba. Then he arranged to have her husband, his friend Uriah, murdered on the battlefield. Later, his and Bathsheba's baby son died, and we become witnesses to his guilt and grief.

So there it is—David's story. What a tangled mess! Why would David want to tell us about this? Why wouldn't he just bury those lowlights instead of writing about them in psalms?

It's because David knew he wasn't the hero of the story.

God was.

And by writing about how God saved him, David believed we would make God the hero of our stories too.

David was clear on his role in his story. He was the sinner. God was the Savior. Where David failed, God prevailed; he restored and redeemed what David couldn't do on his own. David was confident that when people saw what God had done for him, they would recognize that they are the sinner in their own story. If they saw how faithful God was to redeem David's story, they'd also see how faithful God is to redeem theirs. David willingly shared his story out of his thankfulness for what God had done.

Everything in Scripture is there for a reason. God includes David's lowlights as well as his highlights to demonstrate his power as Redeemer and Restorer. And if every detail and every ingredient in David's life story is important because it shows God's power, then doesn't it stand to reason that every detail of our stories is not only important, but redeemable too?

Stop for a minute and think.

What if we were to summarize the highlights and lowlights of our stories? Sure, there are some nice things people would say about us. We've each had our share of glowing moments. But there are a lot of bad things people could say about us, too, because we've each had some dark moments. Those dark moments typically don't make our highlight reels. We don't tweet about them or post them as our Facebook status because we'd rather keep them hidden. We're all a mixed bag of good and bad. Sinner and saint.

But nothing is mixed about God's story. His book is a story of redemption, and he casts himself as the Redeemer. David knew that. I think that is why David so willingly and honestly told his whole story in the psalms—not just the good parts. David truly believed that God could redeem even the corrupt parts of his life story.

God can redeem not only every life, but every season of our life, every addiction, every lie, every failed marriage, every financial crisis, every jealous thought, every bad mood, and every deep, dark secret. He uses our lowlights to demonstrate his power. No matter how deep our pit of sin is, God's long arm of redemption reaches down, pulls us out, washes us clean by the blood of Jesus, and welcomes us home.

When we let others know where we came from and how he saved us from our own pit, we become an extension of that arm of redemption.

So what is your story?

Hopefully, David's story will encourage you to believe that God is the hero of your story, and he can redeem your darkest moments just as he did David's.

But God wants us to go even further.

He wants each of us to share our stories.

I believe God wants to use your story for the salvation of the nations. That sounds like a pretentious claim, doesn't it? It sounds like the kind of charge a preacher or Bible study teacher gives at the end of the lesson. It's something people say at the end of Christian books so readers are inspired, knowing that their story matters, that the negative things they've gone through have a purpose somewhere down the road. It may even sound like something to make you feel good about yourself.

Let me assure you. This isn't an obscure principle, a loose thread buried in the fabric of Scripture. No, this is *the fabric*. It's the core principle of the gospel message, and it is consistently found across the story of the Bible, from the opening pages of the Old Testament to the closing pages of the New Testament.

Let me repeat that, in case you are reading fast and skipped it: God wants to use your story for the *salvation of the nations*.

On page after page of the Bible, we read about God using the stories of his people for the salvation of the nations, for the coming kingdom, and for bringing redemption to the world.

Consider the Samaritan woman at the well. Could there have been a less worthy story for God to use to bring the Samaritans to faith? Yet we know that many people from her town believed in Jesus because of her testimony (John 4:39). What if the Samaritan woman hadn't been willing to tell her story? What if she had run back home and quietly pondered in solitude all that Jesus had told her? Would anything have changed in Samaria? Would anyone have become a believer?

We know it's likely Jesus wouldn't have stayed in Samaria for two days, because the townspeople wouldn't have gone to the well to meet him and urge him to stay. Instead, he and the disciples would likely have rested a bit, eaten their lunch, and then gotten back on the road. As a result, the Samaritans would have missed their encounter with Jesus and certainly wouldn't have become believers that day.

Of course, Jesus wasn't dependent on the woman to get his word out. If she hadn't been willing to tell her story, God is sovereign, and he would have found another way or used another person. But it certainly would have been a tragic loss to the Samarian woman. She was a part of the blessing. She had been redeemed and now had the privilege of helping Jesus redeem her community. Imagine all that she could have missed out on had she not told her story!

Could the same be true for us?

Could failing to tell our story mean we miss out on the blessing of being used by God?

We've all been blessed by David's words. We find such comfort in them that they're often quoted when we need comfort the most. Don't you think he's thankful to have played a part in that, even if it meant publicly sharing his worst moments?

What if David hadn't been willing to write his story? Consider how different our faith would look if David's story, both the highlights and the lowlights, had never appeared in the Bible. Think of how often we turn to Psalms for comfort. What if David's psalms were missing?

We can all think of an instance where someone revealing their story has touched us. Maybe it was a simple connection like Renee and Elaine's. Or perhaps it was learning that we're not alone in our struggles, seeing how God used another person in spite of their lowlights, or finding encouragement in someone who is a few years ahead of us in dealing with grief. Whatever the situation, we've all benefited from someone else's journey.

What if they had never told their story?

What if you never tell yours?

A good friend who is a pastor has a child who is a heroin addict. I'm sure he was tempted to hide his family problems from the church where he worked. He could have withdrawn socially and spiritually from the church and maybe someone would have asked about him, or maybe no one would have noticed as he and his wife drifted into isolation with their secret. But isolation rarely leads to anything good. He knew that to get the support and encouragement he and his wife needed during this difficult time, he'd have to be vulnerable and let people in. But what was the best way to do it?

As we all know, telling our personal stories can be dangerous. If he were to tell his story to people who didn't understand or weren't compassionate, they could blame him for their own child's addiction. They could criticize his parenting or his spiritual life, causing more heartache at a time when he needs support the most.

Fortunately, this minister realized he wasn't the only one going through a trial; parents in his church and community were facing the same issues and needed the same kind of support he did. God used him and his willingness to share his story to form a confidential support group for parents whose children were involved in destructive lifestyles. He wasn't shouting his story from a megaphone on a Sunday morning, and he wasn't doing it in a way that would shame his child. He was privately sharing his story with those who needed to hear it most.

In the group, parents of alcoholics and drug abusers came together and prayed for their children in a faith-filled, understanding, and supportive environment. Think of how many families have been helped because they now have a safe place to discuss their struggles! I'm so thankful my friend knew God could redeem his broken story, and he was willing to be a part of redeeming other people's broken stories.

Imagine how thankful the parents who come to this group are for his willingness to be transparent. He could have started this group without his child being an addict, but think how much more powerful it is when a new couple walks through the door and instead of just saying, "I'm so sorry," he can say, "I've been there, and I'm still here."

He didn't wait for his story to be resolved or to have a happy ending. He shared his story of struggling with a child he loves dearly but couldn't help. His story reminds me that when God uses our stories to heal others they don't have to be finished. They don't have to be wrapped up into a neat, tidy bow with all the answers before God can use them. He can redeem our stories while they're still tattered, and we're still in the brokenness.

I know a lot of people who are in troubled marriages, and they feel as if they have to wait until their marriage situation is resolved before they can talk about it. They either want to wait until it's wildly successful, or there is the finality of a divorce. But more people live in the tension than live in the extremes. When people are willing to share their struggles, they can help others who are living under that same burden.

A friend of mine who volunteers in the music ministry of her church found out her husband was having an affair. She told her husband to leave his girlfriend or leave their marriage. However, her husband wanted them both. He was unwilling to give up the girlfriend, and he wanted to stay married. It was a difficult time for her as she struggled to figure out what to do. Eventually my friend's only option was to divorce him. It wasn't an easy choice. She had three kids to support. But in the middle of all this tension, she was also afraid her church would no longer let her volunteer. One day, she asked the music minister, "Should I stop serving because I'm likely getting a divorce?"

The music minister told her, "No, you didn't do anything wrong. I want you to continue serving because your divorce will be a part of your ministry."

The music minister was right. My friend continued to serve and to worship God despite her broken circumstances. She continued to bless God's name, in spite of the worst thing she could ever imagine happening to her family. Throughout the whole ordeal, she has become such an inspiration to the people around her who have witnessed her faithfulness, despite her trials. It's an ongoing, messy story without a happy ending, but God has used her story to draw others to him.

If you're like me, the testimonies you find the most inspiring aren't those that start out, "I was born a Christian and walked the aisle of my church when I was six . . ." It's the testimonies of those who have struggled and found God faithful even in the midst of their brokenness.

As I wrote already, God can use your story, whatever it is, for the salvation of the nations. I say that, not even knowing what your story is, because that is a principle that comes from the Bible. People hear about the gospel from those who are living out the gospel. They are redeemed when we point them to the Redeemer. They can be saved when those of us who are saved point to the Savior. God wants to use *your* story for the salvation of the nations, as he did David's. Not because of the greatness of your story but because of the greatness of our God.

What trial is God bringing into your life for the purpose of equipping you to do his work? What trials are you going through right now that God is using to equip you for future ministry?

I know there are some hard stories out there—stories that are much harder and more broken than mine. It might even seem unkind to you that I would say, "God is going to use your hard story for good." But I say that, because I have found it to be true. When I try to be the hero of my own story, my story is worthless—but when God is the hero of my story, he can use it in more ways than I can imagine. And I have seen him do it for others too. I have watched God use some of the hardest stories and the deepest wounds to shine his light of mercy and grace on those who needed it most.

C

On January 15, 2013, I played one of the most meaningful events of my career. Several Christian music groups decided to put on a concert in Newtown, Connecticut. This was a month after the Sandy Hook shooter took twenty-six precious souls and left our nation speechless. It was a great honor to be asked, but it was also one of the hardest events I've ever played.

Eight or nine groups were involved, about thirty musicians total.

We all rearranged our schedules and took buses and planes to go where the hurt was still fresh and the wounds still raw. Max Lucado was there to emcee the event and bring comfort to those who attended. We knew we were there to offer our musical talents. But what could we say that could possibly help these people? Expectations were high. The ten-thousand-person arena sold out in thirty-eight minutes.

On the way in, I met a first responder. He told me he was at the school ten minutes after it happened. I couldn't imagine what he saw in those classrooms and hallways, or how it had haunted him every day. I had no words of comfort for him. I just cried with him.

As we gathered together to pray beforehand, Mark Hall with the band Casting Crowns commented that this was the first time all of these confident performers had ever come to an arena of this size and had no idea what to say or do. Then he reminded us why we were there. "At an event like this, there are no musicians. There are no artists. It's just a bunch of us mommies and daddies who didn't know what else to do but come."

We prayed for all of the people who would be in the audience that night. The mommies and daddies, sisters and brothers of the children who were killed. The grandparents. The aunts and uncles and extended family. The friends and neighbors. The first responders and their families. The teachers and the school administrators and all of their families. We also prayed for the people who lived in Newtown and the surrounding areas. We knew that they would be forever traumatized by this event because they had a front-row seat to the horror that took place.

Throughout the evening, we each got up and sang our songs—blubbered through them might be a better description. We all tried to share something from our hearts; but mostly, we just said how inadequate we felt to be standing in the presence of such grief.

The nation was heartbroken and so were we, but we were there to provide hope. While each of us did the best we could, none of us knew what to say.

But there was one person who did . . .

About halfway through Steven Curtis Chapman's set, his wife, Mary Beth, got up to speak. Steven and Mary Beth have six children. The three oldest are biological children and the three youngest were all adopted from China. In May 2008, their five-year-old daughter Maria Sue was accidentally killed when she was struck by an SUV in the Chapmans' driveway.

As Mary Beth took the stage that night, she knew firsthand the grief the audience was feeling. She understood the unexpected timing and horror of it all. She had been living with loss and the ensuing depression for nearly five years. She took the mic and said, "I know you feel like you're not going to make it through this. But you will. God will carry you, because God carried me. I didn't think that God could bring me through it, but he has."

Of all the people who spoke that night, Mary Beth was at the mic for the shortest amount of time. She will tell you she is not really a speaker, but she did what none of us could do. And if I tried to quote her exactly, I couldn't do it justice. Tears are the most vivid memory I have from that night. But when she spoke, a hush fell over the room, tears fell, and God used her story.

I saw her backstage a few minutes later. I hugged her and we both wept.

"Mary Beth," I said, "I hate your story! I wouldn't wish your story on anyone, not even my worst enemy. Yet there is no one in this room who could deny that God used it in such a powerful way tonight to introduce people to the hope that can be found in Jesus Christ. God has used your story to minister to this whole community in a way that none of the rest of us could have. Because you've walked through it, you can give testimony to what God might do, how he might work all things together for good—even this terrible tragedy."

Christian artists can sell millions of albums and reach millions of people with music. Renowned speakers can preach and authors can sell millions of books. But nobody else that night could address the needs of that community in the same way Mary Beth Chapman could.

What trials are you walking through?

Could God be using your trials to better equip you for his work?

What brokenness are you experiencing?

How can God redeem it for his glory?

In every trial you experience, he is closer than you ever could imagine. He doesn't leave us or forsake us. We're often afraid that sharing our story will lead to isolation. The truth is, not sharing our story leads to isolation.

I started this chapter by saying: "Everything I know about God I learned from stories about his people." Like David's story, sometimes those life stories came from the Bible. But often, the stories where I learned about God's comfort, provision, love, protection, and power to redeem came from friends, family, people I met at church, and hurting people I met on the road while traveling.

Like the woman who had the abortion and started a ministry for others who'd also had abortions.

Like Renee and Elaine, who bonded over an introduction.

Like the pastor who started a group for parents of children with addictions.

Like my friend who faithfully served before, during, and after her divorce.

And like Mary Beth Chapman.

I wished my story had started with, "I won the lottery!" and ended with, "And we lived happily ever after." But that is not a story that God can use. And to be honest, is that a story that would comfort or inspire you?

The heroes of the faith I grew up learning about weren't heroes because of their stories; they were heroes because they *shared* their stories. The only thing we're called to emulate is their dependence on God.

In our worst trials, and especially in our extreme brokenness, God is the only hero of our story.

And *that* is a story worth sharing.

MYTH: MY STORY ISN'T WORTH MUCH.

TRUTH: MY STORY IS MY GREATEST OFFERING.

FIFTEEN

TRUSTING MY ROLE

MY MOM WAS IN TOWN, AND WE MET FOR LUNCH AT A
sushi restaurant. As I caught her up on everything going on, I was
overwhelmed with gratitude for my life. After Martin's surgery, I'd
worried about having a job. Now I had *two* jobs and I loved them
both. They gave my life purpose and meaning. The national ministry
provided me the opportunity to work alongside other artists, min-
istering to hurting people. The church job let me be in community
with people I cared about and who cared for me. It wasn't the life I'd
planned, but it was a good life.

"I'm so thankful God gave me this ministry!" I told her. "While
our friends are all starting families, Martin and I are blessed with
this great adventure."

"How do you feel about that?" Mom asked.

"Although we'll never have kids like we wanted, I feel very fulfilled in what I'm doing," I said.

I dipped my sashimi in the soy sauce and then slowly chewed it.
Martin and I had both grown up in great families, and we'd always
wanted to have our own kids. When we got married, we'd decided
that even if we couldn't have children biologically, we would adopt.
But having children was something Martin and I no longer felt that
we could do. Even if we could have kids (which would be a miracle
because of Martin's health situation), I wasn't sure we'd be good

parents. I didn't think it was enough to *want* to have kids. I felt we needed to be responsible and ready for them. I already dealt with enough anxiety over how I would provide for the two of us, and I couldn't imagine adding a third person to that equation. Though the conversation came up between us occasionally, Martin and I didn't spend much time talking about it; the subject was too depressing.

"I've accepted that God's plan for my life is to have this national ministry yet also be plugged into the local church. I think the two complement each other well. I just don't think kids are a part of God's plan for us," I said.

"I hear you, and I think that's beautiful," Mom said. "But I wouldn't rule out having children."

"Really?"

Mom and I hadn't talked about having children for a couple of years, so I was a little surprised that she brought up the subject. "I just don't see that happening."

"Why not?"

"Have you seen us? Somebody should adopt us! We're like two kids who can barely take care of ourselves. I don't see us ever having children," I said. "But I'm okay with that."

Mom reached across the table and patted my hand. "Just don't close the door yet," she said, and the conversation moved on.

Later that night, I thought about what she'd said. She just didn't understand that Martin and I weren't fit to be parents. To be a good parent you needed a surplus of time, energy, money, and love. It seemed we only had deficits. Plus, our marriage was far from perfect.

I was surprised that she brought it up. Mom has always been extremely conservative. She probably thought she could handle four kids—and that's why she only had three! So after all of the time she'd spent with Martin and me and all our issues, I couldn't imagine how she thought we'd make good candidates to start a family.

But there was something more.

Something I hadn't mentioned to anyone—not even my mom.

Though I thought my maternal feelings had long since been dead and buried, they had come creeping back and started showing up in some surprising ways. First, there was a longing in my heart and an ache in my womb when I held my friends' new babies. Then I found myself on the floor playing games with my friends' toddlers and watching their faces as they discovered something for the first time. I imagined playing outdoors with older children and taking them hiking and camping.

I noticed every sweet moment when a child reached his or her arms out to a parent, wanting to be picked up and held. I wondered what it must feel like to have those chubby little arms around my neck or to have the warm smells of a freshly bathed newborn in my house.

Though those maternal feelings had crept back, having children was a dream that had died and was buried at sea. Since I'd prayed about starting a family on our cruise several years earlier, I had accepted God's answer that Martin would be enough. And he was. But since then, God had given me so much more—including an amazing opportunity to travel and minister to others through music.

After the 2008 release of my *Great God Who Saves* album, my touring schedule really picked up. I started traveling with other musicians to play at churches and other venues. We'd load up the tour bus on Wednesday night and head out, sometimes returning early on Sunday for church and other times on Monday just in time for my first meeting.

The groups that asked me to tour with them knew I needed bunk space for two because Martin would be with me. Sometimes he'd help with the sale of merchandise or he'd work the child sponsorship table. He had small roles, but nothing more official than "Laura's husband."

While on the road, I'd met musicians' wives who'd struggled with feeling purposeless and lacking their own identity separate from their husbands'. I could tell Martin was feeling the same way.

204 · WHEN GOD DOESN'T FIX IT

As my time on the road increased, so did his frustrations. He wanted to fit in. He dreamed of being able to meaningfully contribute and get satisfaction from his contributions. I wanted that for him too. I just wasn't sure how to help him make it happen.

"Would you like to apply for a job with the road crew?" I asked one day.

His eye roll betrayed his thoughts. Being a roadie wasn't this former IT guy's dream job.

But he asked anyway, "What would that look like?"

I told him how it would give him a role on the road, a job he could do and feel like he was part of the production. But after a long conversation of debating the merits, we realized it wasn't his skill set or gifting. More than that, he was tired of doing my thing. He'd been either on the road or at work with me for so long that he wanted to do his own thing for once.

The problem was, neither of us had any idea what that might look like or how to find it. Without me at home to drive him to work, how would he get there? And we weren't sure what kinds of jobs would be suitable for him to do. Because of his brain injury, Martin had a hard time reading, as well as comprehending and following long directions. The best way for him to learn something was to do it over and over and over again, until he formed a sort of "muscle memory" that overrode his short-term memory. But where could he find a job where they had the patience to first teach him and then allow him enough practice repetitions to learn to do it on his own?

Martin having a job was like us having children: a dream I knew we'd never fulfill. But the longings for both dreams had returned.

Was God trying to tell us something?

Or were we supposed to just ignore our feelings and hope they went away?

Over a period of several months, I casually mentioned to a couple of close friends that I was feeling that maternal tug again. Each of them encouraged me to have kids.

"How can I do that when I've never had a role model who was a working mom?"

"That's not hard," said a coworker. "There are plenty of working moms at Perimeter. Find one of them to be your role model."

To another, I asked, "What will I do with the kids when I travel?"

A musician who had always traveled with his family said, "Take your kids on the road with you."

"What about the additional expense of having kids?" I asked a friend at Bible study who had five kids.

"Let me get this straight. Are you saying you don't think that if God blessed you with a child, he'd provide for that child?" she asked.

"Martin's disability requires a lot of time and energy from us both," I told a friend who asked if we were planning to have kids. "I'm not sure how a child would fit into that."

"You won't know until you have one," the friend replied.

I heard their encouragement and, despite my doubts, I listened to their advice on how to overcome my objections. As the intensity of my longing for a child increased, I started having conversations with Martin, who had his own set of protestations. Now I was the one countering his objections with solutions.

"What kind of dad can I be when I can't even drive my kid to baseball practice?" he asked.

"Lots of moms I know tell me they're the ones driving their kids to sports, not their husbands."

"What if I forget his or her birthday?"

"We'll put it on your calendar, and I'll make sure to remind you."

After several months of these kinds of conversations, Martin and I agreed it wouldn't hurt to investigate a few adoption agencies to see what we needed to do to be eligible to adopt from them if we couldn't have one on our own. Together we looked at websites and talked to people who had completed international adoptions. But everything we heard was discouraging. We could tell we wouldn't be a fit for their criteria. So a few weeks later, we explored domestic agencies. We were sad to learn that they turned down couples for something as simple as one parent having OCD. We knew our issues would be harder to deal with. Though I'm a musician, I could do the math.

We would never qualify to adopt through an agency.

We sat down with a professional adoption counselor who lovingly told us that we should pursue a private adoption. But of course this is harder to do—they don't advertise online. So when we were introduced to a birth mother and she wanted us to adopt her baby, we were ecstatic! We felt so blessed by God.

But a few months before she delivered, she unexpectedly changed her mind, leaving us stunned. Not only had God closed the door, but he had kicked it shut in our faces.

That was enough for me. The blow of the failed private adoption left me never wanting to try again. We'd faced rejection after rejection and it confirmed everything I'd ever thought. We would be *terrible* parents. If we couldn't qualify to adopt children who desperately needed parents, what did that tell us about whether we should have our own kids?

It was a harsh reality we needed to face.

We weren't going to be parents.

At one of my lunch meetings with my mentor, Sherri, I filled her in on my conversations with Martin and the results of our search. "So we're done trying to adopt," I announced. "I don't care how much I want to have kids; it's obvious God doesn't want us to have them."

"Let me ask you this," she said, choosing her words carefully. "Before you shut the door, is it you who is shutting the door, or is it God? Because it sounds like you haven't really stopped and prayed about this since you prayed on the cruise ship."

"That's true."

"Well, if I remember correctly, God didn't tell you no then."

"No, he didn't. He just wanted me to be satisfied with a family of two. And I am. Martin is enough for me, but I still feel this desire to be a mother."

"Then I think before you shut the door, you should pray and ask God what he wants for you."

As always, Sherri's advice was right on target.

When I got home that night, Martin and I sat down and had a long talk. "I know we've kicked the idea of having kids around a bit recently, but I feel like when we talk about it, we usually conclude that it is a terrible idea. Yet our friends think we should consider it. Because I'm getting older and my biological clock is ticking, I think we need to pray more intentionally about this decision, or it will be decided for us."

Martin agreed, and we began praying about it together and separately.

Then, as we so often did when we weren't sure what God was telling us, we invited other couples into the process. We met with five couples separately, told them of our desire to have children, and gave them all the reasons why we shouldn't. Then we asked each couple to pray and see what they heard God saying. We also invited them to give us their best counsel. "There's no time frame on this. Take as long as you need," I said. "But whatever the outcome, Martin and I just want to be sure it is God's decision, not ours."

During that time, we didn't mention anything to either set of parents, and we didn't ask them to pray about it. We figured they had already given up on the idea of having grandchildren, and we didn't want to put them in an awkward situation where they felt one way, but we heard God calling us in another direction.

It took about six months before all the couples came back to tell us what they'd sensed from God. The message was loud and clear: children are not God's reward for perfect people with perfect marriages.

I remember the husband of one couple asking, "Has Martin's disability hindered his ability to love you?"

"No, not at all."

"Then I don't think his disability will hinder his ability to love a child."

"Will it be hard? Absolutely!" one of my friends said. "But when has hard ever stopped you and Martin in the past?"

Another couple reminded us that with God anything was possible. "Will your family look different from everyone else's family? Yes. But Martin's disability, his inability to drive, and the fact that you work full time aren't deal breakers when it comes to having kids."

One woman asked, "Do you want to have kids?"

"More than anything in the world!" I said.

I still remember her response: "Then don't let the death of one dream lead to the death of another."

It was a unanimous thumbs-up to go ahead with having children. God had clearly spoken.

"We can start trying to have kids!" Martin said later that night.

"I know, it's crazy, isn't it? Just think, nine months from now our life could look very different!" I said.

Nine months later, our life looked exactly the same.

I hadn't gotten pregnant and now the disappointment we felt was worse. We'd prayed. We had others pray. We'd listened and given ourselves permission to believe that we could be parents. But nothing happened, and with each passing month, the disappointment only grew. It was hard to understand how God had given us the green light to get pregnant, yet hadn't blessed us with a baby. And it wasn't just that I couldn't get pregnant; it was that we also knew this was our only option. We would never qualify for an adoption through an agency. If we were going to have kids, they would have to be biological, and my body didn't seem to be cooperating.

I won't pretend I understood what was happening. No theological explanation made sense or made me feel better. We had prayed about having children, but my womb was still empty. Another Christmas would go by without the sound of a child's feet pitter-pattering across the floor, and though it might sound stupid, that was the thing I was holding on to.

One thing that helped distract me was a call from one of my

dearest friends, Marcus Myers. We knew each other well because we'd spent so much time touring together in a band called Silers Bald while I was in college. Marcus and his wife, Katie, had moved to Atlanta and they were temporarily living in an apartment. They wanted us to help them find a safe and cheap place where their daughters—Sadie, age three, and Reece, two—could play outside.

Martin and I met them for lunch one day and got to know their two beautiful girls. After lunch we invited them over to our home. Martin took Marcus downstairs to show him the extra space we had in the basement while Katie and I got something for the girls to drink. When the men came upstairs, Martin said, "Marcus and Katie are going to move in with us!"

"Isn't that a great idea?" Marcus asked.

I glanced at Katie, and she looked as stunned as I felt.

"What happened while you were downstairs?" I asked.

"I showed them all of the extra room we have, and we're not doing anything with it, so I asked Marcus if he'd like to move in," Martin said.

"Let's take a little while to pray about this," said Katie.

"Yeah," I nodded in agreement.

When the girls finished their drinks, we stood in the driveway and said good-bye. As they drove off, I could see Sadie and Reece waving at us from their car seats.

We hadn't been back inside the house five minutes when Katie called and said, "We'd love to move in!"

They were able to get out of their apartment lease and, practically overnight, we went from two in the house to six!

Katie worked as a night nurse in the Neonatal Intensive Care Unit (NICU) of a local hospital. On the nights she worked, Martin and I got to have a taste of what parenting was like. We'd help Marcus feed the girls, get their baths, brush their hair, and read bedtime stories. While they weren't our children, it was still a sweet blessing.

I tried to keep busy burying myself in work, especially on the new album. We were almost finished, but we needed one more song. The problem was, we'd spent all of the money in the album budget so whatever we came up with had to have a simple approach.

"Well, I have this one song I haven't really done much with," I said to my producer. "I just wrote it a few months ago."

"Let's hear it," he said.

"It's called 'Blessings,'" I said, taking my seat behind the piano.

I'd finished writing the song the day after Martin and I arrived in Bentonville, Arkansas, but it was such a personal song that I'd shared it with only two other people. It was a difficult song because of the hard truth it contained, but I knew my producer would tell me if it was a bad idea to include it on the CD. But his words surprised me.

"That's a nice song," he said, as I played the final chords. "We could do it with just pianos and vocals, so it won't cost us anything."

Somewhere along the way, the label decided that "Blessings" should be the radio single. It was a complete surprise to me because I never saw the potential in the song and I didn't think they would choose it. In February 2011, we released "Blessings" as the single, and the album followed in May, debuting at No. 2 on the Billboard Christian Albums chart. A few weeks later, in June, "Blessings" reached No. 1 on the Billboard Christian Songs chart and stayed there for four weeks. We were all dumbfounded how a song about worshipping God during hard times was such a big hit. It was humbling to think that the most commercially successful song I'd ever written was also my most intimate and personal song. While sales numbers were nice because they paid for our groceries, the greatest blessing to me was that every time I sang the song in concert, it reminded me that God deserved my worship, even in my brokenness. And that message was something I needed to hear frequently.

With the success of the new album, I was busier than ever with tours and concerts. Martin began to stay home more and not travel with me as much. It was easier for him since Marcus and Katie were at the house, so he wasn't alone or lonely. We expected them to move out later that fall, but we all enjoyed living together so much that we decided they should stay a couple more months.

"Are you okay with us being here past Christmas?" Katie asked.

"Of course!" we both said. We were thrilled. We loved having them and the girls around as long as they needed to stay.

In December, Katie helped me get the Christmas decorations out of storage. As Katie hung up Sadie's and Reece's stockings, the girls started talking about Santa coming. Their faces lit up as they proudly hung ornaments they'd made on the tree.

Touring kept me busy almost up until Christmas Day. I was more exhausted than usual from the concerts on the road as well as all of the December musical events at church. On Christmas morning, I didn't set an alarm. However, around seven that morning, I heard the Myers family up and about. Apparently the girls had awakened and couldn't wait to see what Santa had brought.

When I heard the sound of Sadie's bare feet on the hardwood floors downstairs, I got up and threw on my robe. Katie and Reece reached the family room at the same time I did. Marcus was already there plugging in the tree lights, and Martin was sitting on the couch and drinking coffee. I could hear Sadie squealing with delight as she found her stocking and presents with her name on them.

"Look, this one's for you, Reece!" she said, bringing her baby sister a package with a big red bow.

I sat down on the couch and Sadie came running over. "Look what Santa brought me!" she said, holding out something pink and sparkly.

"Sorry if the kids woke you," Marcus said. "I know you probably wanted to sleep later."

"Nope. I'm glad I was awake for this. I wouldn't have missed it for anything!"

And it was true. Sitting next to Martin on the couch, watching the girls bounce from adult to adult showing off their new gifts, gave me a deep sense of satisfaction—as if everything was right in the world. They weren't my girls, in the way I'd wanted to have kids of my own, but there was no denying the genuine love I felt for them and the healing they'd brought to our sorrow. I thought back to those moments of depression when I didn't think I could possibly make it through another Christmas without a child, but I had. And I could even say I was happy.

That night, lying in bed next to Martin, I reminisced about waking up to the sounds of Sadie. God had answered my prayers. I'd heard the patter of their feet, and I'd seen the tree lights reflected in their eyes. When I told God that I couldn't make it through another Christmas without a child, he'd sent two beautiful and precious girls to be with us. Somehow, having them with us made things better than I ever could have expected.

God was still faithful, and he still heard and answered my prayers. *Thank you, Jesus, for giving me this gift on your birthday.*

For so long, I thought God needed my help to make his will happen. But I was tired of playing God. For the past three years, I'd tried to control everything. I'd prayed and asked others to pray. We'd pursued adoption agencies and a private adoption, and all of them fell through. And for more than a year, I'd been trying to get pregnant and failed at that too. Though it had still been a magical Christmas, I was emotionally exhausted from trying to figure out God's plan and from trying to help him make it happen.

While lying in bed that night, thinking about Mary, the mother of Jesus, I realized that all of this wasn't up to me. God was the only person who could create life, and he could do it in miraculous ways. *I* didn't have to do anything. God was ultimately the one in control of the timing and the answer to my prayers and my pregnancy if that was his will. He was in charge, not me.

It was only by recognizing that God didn't need my *help* that I truly began to understand my *role.*

My role wasn't to help him provide a baby through phone calls, prayers, or other people.

My role was to trust him.

If God truly wanted us to have a child, he could make it happen in the most miraculous of ways. It wasn't up to me. I had to release my dream of controlling the ways and means of growing our family to him. Perhaps he didn't want us to have children the same way I thought he wanted us to. Perhaps he wanted us to have children in the way we had Sadie and Reece—for a season. I had to be willing to trust him no matter what. So once again, I had to die to self, bury my dream, and let God lead us where he wanted.

Thanks to Sadie and Reece, I didn't feel quite so sad about it. The girls had shown me that even if God never gave me a child, he saw me and heard my prayers. That Christmas, I accepted that there were different ways to create families that didn't look like anyone else's family. More important, I learned that God could, and would, provide for my deepest longings.

It just might look different.

MYTH: GOD NEEDS MY HELP.

TRUTH: GOD WANTS MY TRUST.

SIXTEEN

RESURRECTED DREAMS

WHEN MARTIN AND I WALKED THROUGH HIS MEDICAL trials, we saw a lot of things die. Our vision for our future. Our dreams for each other. Our idea of a perfect family. Sometimes they died all at once; other times, our dreams slowly withered away. When they did, I thought they were gone forever. But occasionally God allows a dream to die so that we can see his power greatly displayed.

In chapter 11 of the Gospel of John, Jesus was traveling with his disciples when he received a message from his friends, Martha and Mary of Bethany, that their brother, Lazarus, was very sick. Though they didn't say so directly, the implication from the women was that they wanted Jesus to come to Bethany and heal him. But Jesus stayed where he was. It took him four days to return to Bethany.

When he arrived, he heard the bad news.

> When Mary reached the place where Jesus was and saw him, she fell at his feet and said, "Lord, if you had been here, my brother would not have died." (John 11:32)

They were upset that Jesus hadn't fixed Lazarus. Jesus understood their disappointment. But these sisters were his friends and not even they fully understood who he was. He was about to show them that death has no power over him.

Jesus is the resurrection and the life. He is the enemy of death, and he alone can defeat it. He resurrects dead things and brings them back to life. He didn't need help or for Mary and Martha to tell him he was too late to raise Lazarus from the dead. In front of the gathered crowd:

> Then Jesus said, "Did I not tell you that if you believe, you will see the glory of God?" (v. 40)

He prayed, thanking God for hearing him, and then commanded Lazarus to come out of the grave. To the surprise of the sisters and the crowd, Lazarus shuffled out, still tightly wrapped in his burial clothes. Jesus did his greatest miracle yet, on his own timetable. Though Mary and Martha had urged him to come sooner and may have felt unloved when he didn't come quickly, those weren't his concerns. Their urgency didn't stir him. And his love for them never changed. He alone could see the future and know the perfect time and the perfect way to answer their prayers.

So what was the sisters' role in this story?

What is our role?

Like Mary and Martha, we can call on Jesus to heal those who are sick. But, if and when Jesus doesn't show up like we think he should, we can't conclude that he doesn't hear us, that he doesn't care, or that he doesn't love us. Nothing Lazarus's sisters said or did could have changed Jesus' timing. And the only thing Jesus asked of Mary and Martha is the only thing he asks of us. Their role and our role is the same.

Believe, and be witnesses to the glory of God.

This is also what Jesus wanted for the crowd that day. He waited four days, so that all of the Jewish mourners who were gathered would know that Lazarus was truly dead. This wasn't some kind of trick. Lazarus wasn't napping. There was no spirit or soul circling his body, waiting to reenter it. Lazarus was four days dead—stinkin' dead.

And through the power given to him by the Father, Jesus raised Lazarus from the dead.

The crowd was there to believe and witness God's glory.

Jesus doesn't raise everyone from the dead. He raises *believers* from the dead to spend eternity in heaven with him and God the Father.

And sometimes, like the crowd gathered that day in Bethany, we can be surprised by seeing Jesus raise things we thought were already dead. This is what Abraham experienced with Isaac. He thought God was calling him to sacrifice his son, but at the last minute, God substituted a ram for the offering.

Is there something you've let go of because *you* couldn't make it happen? Do you believe that if you offered it to God he could raise it or make it happen?

Jesus takes dead things and revives them. He is the life. He is the resurrection. And it is through your belief in him that you will see the glory of God, just as Martha and Mary did. Jesus has the power to resurrect the things we've let die—our hope, our healing, our family, our mind, and our body. And though he doesn't promise to restore everything until we enter Restoration, occasionally we get a glimpse of things we let die being revived. And in that moment we see the glory of God.

I know this, because I have seen him do it.

There were so many things Martin and I had to let die during our brokenness. Martin's desire for a job. My hope to have kids and stay home with them. Or the simple prayer that our path could be easier.

Sometimes we had to let these things die more than once.

Like Mary and Martha, I wanted things to happen my way and in my time. But when I stayed focused on my shortsighted view of the situation, absorbed in my own grief and loss, I missed seeing Jesus, the resurrection, and the life who was standing with me the whole time. He had given me so much, including this wonderful ministry. So I let go of my dreams again, because I knew I wasn't the one who could fulfill them, and I didn't want to spend another minute chasing dead dreams when Jesus offered me eternal life.

ℒ

In late January, I thought my holiday travel schedule had caught up with me. I wasn't feeling like myself and seemed to be more tired than usual. My touring schedule was due to pick up in the coming weeks, so I decided to go to the doctor and get my hormone levels checked out before I got back on the road.

And there in the doctor's office, I saw my Lazarus.

My dead dream had risen again, this time in the form of a pregnancy test.

I was pregnant! Martin and I were going to be parents!

Martin and I were thrilled beyond measure, but we were also a little fearful about telling our parents that they would soon be grandparents. For several weeks we kept the news to ourselves. Only a small group of our closest friends even knew that we'd been trying. Neither of us had told anyone in our family.

When I learned my mom was coming down to spend the weekend with us, I knew it was time to break the news. It had been *three years* since our conversation over sushi, and we'd never talked about it again. I had no idea how she'd feel about us having a baby. No one in our family expected us to have kids. We never talked about it. In hindsight, I was scared people wouldn't think it was a good idea. And I understood why. We weren't sure we thought having a baby was a good idea either.

That Friday, all I could think about was how to tell my mom when she arrived. I considered several ways I could surprise her and make a big deal out of announcing it. But, in the end, I decided it was just best to wait until we were having coffee or a meal. I needed an opportunity to talk with her and find out her true feelings. I realized Martin and I looked like a sinking ship that was about ready to add another passenger. If she didn't think it was a good idea, I wanted her to be able to digest the news in her own way.

Later that evening, Mom arrived with a suitcase in one hand and a bag of goodies in the other. "I've just been to your grandmother's, and she wanted me to bring you some things," Mom said.

"Here, sit down," I said, pulling up a chair. I could hardly look her in the eye. Though I was only a few weeks pregnant, I was sure my stomach was already growing and it would betray the secret I was keeping. *Don't say anything. Wait until the right opportunity comes up.*

"I have some stuff I brought you from home," Mom said. She reached into the bag and started pulling things out. "Here are some muffins your grandmother made, and she sent you some preserves—"

Mom hadn't been in my house more than thirty seconds when I interrupted her. "I have something to tell you," I blurted out. "I'm pregnant!"

Mom stared at me.

She looked completely confused.

Then she looked back in the bag and said, "And I brought these potholders that your grandmother made . . ." It was as if she hadn't heard a word I'd said! She just kept pulling things out of the bag and telling me who sent them.

I didn't know what to do. I expected her to be happy, or maybe even upset. I didn't expect her to have no reaction! She kept talking about my grandmother, giving me updates on her health. She acted as though I'd never even opened my mouth. I knew she'd heard me; I'd seen the look on her face. I didn't know what to say or do.

I finally said, "Mom, you heard what I said about me having a baby inside of me, right? Are you okay with that?"

She started crying.

"Are you mad at me?" I asked.

"No," she said, choking back her tears. "It's just too good to be true!"

I hugged her as she cried, sitting there in my kitchen chair.

Being pregnant was something we all had to get used to. We'd spent so long thinking it would never happen, and now we had less than nine months to know it would. A few weeks later, as Martin and I were once again marveling at the fact that we would soon have a baby, we began to see how deliberate God's timing had been.

For the past year, Martin and I had been able to learn how to take care of little girls from Marcus and Katie. When Katie was working at the hospital and Marcus gave Sadie her bath, Martin would blow-dry Sadie's hair. We watched them parent Sadie and Reece, and we learned how to love a child unconditionally without enabling them, how to disagree with each other as parents but be united in front of the children, how to discipline, care for, and play with kids, and anything else we'd ever want to know about parenting. While we would both be better parents from all that we'd learned by watching Marcus and Katie, this was especially important for Martin. He learned best through constant repetition. For the past year, he'd gotten practice every day, over and over again, as he watched and interacted with the Myers family.

We had been impatient, doing everything we could to bring a child into our lives. But God has a plan from the beginning of time, and once again his timing was perfect. He'd not only resurrected our dead dreams, he'd done it in a way and time frame that was greater than anything any of us could have imagined.

At my next doctor appointment, the ultrasound revealed we were having a girl! God had been preparing our way as parents even before we knew we were pregnant. It was his way of reassuring us that he had a plan for our family and it would unfold in his timing, not ours.

Jesus resurrects believers when they die. At the end of time, during the Restoration, he will resurrect everything that has been dead since the fall.

But occasionally we also get to see him resurrect other dead things. It could be a relationship or a dream we thought was dead. It might be an opportunity we thought was long gone. Perhaps it is someone's faith that we thought had been lost in their youth.

When Jesus raises our dead things, he does it in his timing, not ours.

And he does it for one reason—that we might catch a glimpse of his magnificent power and his marvelous glory.

MYTH: I MUST WORK TO KEEP MY DREAMS ALIVE.

TRUTH: I CAN REST WHEN I RELEASE MY DREAMS TO THE HANDS OF MY LOVING FATHER.

SEVENTEEN

THE BLESSINGS OF "BLESSINGS"

I PRAY EVERY DAY THAT GOD WOULD COMPLETELY HEAL my husband. If you could overhear my prayers, they'd sound something like this: *Good morning, God. Is today the day you're going to heal Martin? Because if you heal him, I promise to give you all the glory.*

Every time I pray that prayer, I feel as if God responds in the same way in my heart: *I know, Laura. I know you will. But what if the healing is a process? What if it's going to be a long road that requires more sleepless nights than you've ever imagined? Or what if it requires more faith than you ever thought you had? Will you still give me all the glory?*

"Blessings" is a song about my prayers. It is filled with the questions I was asking in my personal life, with answers I wasn't sure I believed but hoped were true. It is a very personal and vulnerable song, filled with some hard theology. Sharing it publicly was a step of faith, and the response it received grew my faith. "Blessings" became my most requested song. Since it was hard to separate the song from what Martin and I were living through, each time I performed it, I started to reveal a bit more of our story.

We pray for blessings, we pray for peace
Comfort for family, protection while we sleep

We pray for healing, for prosperity
We pray for your mighty hand to ease our suffering
All along, you hear each spoken need
Yet love us way too much to give us lesser things

I didn't write those lines because I thought it would be a cool, artistic way to minister to someone. I wrote them because those were the very things we had prayed for. But as I released them into the world, I worried that I was sharing too much of my story and that I'd stop getting invitations to play and sing. I think I also feared I was the only one who had these questions.

But what happened was exactly the opposite of what I feared. As the song started getting radio play, my concerts were selling out and I was getting booked into larger venues. Invitations to perform for churches, conferences, and festivals poured in. The media called with requests for interviews. I started receiving phone calls at home. At work, my e-mail inbox filled up as people wrote to tell me about their broken stories. It seemed like the more I shared, the more people wanted to share their stories with me.

Instead of isolating me, the song began to help me see how many other people were also broken, hurt, struggling, or looking for hope. Just like I was.

'Cause what if your blessings come through raindrops?
What if your healing comes through tears?

It's a hard theology—one that isn't talked about much in the church. Yet people seemed to understand God's truth in the lyrics because they were experiencing it in their own lives. They lived it out during their own trials. As they found hope in the midst of their brokenness, they shared their stories with me. I was blessed to hear so many of their stories and to see how the words of the song helped people process their own trials as they discovered blessings hidden in raindrops and tears.

I received an e-mail from a father who founded a nonprofit organization whose mission is to help families in tragic circumstances. He said, "The trials of life definitely can be mercies in disguise, if we open our eyes and hearts to that possibility—even in the worst of situations."

He knows from experience. A few years ago, he lost his young daughter, when his son accidentally discharged a pellet gun and shot her. I can't imagine the horror their family has gone through, but he said they are doing remarkably well despite the tragic circumstances. He wrote, "This may sound strange—I wish my daughter were here right now and none of this had happened, but I'm so thankful for the amazing growth that God has provided. I'll never be the person I was before, but now I have a heart for the suffering that drives me each day."

Despite his own tragic circumstances, he believes his suffering has changed him and helped him to grow closer to God. If he believes that after all he's gone through, then how could I believe anything less?

Likewise, when I think of all the sleepless nights I've endured with Martin, I think of people like Jane and her husband who've probably had many more. Fifteen years ago, Jane and her husband were expecting identical twin boys, but at almost thirty-eight weeks, the baby who kicked her most fell deadly quiet. Apparently, the umbilical cord got twisted into a knot, which tightened and cut off his blood supply from the placenta, ending his life. Tragically, the drop in blood pressure resulted in permanent brain damage to his twin, Thomas. For Jane and her husband, what was expected to be a joyous birth of identical brothers, turned into a traumatic birth experience, followed by the grief of losing one of their sons.

Thomas, the surviving twin, was inconsolable. The only time he stopped crying was when he was asleep. Despite their loss, the young couple in their twenties were told that they should "be happy" because they were "lucky to have a healthy boy."

But at eighteen months, an MRI revealed that Thomas wasn't

healthy. The brain injury had left him with a visual impairment, feeding problems, severe social and learning difficulties, and life-threatening seizures. Thomas would never speak. Jane and her husband would never hear "I love you" from their son. Their lives and their marriage were ripped apart by the grief, heartache, and shattered expectations. They sought help to keep their marriage together, but things didn't look good as the emotional scars and grief were so profound.

Thomas was a poor sleeper, and with his constant wailing, Jane found it difficult to cope. "I was so full of anger, I used to rant at God, saying, 'I'm not asking you to heal him, or even make him eat. Just make him sleep!'" Jane wrote. "I had prayed for the safety of my twins every day, and my greatest struggle was reconciling God's goodness to me." Who could blame her for feeling that way? Most of us have been angry with God for much less.

But one day while Jane was ironing, "Blessings" was on the radio and she heard the words:

What if a thousand sleepless nights
Are what it takes to know you're near?
What if trials of this life
Are your mercies in disguise?

"Suddenly I got it," Jane said. "If this is what God has for me, and if Thomas wakes up every night for the rest of his life, then that's fine, because God is God, and I'm not. He has done everything for me, yet I want more from him. My place is to trust him and serve him."

From that point on, Jane reported that she changed her prayers. Soon Thomas started sleeping through the night. When he did wake up, Jane was no longer annoyed; she saw it as God asking her, *Is it still okay when he doesn't sleep?*

"I still have questions," Jane said, "but Thomas is such a happy boy. He's the most affectionate and engaging teenager you could ever wish to meet."

Jane saw other blessings too. Jane says her relationship with the Father is so much deeper, and her once-troubled marriage is now strong. She and her husband have two more wonderful children who adore their brother and look forward to one day meeting his twin.

Many people who hear the song have questions. That's not surprising because I had so many questions when I wrote it. In fact, the whole second verse is full of my doubts about God's goodness and whether he was present in our trials.

> We pray for wisdom, your voice to hear
> We cry in anger when we cannot feel you near
> We doubt your goodness, we doubt your love
> As if every promise from your Word is not enough
> And all the while, you hear each desperate plea
> And long that we'd have faith to believe

When I wrote the second verse, I was confessing my faithlessness. Yet, somehow, God used my faithlessness to instill faith in other people—people like Didi.

Didi started praying to God for a baby when she was only eleven. By the time she was a teenager, she was begging God for children and already thinking how she'd space them out and what she would name them. When she got married at twenty-five, she thought she'd get pregnant on her honeymoon. But five and a half years later, she still hasn't conceived.

Like so many people I've heard from, the first time she heard "Blessings," she had to pull over to the side of the road because she was crying so hard she couldn't continue driving safely. "I was so overcome that even though my deepest desire wasn't being fulfilled, God still loved me. God still had a plan. And as lame as it sounds, I was so filled with hope by the idea that other people who love Jesus more than me and obey better than me ask the same questions and have the same struggles."

Didi is right about many of us asking the same questions and having the same struggles. I discovered that God loves using broken people and broken things. When I had doubts about sharing my story, he'd whisper to me and say he wanted to use the broken things in my life to minister to the brokenness in others. I didn't need all the answers for him to use my story. It was the beginning of my doing ministry in a more vulnerable way than I ever had before. My vulnerability went viral, and people like Becky in turn shared their stories with me.

Becky's first pregnancy ended in a miscarriage. She asked that "Blessings" be played at the memorial service. She wrote me recently and said, "Two days ago, I miscarried again. Even though I have so much pain, anger, and fear to work through, I still cling to the promise that God has a purpose for my suffering, and I now return with an even deeper understanding and appreciation for the truth in your song."

These are hard truths to learn, and it seems that the path to that deeper understanding is often paved with heartbreaking pain. No matter what it is that we are praying for, a time will come when we bump up against what we think God should do and what he allows.

Robin had been married for twenty-seven years when I met her at a ladies' ministry event. Her husband had recently left her, and she said the only way she was making it was on God's strength. But that didn't mean she still didn't have questions.

"I've accepted that I'll never understand how my husband could give up a loving family for what he calls freedom, because that makes no logical sense to me," Robin wrote in an e-mail. "And I'll never understand why God allowed it when he is sovereign and could have prevented it. My finite brain can't comprehend his ways. But I've accepted that I don't need to understand why it happened. Like Job, God doesn't owe me an explanation. I just need to focus on how I will respond. And, right now, I want to shine his glory and accept his blessings, in whatever form they come."

When friends betray us, when darkness seems to win
We know that pain reminds this heart
That this is not, this is not our home
It's not our home

Elizabeth wrote, "I have struggled with friendships, and this line really helped me get through the tough times. It reminds me that all the tears I have shed over being hurt and betrayed by friends are not okay. But it gives me hope that even when bad things happen, God hears me. I thought the tears I shed were a waste, but they were helping me. I saw hope in my sleepless nights of crying out to God, and it's what drew me into his arms. The truth in this song gave me hope in the darkest times of my life. When I didn't know what to do, I played this song, and it got me through. It spoke to me, and blessed me."

It's not wrong for us to hope for healing, comfort, and peace. Those are characteristics of who our Father is. But when I wrote those lines in the song, they were meant to remind us all to hang in there because we're not complete. We were created to live in a world where sin doesn't exist and where there is no separation from God, but we're not there yet. Sin exists on earth, and we see bad things happen as a result of it.

Rebecca knows what happens when sin takes over. Her husband turned forty, lost his job, lost his grandfather, and then lost his mind. He started drinking and would go for days without sleeping. When Rebecca was asleep and snored too loudly, instead of nudging her, he'd take a pillow and try to smother her. Eventually she had to leave her home, not to save her marriage but to *save her life*! At the time she wrote me, she was still healing physically from the beating he gave her the night she left.

She wrote, "I had a love-hate relationship with 'Blessings' when it came out. On one hand, it validated the suffering I was going through and spoke of a future with a hope. On the other hand, it was a daily reminder that I had to accept, even embrace, the deepest pain I'd ever experienced."

She says she doesn't sing the song lightly because she knows how deep her suffering goes and how much the raindrops stung when they fell on her day after day. And her pain continues. Her husband is now in a nursing home. Rebecca says her husband doesn't remember she exists. "He, like Nebuchadnezzar, has lost his mind," she wrote in a recent e-mail. "The alcohol took his mind, my best friend, and our marriage."

Yet Rebecca wrote in her blog about a trip to Kenya, and the discoveries she's made since the loss of her marriage. "There is a breathtaking beauty found in suffering that you can't know until you risk looking for Jesus in the midst of it. That beauty is *so* moving, you gasp in awe of the Creator who gives us beauty for our ashes." Rebecca's story isn't over, but her path toward God continues. On that same trip, she later told a crowd at the church, "God is worth the wait. He is good. He is kind. He is faithful, and he is with you in the middle of whatever you are going through."

Some of the stories I heard were like ours—people left in limbo with no tidy bow to tie up the last half of their story.

Ben and Amanda have one of those stories. They have been married for nine years and have four kids, aged seven and under. Ben has had health problems since birth. He was born with a defective heart and wasn't expected to live to adulthood. At eighteen, he received a heart and double lung transplant. Ten years later, he received a kidney transplant. But now, after twenty years, his lungs are failing again, and he needs another transplant. While doing his transplant evaluation, the doctor discovered additional complications and let Ben know it would be an extremely risky surgery. So what do they do? How does a story like this end?

"We are still waiting to see what God's plan is for Ben," Amanda said. "Each day we live with the uncertainty of not knowing if I will grow old with my husband, or how much time we will get to spend together as a family of six. So much is unknown, but the song 'Blessings' has been a great reminder that God uses all of this for good, and that we are blessed because God is walking with us through this major trial."

Rachel has been on the heart transplant list for sixteen months. Born in 2005, she was found in a basket at a bus stop in Shanghai, China. Tests revealed she was born with only half a heart. They declared her "terminal" and sent her to an orphanage to die. Despite her severely damaged heart, Rachel persevered. While in the orphanage, she experienced tremendous abuse and witnessed tragedies too terrible to write about here. In September 2011, at age seven and a half, she was adopted by the McCary family. Her mom, Lori, wrote to tell me that for her eighth birthday—her first birthday in her new home—Rachel wanted an iTouch. Lori purchased one off of Craigslist, deleted everything, and loaded it with Rachel's favorite apps. She didn't have time to load music on it and promised she would soon. But in her broken English, Rachel said the iTouch already had music, and it was her favorite song. Lori knew it was impossible because they had erased everything on the iTouch, but Rachel insisted. She even knew the words to the song because she had listened to it over and over again—the song was "Blessings."

Rachel seemed to understand that she might not get the heart she needs. A few months ago, while in the car, she suddenly announced, "This is not our home!" The announcement took Lori by surprise as it seemed to come out of the blue, but Rachel just repeated, "This is not our home! Heaven is! This is just our temporary home!"

One evening, Lori had to break the bad news to Rachel that her friend, Teresa, who was undergoing her own transplant, had just died. Wanting to make sure her daughter was okay, Lori asked Rachel if she thought Teresa's death was a good thing or a bad thing. Rachel said, "Oh, it's a good thing for Teresa, but not good for her mommy!"

"I cry even as I type these beautiful words," Lori wrote. "From down the hall, I can hear the song playing for Rachel as she drifts off to sleep. What are the chances that a single song was left on Rachel's iTouch, and that single song was 'Blessings'?" Lori believes that "God, in his providence, had left it there just for her. He has used it to speak deep truths into her failing heart as she nears the end of her battle without the heart she so desperately needs."

It seems that for so many of us going through trials, the unexpected ones are the hardest, but they are also the times we need God the most. "When we know something is coming, we can get prayed up for it," Charlene wrote. "When things catch me off guard, I kind of go into a controlled panic mode where I feel nothing and just try to get through."

This has happened to Charlene twice. The first was when her thirty-year-old husband underwent open-heart surgery for a congenital heart defect. Then five years later, when he was diagnosed with a brain tumor and underwent a twenty-six-hour surgery!

I can't imagine how she made it through that. It was hard enough on me for the few hours we waited on the results from Martin's surgery. But Charlene wrote, "The song 'Blessings' has really spoken to me because I feel I have received so many blessings through that time. Although it was not a good time, God has used this song to really minister to my spirit." As Charlene and her husband continue with his radiation and other treatments, she said, "I know that God has not forgotten me, despite the difficulties I have gone through with my husband."

I was so thankful that God was able to use the words of my discomfort to bring comfort to those who, like Martin and me, were praying for healing. But even more than that, I marveled at how God was able to use the words of my unbelief to help others believe in him.

One young man said he was a heavy drug and alcohol user while he was in high school and his mom was very worried. "She would pray over my car every day," he wrote. One day while he was in the car, the cord to his iPhone quit working. The only station he could get on the radio was the local Christian station—and the song "Blessings" was playing. "I teared up," he wrote. "The words hit me and I realized who I was becoming. I went into rehab that day and changed my life. I knew God was with me." He thanked me for the song and said, "I'm not sure where I'd be without it."

In moments like that, I know it's not because it's a great song, or I am a great songwriter. It's because we have such a great God. Who else could take my ramblings, questions, and doubts, and use them to turn the heart of a teenager? Only God could do that. I couldn't do that if I set out to.

Pam knows how different her life would be without God because she lived apart from him for many years. After some financial setbacks that required her to go to work for the first time in thirty years, Pam took a hard look at her life. "I realized I had walked away from God. Not all at once, not intentionally, but I had slowly wandered off. I felt guilty. It didn't feel like I could go any lower."

On her way to work, she started listening to a Christian radio station, where she frequently heard "Blessings." "I looked up the lyrics and heard the voice of God," Pam wrote. "I sang the words and felt the healing begin to come. I realized God had not changed or walked away, and the circumstances of my life were not punishment."

There was no magic restoration of her finances, and no quick fix in sight. But Pam began to understand that the promises of God weren't for earthly riches. And they weren't always easily understood. "Through the torrential rains in my life, I could see God was still standing right where I left him, waiting for me to turn around. My heart was eased; my soul was comforted. No matter what happened next, he would be with me. I needed to let him pour out the blessings."

Pam says things are financially better now. "I feel a peace that I doubt I could have found without the rain and the heartache." She wonders if she would have been further sucked in to "the bigger, better, shinier lifestyle" she wandered into when she walked away from God. "The consequences of my choices were painful, disappointing, and full of grief. But God showed me his love and grace, and assured me this life will always be difficult, but I never have to walk it alone."

That's an amazing promise, isn't it? No matter what we go through, God will be right there with us. Even when we can't see him or feel his presence, he is there with us.

After a show in Old Orchard Beach, Maine, I met another Amanda. In the summer of 2011, she thought she had her whole life together. She'd just started a new job and had gotten her first apartment. Then on the Fourth of July, she learned her grandmother had passed away from ALS. Amanda and her grandmother were very close. As she drove from New Hampshire to New York for the funeral, she plugged in her iPod and listened to a CD a friend had given her. "Blessings" started playing. "In that moment, I wept harder than I ever have. I gave my life to the Lord. I saw my grandmother's joy and said, 'I want that.'" A few days later, Amanda sang the song at her grandmother's funeral. "I miss my grandmother every day, but I know that without her passing and hearing the song on my iPod that day, I wouldn't be who I am today."

So many people have sung "Blessings" at their church, at a funeral, or at a memorial service for a loved one. Leslie has probably sung it in as many unique places as anyone could imagine. She attended one of my sessions at a National Worship Leader's Conference, but the line was long, and I didn't get to talk to her that day. She later wrote and told me her story.

In June 2011, Leslie and her husband were preparing to help their meth-addicted adult son move out of their home and into a place of his own—but he was injured at work. Since he'd be on extended leave, Leslie and her husband decided to let him stay on at their house. But a professional counselor challenged the couple. "You are *killing* your son by allowing him to continue to live at home!" His words stung but eventually caused Leslie and her husband to see things in a different light. When their son began using drugs again, they found the strength to let him go. They put their son out on the street with no job, no phone, and nowhere to go.

"But we knew it was the right thing to do. After almost eighteen years of fearing he would commit suicide, we realized we had done everything we could to give him a better life, but we couldn't do it for him. He would have to master his life on his own. We made sure he knew we loved him, we explained we would always support him in recovery, but we could not support him in his addiction," Leslie said. Then God did for Leslie what he had done for David and for me. He *put a new song* in Leslie's mouth. She started singing "Blessings."

"I sang it at my family reunion with my son present. I was yet to grasp the message. After we had to release our son to God, I sang it at one of our Families Anonymous meetings, and then I was asked to sing it at a Parents Helping Parents meeting. I have sung 'Blessings' at a Chamber of Commerce meeting where a few other parents and I shared our stories. I have sung it at church, at funerals, to friends facing divorce, and even to a patient in a doctor's office who was dealing with a cancer diagnosis. It seemed this had become *my* song, and I shared the message with many. I believed the words and believed the message."

Life is still full of ups and downs for Leslie, but she continues to sing. I also love how she calls it *her* song, though Ginny would disagree. Ginny says it is her mom's song, because after her father had a series of strokes, her mom took comfort in the song in those moments when her father no longer recognized her. "Blessings" comforted her with God's truth.

So many people ended their letters by thanking me for helping make them aware of their blessings. But I should thank *them*—along with every person who has told me their story through e-mail, phone calls, letters, packages, notes, meetings at conferences, signing lines after concerts, and at so many churches. And especially to all of you who call it *your song*. It's certainly not my song. I truly believe it is God's song, and I am blessed just to get a taste of what he has done with it.

Christian songwriters don't write songs about the truths we've mastered. We write them about the realities we're grappling with.

That's why it can be so affirming to us when we see how others connect with our music.

> What if my greatest disappointments
> Or the aching of this life
> Is the revealing of a greater thirst
> This world can't satisfy?
> And what if trials of this life
> The rain, the storms, the hardest nights
> Are your mercies in disguise?

Every night on tour I sang the lyrics I so needed to believe were true. And over time, I did believe they were true. Not from hearing them echoing around the room, or even from having them stir my mind and spirit, though both of those played a part. What finally convinced me that the words were true was when I heard them back from other people, many of whom were grappling with the same truths and living them out. I was amazed to see their stories give flesh to God's truth. After meeting so many of them night after night, I began to see all of *my* raindrop-blurred blessings and tear-stained healings. The people who shared their experiences with me were returning my vulnerabilities, questions, and stories with their own vulnerabilities, questions, and stories. That helped me to see and know that God's promises are genuine, and genuinely mine.

Somehow God had taken the broken parts of our stories, intermingled them, and used them to draw us all closer to him. And somehow, this mess of brokenness that we created together began this huge work of healing in my life and in the life of my family.

We still experience days when Martin and I look at each other, and while we're overwhelmed with gratitude for the way God has used our story, we still ask, was it worth everything we've gone through? Was it worth Martin losing everything he's lost? There are days we say absolutely yes!

But some days we say absolutely not! But what "Blessings" taught us both is that this is our story, and even in the midst of our hard and broken situation, there are unique blessings that we get to be a part of and the final "Was this worth it?" score won't be tallied until we see God face to face in heaven. And I suspect at that time, it won't matter.

But what does matter is telling our story here and now.

I think that with God's help, we can do more. If sharing my story has blessed you, and if all the fans who shared their stories were a blessing to me, what might happen if we shared them with others? What if telling your story at church would not only be a blessing in disguise for you, but a lifeline to someone who needed to hear God's hope and truth? What if sharing your trials through a blog post or a Facebook status encourages others who are going through their own trials? What if seeing how you've turned to God helps someone else know him?

I know, I hear your objections.

You don't feel that you're prepared to do that. Your story isn't finished. It doesn't have a happy ending. You have too many questions. You're not sure what you believe.

All I can tell you is that every objection you have is an objection that I've had too. Yet, despite my brokenness, this chapter is a testimony not to my song but to what God can do with broken lives.

What could he do with yours?

Sometimes, the things we pray for, like healing, peace, and comfort, are given to us just as we requested. Sometimes, they are withheld. But it's not because God is punishing us.

It's because God has something else for us.

The blessing of "Blessings" has been that while I searched, God used the song to help others identify their blessings, and each time they found theirs, I found mine. If your story is unfinished, broken, or messy like mine, if you feel as though God doesn't answer your prayers, then perhaps it's because he has something better for you. The only way you'll find out is to trust him with your story. I learned that when I was willing to share mine, God used it to heal others emotionally, physically, and spiritually.

And that's what healed me.

MYTH: GOD IS WITHHOLDING WHAT I WANT
BECAUSE HE IS PUNISHING ME.

TRUTH: GOD IS WITHHOLDING WHAT I WANT
BECAUSE HE HAS SOMETHING BETTER FOR ME.

EIGHTEEN

ABUNDANTLY EXTRAVAGANT

FOR ME, BEING PREGNANT WAS DAUNTING. I FELT LIKE I never had a handle on things and there was so much I was unsure of. How would I get to the hospital when I went into labor? Martin couldn't drive me. What would happen if, while I was giving birth, Martin had to leave the delivery room to go to the bathroom? How would he find his way back? What if the baby needed special care? Could we afford it? The questions kept coming, and my fears remained the same: *You're not good enough to be a parent. You don't deserve to have a baby. You never should have gotten pregnant.*

A few weeks after I became pregnant, Martin and I got into a huge fight. I was so scared, sad, and lonely that I curled into a ball on the floor of our guest bedroom and lay there crying. How in the world could we be parents? We couldn't even manage our own marriage! Whether it was hormones from the pregnancy or anxiety over what was about to happen, it didn't matter. All I could think was that my getting pregnant had been a terrible idea. I felt alone, as my tears dampened the carpet. *I can't do this on my own. I need a plan.* I called Sherri, my mentor, to see if she could help.

"This was a terrible idea!" I said when she answered the phone.

"What was a terrible idea?"

"Getting pregnant," I said, sniffling. "Martin and I just had a big fight, and it reminded me what a huge responsibility it is to have children. I don't think we can do this. This baby deserves to have a good home, with good parents, who are better equipped to take care of a child than we are."

Sherri took a deep breath and let out a long sigh. "Laura, children are a gift from the Lord. They are *always* a gift from the Lord. Think about how many friends you have who can't get pregnant. Do you really think it's an accident that God has allowed you and Martin, against all odds, to get pregnant?"

"Well, when you put it that way, I guess not," I said.

"If God didn't want you to have this baby, he would not have blessed you with one."

We talked a while longer, and Sherri reassured me that we didn't have to be perfect to be great parents. She also reminded me that my doubts could be a form of spiritual warfare. Satan would love nothing more than to tear our family apart. By the time I hung up, I'd stopped crying and felt better. We hadn't "accidentally" gotten pregnant. God had *blessed* us with a baby, and *he* would help us raise our child.

Just as Sherri's words and advice meant so much to me, Bill was doing what he could to prepare Martin to be a father. Still, we needed to figure out a lot on our own, and our friends and family recognized that. But in an effort to be helpful, sometimes they made things worse. For example, they'd ask Martin well-meaning questions that he couldn't always answer. Or they would point out how much our lives would change and how much harder it would be with a baby in tow.

Martin began to question himself and his ability to be a good father. He wanted to provide for our baby financially and emotionally. He also worried that, due to his memory limitations, he might not be able to remember all the secrets a little girl tells her daddy. That's when I reminded him there were many kids whose fathers didn't live with them or were too busy to pay attention to them. For some of them, the only time they spoke to their father was when they were in trouble. Children who grew up in homes like that sometimes felt ignored by their fathers. I knew that would never happen in our home.

"I am so thankful our daughter will never feel that way," I said to Martin. "You will always be there for her, and she will always feel loved and cared for by you. That's a precious gift that many fathers can't, or don't, give their children. You have the opportunity to do that."

℘

On September 14, 2012, Josephine Grace Elvington entered our world with a cry that announced healthy lungs. She was the coolest baby ever! We didn't know it was possible to love a little one so much. We oohed and aahed over everything she did and couldn't believe we got to take her home with us a few days later. She was the greatest blessing Martin and I never thought we would have! And she was going to teach us everything we needed to know about being parents.

We had a few hiccups getting settled as a family. One day, Martin answered the door and told friends who had come to see our baby that I was upstairs changing Josie's diaper, and I'd be down in a minute. A few minutes later, I came down the stairs holding a basketful of laundry, with no baby in sight.

"Where's Josie?" Martin asked. "I thought you were changing her diaper."

"I thought you were rocking her to sleep," I said.

We backtracked our steps to find Josie sleeping soundly in her crib. One of us had rocked her to sleep and forgotten that we'd put her down. You might think that a mix-up like that was the fault of Josie's memory-impaired father. You'd be half right. Memory lapses were equally likely to happen for Josie's sleep-deprived mother!

After the initial adjustment, Martin and I, along with Josie's help, got our parenting act together. Just as we'd done with his medical needs, we developed and followed routines for everything Josie needed, from feeding to diaper changing, from bath to bed. So many times, it would have been easier for me to just do it myself. But that wasn't what was best for Martin, for Josie, or to keep me from becoming resentful because I had to do everything. We always performed the same actions in the same place. I organized diaper changing and feeding supplies, so they were always visible to Martin, serving to remind him what needed to be done. Developing these kinds of routines helped him fully be a part of Josie's care. Josie even cooperated to give Martin the repetition he needed to get good at the job! Every couple of hours she'd either need to eat or have a diaper changed, so we *both* had plenty of practice. Eventually, Martin was able to stay home with her for short periods of time. But most days, I took her to work with me swaddled in a baby wrap.

$$\mathscr{L}$$

After Josie was born, several friends warned me about going out on tour. In subtle and not-so-subtle ways, they suggested I might want to give up traveling and performing. I didn't think my lifestyle would change much even with Josie in tow—until we took our first trip.

Josie was only eight weeks old the first time we set out on tour. I took everyone with me—Josie, Martin, my mom, and my manager, Nicole. We flew to Omaha for our first stop, where we were scheduled to play a church the next day. I checked everyone into a nearby hotel. The following night, after we played in Omaha, the bus would pick us up and we'd travel to a few other cities before ending up in Denver, where my brother lived. My dad had rented a condo in Vail and was flying out there to meet us where we would spend a few days together as a family in between our tour dates.

As soon as we checked into the hotel and everyone got comfortable, my manager received a call saying the tour promoter had canceled the entire tour! I was stunned. Fans had already bought tickets and were expecting a show the next evening. I didn't know what to do.

When something like that happens, no one blames the promoter; they think the artist canceled, so the ramifications were huge. I didn't want to disappoint the families who had already bought tickets, and some of the other artists were already in Omaha, so it made sense to do the show anyway and just do it for free. But after the concert, Nicole came to me with more bad news.

"The bus driver just arrived and he was expecting a check and a hotel room. The promoter took the ticket sales receipts and now there is no one to pay the bus driver. I used my credit card to get him a hotel room, but he's refusing to drive without payment."

"Are you kidding? The bus was supposed to pick us up after the show."

"I don't think there is going to be a bus, because there is no money."

"What do you mean there's not going to be a bus? What are we going to do?"

"We'll have to spend another night in Omaha until we get something figured out."

"We still have our reservations, right?"

"Well, not exactly. They weren't paid for either."

"What am I supposed to do? I have my whole family here with me."

"I don't know what to tell you right now other than I am working on it."

So we were stuck in Omaha without transportation, a tour, or a paycheck that I was counting on. I needed to figure out something fast because every day I wasted, more money was sailing out the door. Nicole spent most of the night trying to get answers from the promoter, who we were told had filed for bankruptcy and was no longer responding to our calls and e-mails. She also tried to salvage my reputation with the venues and radio stations that had promoted the tour, while I tried to figure out what to do with my family. After talking with my mom, and having several phone conversations with my dad, we finally decided it would be best for us to travel on to Denver. We arranged to get into the condo in Vail a couple of days earlier than planned, and once that was settled, I ordered airline tickets for the four of us—Mom, Josie, Martin, and me—to fly out the next day.

Traveling with a child was definitely harder in some ways—the most pronounced way being how such a little person could require so much luggage. Josie needed her own entourage to get her checked in at the airport! Fortunately, we were able to board early and get settled. I handed the ticket agent our tickets, she scanned them, and my phone rang. I motioned with my hand for the rest of them to keep going, while I took the call in the Jetway.

"Laura, I'm trying to see if they still want you to do the St. Louis concert," Nicole said.

"I thought the whole tour had been canceled."

"It has, but Steven Curtis Chapman has agreed to do it for free because five thousand tickets have been sold and he doesn't want to disappoint the fans, and I know you don't want to either. That's why I'm trying to get you on this show as well."

"Are you kidding me? Of course I want to help, but I'm walking down the Jetway, with my whole family, to get on the plane to Denver."

"Can't you just get off the plane?"

"Our bags have already been loaded. And my family members are already sitting in their seats. Is this concert a for-sure thing?"

"No."

"Well, then, I've got to get on the plane."

I hung up and flew to Denver with my mom and my family. As soon as I landed, I saw I had a voice mail. It was Nicole with a short message: "If you're up for it, they want you in St. Louis tomorrow."

I called her back and got the details, and then rented a car to drive the four of us to Vail. It was a two-hour trip. We arrived, ate dinner, and went to bed. The next morning, Josie (who was still nursing) and I drove two hours back to Denver. From there, the two of us flew to

St. Louis, where we met Nicole, played a concert that night, slept for a few hours in a hotel, then got up the next morning, flew back to Denver, and drove back to Vail. It was a grueling trip, complete with meltdowns by both Elvington girls.

Mine happened even before we left Denver that morning. I was so stressed and exhausted that I developed a migraine at the airport. I'd never had one before, and I wasn't sure if it would ever go away. The chairs at the gate were filled with people, and I couldn't find a place to sit. Josie was asleep on my chest, wrapped in a baby carrier. I sat on the floor and started crying, trying desperately not to let my tears hit her head so she would stay asleep.

Later that night, it was Josie's turn. After the concert, we were traveling in a van on our way to a hotel, but because the tour had fallen through, so had all of our hotel reservations. So, like the Bible says, there wasn't any room for us at the inn. Or the Holiday Inn. Or the Hampton Inn. Or any other inn. It took what seemed like hours for us to finally find a place to stay. While we worked out our lodging details, Josie began to cry. Soon her crying turned to screaming. Unfortunately, we were in a moving vehicle, and I couldn't take her out of the car seat to hold her.

It had been a long day for both of us, and I began to cry too. I couldn't help but feel sorry for myself and for Josie.

"I am a horrible mother. What am I doing out here in the early morning hours riding around without a place to go with my baby?" I asked Nicole.

She tried to comfort me. "It's okay, and there is no mommy guilt here. Josie won't remember what a horrible day this was."

This is not how I expected my life to turn out. I thought back to my days in Columbia when I was learning how to use my musical talents and gifts to tell people about Jesus. No one told me this was going to be a part of it. I reached into my bags looking for a bottle or a toy to satisfy Josie. Then I started thinking of some of my classmates. Many of them had become full-time missionaries in foreign countries. They were raising their kids without many of the things I took for granted.

"What am I doing complaining?" I asked Nicole. "I am in a nice, heated van on my way to a hotel. I have friends who are raising their kids in far worse conditions in Africa."

I found a bottle and tried to warm it in my hands. "Josie, I know how hard this is on you right now. But you will never know a day in your life when you didn't serve the Lord." I didn't need to apologize to Josie for what we were doing. The fact that she will never remember a day in her life that wasn't lived on mission for the cause of Christ is a *good* thing. It had been a ridiculous amount of travel, but this was the life God had called us to. And so when family and ministry seemed to collide, I relied on God.

God had called our family to this ministry.

Though our family didn't look like anyone else's, this is what we did. As I tried to soothe her, I remembered something that a pastor friend said to Martin and me when we went through premarital counseling. "You should never sacrifice your family for ministry. But you know your family will always make sacrifices for ministry."

Though the trip seemed to be a fiasco, several good things came out of it. First, I had a fresh understanding of another couple who had to travel during the holidays—they also couldn't find room at the inn. But I also got to play with Steven Curtis Chapman, and he would later ask us to go on tour with him, which opened up new opportunities for both of us to minister together. What seemed like a failed travel itinerary had been a part of God's plan all along! It was another blessing in disguise.

ℒ

Two months later, when Josie was four months old, we tried it again. I took my entourage of Martin, Josie, and our nanny out on our spring tour. We embarked with hesitation, but unlike our last tour fiasco, this time it was a huge success. We all had a blast! It was such a sweet time together for our family. It was as if God had perfectly designed our family for this kind of lifestyle.

Our first tour was with Mandisa and Brandon Heath. Right away, Josie became the hit of the tour. The other artists were soon calling themselves "Aunt Disa" and "Uncle Brandon," as they fought over who got to hold her. Before Brandon went onstage every night he'd say, "I have to kiss the baby's head for good luck!" She became our beloved little tour mascot.

Even as a baby, Josie liked being around the lights and the sounds. I even have pictures of her sitting behind the lighting board, bouncing on the knees of the crew. It was an adventure, and she loved it.

As she grew, she loved to see me onstage. Sometimes I would bring her out to introduce her to everyone in the audience. There's nothing better than a toddler drooling on a mic to make an audience swoon. When I was onstage, Martin or our nanny typically took her to the church nursery. Since she was the only child there, she had full reign of all the toys. To her, each venue was like a new toy store, and she could play with anything she wanted without having to share it. If she had any adjustment problems from being on the road, it was usually on Sunday mornings at Perimeter when she had to share the toys with other kids in the nursery!

To her, our life was normal. She just assumed that everyone ate catered meals with thirty of their closest friends. And she wasn't picky. If you had fries, you were her friend. She'd climb down from her chair and beg, "More fries?" Instead of play dates with the kids from the neighborhood, she played peek-a-boo and hide-and-seek with the crew. It tickled me to see those big, hairy, calloused guys talking to her in baby voices. She spread joy wherever she went, and she loved meeting new people. Even after I finished a tour, we'd get calls from band members who'd say, "We miss you, but we *really* miss Josie. Can she come on tour with us?"

We're probably raising Josie differently than most people think we should, but differently doesn't mean better or worse. By the time she was four months old, she'd already been to ten states; and by the time she was a year, she'd probably visited thirty more. When we are on the road, I get to spend more time with Josie and Martin than any other working mother and wife I know. Though there are things I'd like to give her and can't, our days together are the blessing I never thought I'd have.

Before we started touring, I'd always pictured Josie as a left-out child whose mother couldn't be on Pinterest and at play dates because she was working. But nothing could have been further from the truth. I don't go to Pinterest to find out how to throw a one-year-old's birthday party, because no one on Pinterest tells you how to do it on a tour bus. So we make up our own rules, we have our own fun, and every day is truly an adventure.

By being exposed to so many people on the road, Josie has learned how to be strong and independent. She is also compassionate toward those with disabilities. God is the author of Josie's life story, and he's writing her story the same way he's writing Martin's and mine.

Despite everyone's warnings to the contrary, the biggest surprise for me as a working mom was that once Josie started touring with us, I *loved* touring even more than I did before I had her! Having my daughter with me on the road was not a hindrance or an obstacle; it was pure joy for me.

$\mathscr{L}$

Martin's job story is still a work in progress, but we've seen some amazing developments and he's had some really cool experiences. Five months after Josie was born, Martin stepped out on his own and found a part-time job coaching baseball for a season. As a former high school player and a huge fan of the game, it was something he was passionate about. He's had other opportunities, too, like serving at a church.

With each new opportunity, I had to set another piece of him free. First it was his schedule. He'd been traveling with me since we'd gotten married. I couldn't imagine going without him. But as opportunities came up for him, they sometimes clashed with my tour schedule. In the past, every time I went on tour, I'd expected Martin to stop whatever he was doing and follow me because I was the bread-winner. But having something of his own was important to him, so with the help of Sherri and Bill we found ways to make it work without us being separated for long periods of time.

Discussing these matters with Sherri and Bill helped me see that I still had other underlying issues and concerns to work through. Was I afraid to leave him home alone? Did I not want Martin to work because the logistics were harder on me? Was I scared of him failing in public? And what *if* he failed? How would that make me feel? What if he got hit by a baseball or had trouble remembering the kids' names? It was a scary world out there, and I feared what could happen. But rather than let my fears stop us, Bill and Sherri helped me use them as motivation to prepare Martin to do more on his own.

C

Getting Martin ready to stay alone meant coming up with new routines and ways of doing things. Martin would have to learn to be independent at a whole new level. On days someone couldn't pick him up and I wasn't there to drive him, Martin would ride his bike.

The Monday before I was scheduled to leave, we sat down and talked about the weekend. "I'm going to be gone all weekend, so you're going to have to get your own food and take medications on your own. You'll need to remember to charge your phone each night, so you can get in touch with someone if you need to."

I felt like a mother sending her firstborn off to college. There were so many details to remember, and I was afraid I'd forget to tell him everything he needed to know. Or worse, that he'd forget everything

I told him once I was gone. I was nervous that weekend, and I checked my phone constantly to make sure he hadn't tried to call.

But everything worked out fine! In fact, I think it was ultimately a *good* thing for our marriage. For more than seven years, we'd been together pretty much every day. But that Sunday night when I got home and we sat down for dinner, for the first time, I was able to say, "Tell me about your weekend. What did you do?"

Some days, he was better at remembering than other days, but I typically knew enough to elicit a response from him. "You mentioned you were with John. What did you guys do?"

"We went to the movies."

"What did you see?"

"Hmm . . ."

Then I'd name a few movies, and he'd say, "Nope," until I hit the one he'd seen. Then he'd say, "Yeah! That was it."

"Did you like it?"

"I don't know. I don't remember."

It was a huge thing for us. We'd never had a conversation like that before he started working, and now we were having one every Sunday night!

I tried to stay out of the details of these opportunities and allow Martin to do on his own without doing my own reconnaissance on it. For example, I had no idea what he did when he went to a practice, if he contributed to the boys' baseball skills, or if he was there to inspire team morale. A few months into the season, he came home and told me he'd been hit in the head by a ball. He hadn't seen it coming. I wanted to say, "I'm completely in support of your recovery, but it would be a lot easier if you would just stay here and not do anything dangerous." But was that best for Martin, or what was best for me?

Instead, I made sure he was okay and then asked how the rest of practice went.

I had to let him go.

X

Martin had been helping the team for several months when they had a weekend tournament including a game on Sunday—Father's Day. Josie and I attended to cheer on Martin and his team. I was so proud of him as I watched him interacting with the boys.

After the game, one of the boys gave Martin a Father's Day card. It said, "Thanks for being like a dad to all of us on the team." At that moment, I had a glimpse of what Martin was *really* doing. Most of the high-school-aged young men came from extraordinarily successful families with high-achieving dads who could afford to pay the expensive travel team costs for their sons. But because of their responsibilities at work, many of them didn't attend practices, or even games. When they did, they often had unrealistic expectations of what their sons should be able to do on the field, and they weren't shy about expressing their disappointment when their sons didn't live up to their expectations. Most of the boys just wanted to throw the ball around with their dad.

Martin showed up at the fields each day and played catch with these kids. But more than that, he loved on them. In turn, they loved and respected him as a coach and a loving father figure. Everyone I talked to at the fields that day told me Martin is a great encourager. He's not the kind of coach who gets mad and yells at the boys. Martin is the one who says, "It's okay. You'll get it next time. You just need to work on it a little more." Or, "You gave it your all! Good try!" He was always loving and encouraging. He wanted to help the boys do their best.

My greatest fear for Martin is that he will get so caught up in his disabilities that he won't see his abilities. Sometimes he worries that he can't work a forty-hour-a-week job because he doesn't have the brain stamina or organizational skills to do the kinds of jobs he trained for in college. But he doesn't see all that he has to give. I found it ironic that several of the baseball players had dads who were executives at software and technology companies. They were doing jobs Martin would have loved to do but couldn't. When the player gave him that Father's Day card, it was an affirmation of what Martin *could* do.

My greatest desire for him has always been that wherever he served, he would serve with all of his heart and make an impact. The season he worked with the team I saw him do it with the boys, and since then I've seen him do it in his other opportunities.

Being outside of the home isn't easy for Martin. He has to work hard to remember the names of the people he works with. He uses memory tools like taking a piece of paper and writing down names and descriptions such as "Josh—tall, dark hair." "Carrie—short, blonde hair." It can take him months to learn everyone's names, but I am so proud of how hard he works to do what comes easily to the rest of us.

Whether he's working with a team or helping out our friends, I love seeing Martin through someone else's eyes—someone who appreciates him for who he is and what he can do, not for who he was or what he can't do.

Seeing him that way is an *extraordinary* blessing to both of us.

✐

Jesus had resurrected some of the dreams that Martin and I had let die. And he'd done it in the most beautiful and unexpected ways. Not only did we have a daughter, but before we had her we had the training we needed to take care of her. And when she came, she had the perfect personality to take on the road. In addition, God had given me a ministry that had grown through a song I wrote about my doubts. He, in turn, used that song to give hope to so many. Now, Martin was getting opportunities to do things outside of the house, to use his gifts and abilities to minister to others like he had when he led a college Bible study before we got married.

None of these were things that we could resurrect on our own. But God could.

So many times, we think God is sufficient. And certainly God provides for our every need. But there is also evidence that he does abundantly more than we could ever hope for or imagine. When we submit our prayers to him, trusting his wisdom and timing for the answers, we can see the extravagance of the blessings he bestows on us. Our life was an example of that. Though we continued to live through the trials, we'd been extravagantly blessed along the way.

God didn't answer every prayer.

He didn't give us everything we asked for.

But he has always been with us, loved us, and blessed us beyond anything we could ever imagine.

When we go through trials, it's easy for us to pray for protection from harm, for our health, for our safety, and for our own happiness. But I think God has more planned for us than those things. He's asking us if we'll still believe and have faith even if our life isn't comfortable, our days are filled with trials, our prayers aren't answered the way we like, and our dreams die. He's asking us to have faith, even during our trials, because he has more good planned for us than we could ever hope for or imagine.

In 2 Corinthians 9:8, Paul said, "God is able to bless you abundantly, so that in all things at all times, having all that you need, you will abound in every good work." Why wouldn't God bless us abundantly if we're faithful to give him the credit? His blessings are given to help us do his work.

Ephesians 3:20–21 says, "Now to him who is able to do immeasurably more than all we ask or imagine, according to his power that is at work within us, to him be glory in the church and in Christ Jesus throughout all generations, for ever and ever! Amen."

Our trials are part of a bigger plan that we might not see unfolding until years, or maybe even generations, later. That's why our stories are so important. They're part of a much bigger story—God's story. While he doesn't always answer our prayers the way we would like, God gives us everything we need to abound in the good work he has for us. And when we do, our story will bring God glory because he can do immeasurably more than we ask or imagine.

Martin and I have been through trials—we're still going through them—but we came to see that even in the midst of our trials, not only was God there, but he was blessing us. When we submitted our dreams and our prayers to him, we often found his timing and answers weren't in line with our expectations. But neither were the blessings. They were always more extravagant and abundant than we ever thought possible. Nowhere did we experience that more than when we started praying for a brother or sister for Josie.

$$\mathscr{L}$$

I'm sure that many people thought we were foolish to want to add another child to our family. But even before she was born, we knew we wanted Josie to have a sibling. We often joked that she'd need a sibling to go to therapy with her when she was older to verify all of the crazy things that happened in her life!

When Josie turned one, Martin and I started trying to get pregnant again. We firmly believed that this time, it would be without all of the drama and anxiety we had with Josie's pregnancy and birth. We knew parents didn't have to be perfect to be good, and we knew that children were a special gift from God.

But God had even bigger plans in mind. He wanted us to trust him, so he gave us twice as many opportunities to do so. After I got pregnant, a doctor appointment revealed that God had exceedingly and abundantly blessed us with twice as many reasons to trust him.

I was pregnant with twins!

God truly blessed us with immeasurably more than we had asked for, and so much more than we could have imagined. It was just *two* more reminders that we weren't writing our story. He was.

I couldn't create life or bring a life safely into the world. I couldn't take my doubts and use them to minister to people. I couldn't find Martin a job where people loved and respected him for who he is. And on my own, I certainly can't be responsible for two more lives and mouths to feed.

But I don't have to.

Because my God can.

What can he do in your life through the abundant blessings he's given you?

MYTH: GOD IS INDIFFERENT TO THE
DESIRES OF OUR HEART.

TRUTH: GOD IS ABLE TO DO ABUNDANTLY
MORE THAN WE ASK FOR OR IMAGINE!

NINETEEN

A BETTER BROKEN

"CINDY" AND I MET AT A RADIO STATION IN TEXAS. WE were both on a talk-show panel about brain injuries. It had been more than seven years since Martin's brain tumor diagnosis, but Cindy's husband had been injured in a motorcycle accident just a few months earlier. I could relate to all she was going through. Everything she described as his full-time caretaker was what I had experienced, or was still experiencing, with Martin.

While we were on the air, Cindy talked about how difficult her days were. Her husband was struggling with depression and had a short-term memory deficit. Their youngest was a three-year-old daughter, but she couldn't leave the daughter at home with her husband because he was crying all the time and had lost interest in his children because of the depression. No one knew what she was going through because he looked fine. It wasn't as though he had a cast on his leg; no one could see the mental and emotional wounds from his injury. Since it was an ongoing problem (he wasn't going to die from it), people either couldn't see or didn't know that she needed help. But it was obvious to everyone on the panel that she was really struggling. When the interview was over, another woman from the panel thanked Cindy for sharing her story. "Hang in there," she said. "I'm praying for you, and I really believe things are going to get better and your husband is going to have a full recovery."

After she left, I hugged Cindy and said, "I'm not going to say that I think things are going to get better. Hearing your story, I think it's quite possible that things might get *worse*. But even though your circumstances may not get better, I believe *you* can get better."

It's a hard truth to hear that our circumstances might not change and God might not fix the broken things in our lives. But I know personally that even when our situation doesn't change for the better, *we* can change for the better.

In fact, that's the primary reason I wrote this book. Whether I'm at Perimeter or out touring with my music ministry, I'm frequently approached by people of all ages who tell me about their broken circumstances, their seemingly unanswered prayers, and their disappointments with life. They want to know how I got to be "okay," or how I "made it through to the other side."

What I always want to say, but rarely have the time to explain in detail, is that I'm not okay. We're not through to the other side. We're still knee-deep in it and likely always will be. If I had more time to talk to them, I'd say that despite the fact that Martin and I are still hanging on every day, what they see in us is how God has been evident in our story, time and again. He has used it in powerful ways. And he has used it, not because we were special, or famous, or even great examples of people experiencing brokenness in a way that God approved of. I believe he used our story for the same reason he uses others' stories: because we were willing for him to use it. And in our weakness, we were willing to give him the glory.

I believe he wants to do the same for you through your broken story too.

Even though our situations aren't going to get better, there are ways *we* can get better. Our marriages can get better. Our relationships with our children can get better. Our attitudes can get better. Our grief can get better. Our intimacy with God can get better. Though we're still broken, it can be a better broken.

So how do we do that?

I don't know.

Unfortunately, there is no single, easy answer to find purpose, meaning, and even joy in your trials. I'd be a fraud if I tried to offer you a seven-step program, a learn-by-example program, or any other kind of program, because there isn't one. I didn't write this book because I have ten easy steps to happiness or a quick fix for whatever ails you. Each of us is broken in different ways. Our trials and our circumstances are unique. What we have to individually figure out is what it looks like for us to get better even when our circumstances don't. Now, before you get frustrated that you've shelled out money for this book and spent hours of your time reading this far only to find out that I don't have all of the answers, let me explain.

We're never going to have all of the answers this side of heaven.

The Bible doesn't promise us that.

God doesn't promise us that.

♌

One of the ways I got better was to reexamine the things I thought I knew in light of what Scripture says and the various trials I was going through. Throughout this book I've outlined some of the myths I previously believed and the truths that I've discovered. I found that some of the things I believed stood up to Scripture and some of them were a little off. A few were way off. Maybe you've believed some of those lies too. Or maybe you grew up believing your own set of lies. To get better in your brokenness, you need to replace those lies with truth. Relying on the truth of Scripture will definitely help you get better.

For example, one of the lies Martin and I believed for years was that the biggest problem in our marriage was Martin's disability. Maybe you think the biggest problem in your marriage is your spouse's job, your mother-in-law, your prodigal child, or your lack of finances. If you're like us, you blame everything that happens on that one issue. If Martin and I got into a fight, it was because of his disability. If we wanted to do something but we couldn't afford it, it was because of his disability. If we had a hard time communicating, it was because of his disability. If our marriage wasn't good, it was because of his disability.

But that was a lie.

The biggest problem in our marriage was our sin.

Whether it was our need to control or assign blame, our selfishness, or our pride, sin was the real problem. The disability wasn't the problem; it was just the mirror to our sin. Disabilities don't cause relationships to fall apart; it's how our sin manifests itself in that disability setting. But as long as we blamed all of our problems on something that was broken and couldn't be fixed, we didn't have to deal with the problems. If Cindy and I had stuck around the radio station a little longer, I would have told her what this looked like in our marriage.

For example, some days Martin asks me the same exact question five times in a row. When he does that several times a day, it makes me want to punch my fist through a wall! For years, I blamed my anger and mounting frustration on his disability. So did he. If only he were healed, we'd think, we wouldn't have these problems in our marriage. We'd get along better as a couple.

Nothing could be further from the truth.

If he didn't have memory problems, I'd still have a sin problem, and I would just get annoyed at him for something else.

It was my selfish, sinful nature that didn't want to be inconvenienced by answering the same question five times. So when he asked the same thing *again*, I got annoyed and felt put out. Then I'd justify my actions by making a list of all the other things that annoyed me, like having to be the primary breadwinner. And I'd blame that annoyance on the disability too. Even if Martin didn't have his disability, it's not as though we'd suddenly become wealthy. There's a good chance I'd still have to work, even if he had a job. Today, it often takes two incomes for families to make ends meet. Plus, I love my jobs and consider them a blessing from God!

When Martin asked me the same question for the fifth time, he wasn't doing it to get on my bad side. He was doing it because he needed the answer, and he couldn't remember I had already answered it patiently the first four times he asked. All he knew was that when he asked the question the last time, I blew a fuse. He had no idea why I was so upset with him, because he couldn't remember asking the question the previous four times. I can't imagine how he must have felt to ask a simple question and have his wife blow up. It must have been so unnerving.

Martin's disability wasn't preventing our marital happiness.

In that situation, my sinful behavior was.

Martin's disability was purely an opportunity. It could either bring tension into our marriage—like when I get frustrated at having to answer the same question. Or it could bring grace—like when I realize how blessed I am to be able to serve my husband five times more than any other wife. The problems in our marriage are caused because I am selfish, and I choose anger instead of grace. There are so many choices I could make that will bring us closer together, and a few that, over time, tear us apart. His disability offers me more chances to get it right (or wrong) than most other people get in their marriage.

No matter what we've gone through, each of us has some expectation of what our life should look like. Maybe you are single and think you should be married by now. Maybe you are married and thought you would have kids but don't. Perhaps you're divorced and you think you should still be married—or remarried. Or maybe you or a loved one is sick and you think you should be healthy.

What are your expectations about your life?

Where has your life fallen short of those expectations?

For Martin and me, his disability means we fall short of the expectations we had for our lives. For others, the issue might be an addiction, an incurable disease, or grief after the loss of a loved one.

In fact, you probably started reading this book because something in your life didn't look the way you thought it should. It's broken and it's never going to get better. To be better in our brokenness isn't to remove the brokenness; it's to remove the selfishness, pride, impatience, or other sinful behaviors we blame on the brokenness. When we stop blaming our situation on the brokenness, we begin to see that the brokenness is a trial designed specifically for us.

Now don't mistake what I am saying here. God did not give Martin a brain tumor so I would learn how to be more patient, or so we would learn how to communicate in a healthy way. Brain tumors entered the world when sin entered the world. But God wastes nothing. So, despite the fact that God hates brain tumors as much as we do, he can use our circumstances to teach us to have patience, to give grace, to withhold anger, and a thousand other things that make our marriage stronger than it would be without our trials.

I've also learned that I can't overcome my sinful tendencies on my own. I rarely choose patience and grace over anger and annoyance. Yet I've learned that even though they aren't my automatic response to situations, the more I practice patience and grace, the better I get. So why wouldn't God use the trials in my life to teach me patience? Why wouldn't God, who gave us perfect grace and who wants me to give and receive it, give me an astounding number of opportunities to learn how to give and receive grace? If God, who wants what is best for me, knows that means learning to depend on him more than I am capable of, why wouldn't he design circumstances in my life to teach me how to be totally dependent on him for everything?

Why wouldn't he design the trials in your life specifically for you?

To reach you?

To teach you?

And to draw you closer to God?

"I can't do this anymore," a lady said to me after a conference.

"You know, you're right," I said.

"This life is too hard for me," a teenager who was contemplating suicide said.

"I know," I replied. "It sure is."

"This is the hardest thing I've ever done," said a middle-aged woman responsible for her elderly mother's care.

"I believe it is," I agreed.

But to each of them I also said, "But Christ can do it through you." And then I told them how he'd helped me live through days that were impossible on my own.

Many caretakers don't feel appreciated. They feel unloved. They work so hard to care for someone but feel disrespected. When I point them to Scripture, they often feel like the Bible is another rule book they can never live up to. They think the reason this hard thing is happening to them is because they have failed God in some way— they didn't pray enough, read enough Scripture, serve enough, or have morning quiet times.

It's a lie that I mentioned earlier because I once believed it too.

But their brokenness isn't a punishment. And the Bible isn't just another high standard that they can't keep. So I take time to help them really understand what Scripture is.

It's a love letter to them.

It's from the God who created them, the same God who designed them to need him.

God has so intricately designed us to be in relationship with him that if we try to do life on our own, we can't. It's impossible without him. No wonder people say it's the hardest thing they've ever done, that life is too much for them, and they can't do it anymore. The truth is we can't. But he can.

So many of us say we want to follow Jesus, but we have a list of reservations about doing so. "As long as I am in control of my circumstances, I will follow him."

"I will follow him as long as I am healthy."

"I will follow him as long as my child is obedient."

"I will follow him as long as the pain goes away."

"I will follow him as long as it doesn't require too much from me."

I will follow him as long as it doesn't look like he's headed toward the cross.

In Scripture, we see that, despite their circumstances, the people who follow Jesus consistently demonstrate love. They have joy and a tremendous passion for life, which is something we all want. To have a better broken, we need to reconcile that those two things can happen simultaneously—we can face trials, and we can still have joy.

Joy doesn't come from our circumstances; it comes from our God. And since God is with us during our trials, it is possible to have joy even in our trials.

Joy is in the Lord. Brokenness is in the world. As long as we're alive, both will coexist on earth.

And that can trip up a lot of people. They don't understand the difference between momentary happiness and a deep-seated, God-given joy. In fact, most of us have an expectation of what a "happy life" looks like. But it always seems just a little beyond us. I've heard people say things like, "If only God gave me this, then I'd be happy." Or, "If only God took this thing away, then I'd be happy."

I've said things like that too. I thought if only Martin were healed our lives would be happier and our marriage would be better. When Martin was sick, I thought we'd be happy if we just had a diagnosis. Then we had a diagnosis of a brain tumor, so I thought we'd be happy once it was removed. Then it was removed, and I thought we'd be happy once he had recovered. And then he recovered, but not fully, and I thought we could only be happy if he was fully healed. But it has almost been ten years now, and it doesn't look like we'll *ever* reach that bar.

But if we did, I bet the bar would move again. That would be a lot of years of unhappiness based on our circumstances.

Maybe your moving bar looks something like this: *If I get married, I'll be happy.* And then you get married but decide you need a better-paying job or kids to be happy. You get the job, the kids, the house, and the dog, and now you're sure you'll be happy once the kids are gone, and you can retire from the job you once wanted so badly. But joy doesn't have to be "out there." We can have joy even in the worst circumstances.

I'm sure Martin doesn't have joy all the time. I also see how he inspires so many people, including me, to never give up. How can I complain about all I have to do on my busiest days when I think how Martin can't remember the details of his quietest days? How can I call myself forgetful for not remembering a volunteer's name when Martin spends six months memorizing the names of the boys on his baseball team and celebrates that as an accomplishment? Martin has joy that contradicts his circumstances, but that joy is completely consistent with his God.

It's a deep joy that comes from making intentional choices about how we're going to live our lives despite our circumstances. Despite the darkness of our circumstances, joy does come in the morning. But I have met people who have turned their back on the joy that could be theirs. They're convinced that unless God answers their prayers exactly as they've prayed, then God isn't all that helpful to them. It's another lie that trips up most of us. We think that if we just had an explanation as to why we're in these circumstances, we'd be able to accept them. But it's a lie that comfort, satisfaction, and joy come from an answer to "Why is this happening to me?"

✐

Consider the apostle Paul. He never got an answer to why he had to endure the things he did, yet he talked a lot about joy. In fact, while he was imprisoned, he wrote a lot about joy. His story is unlike any other. He was one of the greatest Christian persecutors of his time. He hated the church and went house to house, where he dragged out the Christians and had them thrown in prison. When the movement continued, he decided it was time to go after the originators. So one day Paul set out for Damascus to hunt down the instigators of the Jesus movement—the disciples.

But on the road to Damascus, Paul had an encounter with the risen Jesus. A flash of light blinded him and, as instructed by the voice of Jesus, he waited in Damascus until Ananias was sent to baptize him and restore his sight.

This may have been the most dramatic conversion ever!

While there was initial skepticism about the changes that took place, it soon became apparent that his zealousness against Christianity had been replaced with a zeal for Christ. Instead of stopping the spread of the gospel, Paul became the greatest Christian missionary and evangelist in the history of the world. It was Paul who took the gospel to the Gentiles and is the primary writer of the New Testament.

Despite his beginnings, Paul grew to deeply love Jesus and his message.

To have a story like that, there is no doubt that God deeply loved Paul. But that didn't mean Paul was exempt from the trials of this life. In fact, Paul had at least one glaring problem that prevented him from doing all he wanted for the cause of Christ. He referred to it as a "thorn in the flesh."

"Therefore, in order to keep me from becoming conceited, I was given a thorn in my flesh, a messenger of Satan, to torment me" (2 Cor. 12:7).

We're never told what Paul's thorn in the flesh was. Some have speculated it was a physical problem. Others have suggested it was a character flaw. Frankly, I am glad we're never told. That way we can relate our own thorns in the flesh to Paul's situation. So I like to think that perhaps Paul had a brain tumor or a head injury. Perhaps you might think of it as grief over a lost loved one, an addiction, or an incurable disease.

What matters about Paul's broken condition is not what it was specifically; what matters is what he did about it. Paul remarked that it was "given to him," with the implication that God was the giver. So did Paul just blindly accept it? Did he get angry and say, "Why me?" Did he turn his back on God?

Paul did none of those things. Instead he prayed about it: "Three times I pleaded with the Lord to take it away from me" (v. 8).

More than just a casual prayer, Paul begged God to take it away. Whatever this ugly, broken thing was in Paul's life, Paul couldn't make it go away on his own. He needed God to step in and make something happen. So Paul prayed once and didn't see anything happen. Like so many of us who think God didn't hear us the first time, Paul prayed a second time. Maybe the second time was a little louder or a little longer. Yet still no discernable response. So he prayed a third time.

We've done exactly the same thing, haven't we?

We've asked God to heal the illness, fix the marriage, cure the addiction, repair our credit, and prevent the miscarriage. When it seems God doesn't hear our prayer the first or second time, we ask again, *pleading* our case before him.

Which is exactly what Paul did too.

Paul wrote, "But he said to me, 'My grace is sufficient for you, for my power is made perfect in weakness'" (v. 9). It's an astonishing answer. God said to Paul, and therefore, perhaps to all of us, "I'm going to leave your brokenness there, and I'm not going to fix it, because my grace is enough for you. Not only that, but my power is perfected when you can't do anything to get rid of it yourself."

Paul would have much preferred to have the thorn removed and make everything okay. He wanted God to fix it.

But God wanted the thorn to remain right where it was.

Stuck firmly in Paul's side.

Maybe you've prayed to have something fixed, healed, taken away, given to you, restored, or repaired but you didn't see anything change. So you prayed more. You pleaded. And then begged. But nothing changed; things remained right where they were before you prayed.

Maybe you thought God didn't hear you.

But perhaps God heard you and his answer was the same as his answer to Paul. He left your brokenness right where it was.

If that is how God has answered your prayer, he's not ignoring you. He's not punishing you. He's not demanding more from you. He just wants you to know he is sufficient for you and his power is made perfect in your weakness.

Can you think of any prayer you've prayed where you thought God didn't answer? Looking back, can you see that perhaps his answer was, "No, I'm not going to take that thing away. I'm going to leave it right where it is"?

If that's happened to you, let's pause here to make sure you understand what God didn't say to Paul. He didn't say, "I'm going to leave it there because you were a terrible person in the past, and you don't deserve to have it taken away!" God didn't say, "I wish I could take it away from you, Paul, I really do. It's just that I'm not strong or powerful enough to take it away." And God didn't say, "Stop your whining! The reason I'm not removing your stupid thorn is because I don't care about it, and I don't care about you!"

Paul wasn't being punished. Paul was loved.

And neither are you being punished. You are also loved.

God loves and cares for Paul despite anything he had done in the past or would do in the future. And God certainly has the power to remove this unknown thorn anytime he wants. But God is saying, "For now, I want to leave this thing with you because my power is made perfect in your weakness. And even though it hurts and you're suffering because of it, my grace is sufficient for you regardless of what it feels like."

Could God be saying something similar to me?

And to you?

If so, what should our response be?

Maybe it should be the same as Paul's—:

Therefore I will boast all the more gladly about my weaknesses, so that Christ's power may rest on me. That is why, for Christ's sake, I delight in weaknesses, in insults, in hardships, in persecutions, in difficulties. For when I am weak, then I am strong. (vv. 9–10)

Instead of being upset that his prayer to have his thorn removed was denied, Paul accepted God's explanation. Rather than running and hiding, Paul delighted in this stumbling block. He's like, "Bring it on!" It's as if Paul was *celebrating* his broken parts because they were opportunities for others to see God's glory through him. God's strength was made stronger in Paul's weakness, so Paul didn't want to cover up, hide, or excuse his weaknesses. Paul wanted everyone to know he was weak!

We said earlier that if we could handle all of our problems in life, we wouldn't need God. But because we can't, he is the hero of our story. What Paul says that he delights in is exposing all of the broken things in his life because it shows how big a hero his God is. Paul wasn't embarrassed to talk about his thorn in the flesh because God was magnified by it. Paul's thorn was an excuse to talk about God's power and glory.

When was the last time you celebrated what was broken in your life because God was magnified by it? How could your weak and broken parts bring glory to God?

For me, it was sharing my doubts and fears. For someone who is employed as a music minister at a prominent church, my doubts about God were downright embarrassing. Yet God used my thorn in the flesh—my weakness—to create a song that ministered to many broken people.

Finally, Paul noted that when he was weak, then God was strong through him. That is what makes Paul strong. So when Paul was weak, he was strong in God's power. It's one of those juxtapositions we don't really understand until we've lived through it.

When I look back and see how young and naive Martin and I were when we started on this journey, it's obvious we were weak in every area. Neither one of us had ever faced a health crisis like this in our family. Our marriage was barely a year old when Martin started having symptoms. While our faith was real, it surely wasn't strong enough to survive the doubts we encountered.

But in our weakness, God was strong. And the reason we tell our story is because God is the hero. We give him all of the glory for what he's brought us through. Our marriage is closer than it ever would have been without the trials we faced. We are so thankful for the opportunities we have to serve, and we know that without the things we've experienced, we wouldn't be serving in these areas. And our relationship with God has become more intimate, with more layers of trust than either of us ever could have imagined.

Paul's weaknesses are his ministry. When he boasts of them he boasts of God.

Martin and I both serve out of our weaknesses and so to share our story, we can only boast of God's great glory and strength.

So let me ask you a question.

Could it be that the broken parts of your life, the trials you are facing or have endured already, are places where God can reveal his strength through you?

And if so, are you willing to tell your story?

Will you gladly boast of your weaknesses to show God's strength?

Can God meeting you in your trials be your strength, or even the beginning of your ministry?

Just to be clear, Paul did not believe that suffering was the only way to exhibit Christ's power. Nor was he a masochist who invited more pain so he might somehow receive more power. Paul had an affliction that he preferred God remove, which is why he prayed for the thorn to be taken away.

Likewise, Paul's prayer wasn't the power of positive thinking. He didn't repeat a mantra over and over. Nor did he boast about his suffering because he was a happy little martyr. Instead, Paul deferred to God's wisdom and power. He told God and anyone else who would listen that as long as he must endure this affliction, he knew that God was sufficient and therefore he would boast of God's ability to work in and through him despite the thorn.

To put it in a more modern context, Martin and I didn't "believe" through the power of positive thinking that the consequences of his brain tumor surgery would just disappear. We didn't deny there were consequences and try to put on a happy face and ignore his faulty memory. Neither did we welcome all of the trials we've been through because of it.

Instead, we've prayed every day for Martin to be fully healed; for all of the consequences of the tumor and surgery to be gone. Our desire always has been and always will be for God to heal Martin completely. And we believe our God has the power and ability to do that.

But when God chooses not to, we can still give him glory, and we can still boast of his strength in our weakness, and we can still find joy in his presence. That doesn't mean we pretend as if we like what is happening to us. It's just that we acknowledge God is God and we are not. Even in the midst of our unchanging circumstances, we can still give him praise and glory. We can still tell others how frail and weak we are, while saying how strong our God remains. We can be content and even find joy in our tragedy, not because we *will* ourselves to be or we have some kind of extraordinary mastery over our feelings.

I have a friend who longs to be married and doesn't understand why God hasn't brought her a husband yet. Every morning when she wakes up, the first thing she does in her quiet time is pray for her husband. The second thing she does is pray that God makes the most of her singleness for that day.

She lives in the both/and.

She doesn't roll over and say, "I'm happy and content right where I am," when she's not happy or content. Instead, she prays fervently that God will bring her a husband. But she also recognizes the fact that every day she *is* single, God has a purpose for her in her singleness.

We can be content and even have joy because of God's grace.

Paul didn't call us to suffering.

In fact, Paul called on God to remove his suffering.

But what Paul knew, and what Martin and I have learned, is that God is *more* than present in suffering.

He is sufficient.

So when I talk to someone like Cindy, I remind her that Paul's circumstances didn't change. His thorn was not removed. He spent lots of time in prison, which went against every expectation he had for his life. But if there ever was an example of someone whose attitude could change, it was Paul. He went from Christian killer to Christ follower. From anger to joy. From doubt to belief. And from weakness to strength in Christ.

While our broken circumstances may not change, we can. We do this by clinging to Scripture, discovering who God truly is, being willing to share our story even in the trials, and looking for blessings in our brokenness.

We are all broken, but we can have a better story.

And a better story begins with using our brokenness.

MYTH: THINGS HAVE TO GET BETTER
BEFORE I CAN GET BETTER.

TRUTH: MY SITUATION MAY NOT GET
BETTER, BUT I CAN GET BETTER.

TWENTY

MESSY ENDINGS

I HAVE WON SEVERAL AWARDS FOR MY MUSIC, BUT ONE award I'm pretty sure I'll never be nominated for is Mother of the Year. Take for example one Wednesday morning when Josie was thirteen months old. We woke up late for a Bible study I was leading with only enough time to get one of us dressed. Since I was teaching the class that day, I decided it needed to be me.

Josie stayed in her pajamas.

We arrived at Perimeter before child care opened, so I took Josie with me to the fellowship hall while I did a sound check. Josie began toddling around, running in circles, and trying to be a big girl while climbing on the hardwood stairs to the stage.

That's when it happened.

I turned away just for a minute, and she took a tumble, falling flat on her face and busting her lip. She started wailing, catching the attention of everyone (including me) who was setting up the event. As we all raced toward her, she stopped crying. Sensing she was the center of attention, she forgot all about her fall and bloody lip. And since she has grown up around musicians, she understands that when you have an audience, it is time to perform. She had just learned how to blow kisses, so she started blowing bloody kisses to everyone. Her face was all sweetness and smiles, but blood was going everywhere! "Oh, I'm fine," she seemed to be saying, as blood dripped onto her Hello Kitty pajamas. I picked her up and she buried her face in my blouse—the pretty white blouse that I purposely wore to convince the newcomers that I was the one in charge. As I carried Josie out of the fellowship hall and to the nursery, she continued blowing bloody kisses over my shoulder as the horrified staff looked on.

I arrived at the nursery and stood in line with all of the "good moms" who had decked out their little girls in perfectly pressed, hand-smocked dresses with matching hair bows. I caught a glimpse of us in a mirror near the door, and Josie and I looked like characters from the set of *Texas Chainsaw Massacre*. But what could we do?

When we reached the front of the line, the nursery worker actually recoiled and grimaced at us.

The director walked over and, seeing that it was me, handed me a beeper. "Aren't you speaking this morning?"

"Yeah, I'm supposed to start in fifteen minutes."

"What if something goes wrong and we need to beep you?" asked the director.

"Yeah, I'm probably not going to answer it," I said, handing Josie to her.

"But what if there is an emergency?"

I pointed at Josie, who was now blowing her bloody kisses onto the director. "Look at her. She's still in her pajamas and bleeding. Whatever emergency comes up, clearly y'all can do a better job than I can!"

On my way back to the fellowship hall, I made a quick stop in the bathroom, where I wet some paper towels and attempted to make the bloodstains a more flattering shade of pink. As I scrubbed brown bits of paper towel into my blouse, I thought, *What am I doing here?* I was a mess, my kid was a mess, and unless I got it together, I was about to make a mess of the Bible study I was getting ready to teach.

As I looked at the other moms coming in and out of the bathroom with cute clothes, matching jewelry, and manicures, I couldn't even wrap my head around how they all looked so put together. But that is when I had a realization: *I am so thankful God has not called me to a tidy, well-put-together life for the glory of Laura.* Instead, he has called me to this messy, unmanageable, and totally dependent on him life for the glory of God.

That morning was a turning point for me. For the past several years, Martin had been on a physical journey, relearning how to do some of the most basic things—like walk and eat. Simultaneously, I had been on a spiritual journey that caused me to examine and redefine some basic spiritual practices—like the importance of depending on Scripture. But now, we were on a new journey together, redefining family and parenting. Just like it wasn't fair for Martin to compare himself to his "before" self and expectations about life, I couldn't hold myself to the ideal images of motherhood that I'd experienced growing up either. Our lives were different than we expected them to be, but that didn't mean they weren't exactly what God had planned for us. If because of our circumstances we would have to be more dependent on Jesus than other parents, well, that was a good thing.

Fortunately, God's expectations of me didn't include hosting the perfect two-year-old birthday party, hand-smocking a dress, or teaching Josie the alphabet by the time she was eighteen months old. Those were expectations *I* had placed on my self. But God didn't create me to be like every other mom. He created me to be me, and he loves me just how I am.

When songwriters are trying to figure something out, they often write a song about it. The song I wrote was called "I Can Just Be Me."

The lyrics begin with me trying to do everything but not measuring up. Then in the chorus I ask God to be everything that I can't be.

I've been doing all that I can
To hold it all together
Piece by piece.
I've been feeling like a failure,
Trying to be braver

Than I could ever be.
It's just not me.

So be my healer, be my comfort, be my peace.
Cause I can be broken, I can be needy,
Lord I need you now to be,
Be my God, so I can just be me.

So be my father, my mighty warrior, be my king.
Cause I can be scattered, frail and shattered,
Lord I need you now to be,
Be my God, so I can just be me.

And be my savior, be my lifeline, won't you be my everything.
Cause I'm so tired of trying to be someone
I was never meant to be
Be my God
Please be my God
Be my God
So I can just be me
So I can just be me
I can just be me.

And as I worked through the ideas behind the song, I realized that when we're living in brokenness we can sometimes feel as though we're less than or not good enough. Sometimes that leads us to trying harder. Often it leads to us failing further. But we have to give up that idea and settle into who God created us to be.

Looking in the mirror that morning, it was clear I wouldn't win a Best Mom trophy, but that was okay. I was finally able to embrace the fact that I am a working mom whose daughter might climb more catwalks in an arena than trees on a playground. She'll start trends by wearing her pjs to church and blowing kisses (though they might be bloody) to her audience. But she'll also know that there was a man who shed his blood for her when he died on a cross. And she'll never think of church as a place we go, but something we do wherever we are.

Mine is motherhood redefined with God at the center rather than my achievements at the center. But it is a center that is always in flux.

Just when we started to get good at being Josie's parents, our little family of three added two more. On September 18, 2014, we welcomed Josie's new little brothers, Benjamin Cary and Griffin James, who doubled not only the joy in our house but also the chaos.

Their birth was a reminder to me that good and beautiful things can come from pain. My labor was roughly eight hours long, and I said Jesus' name a lot—not in vain, but in pain. Of course, I would go through every minute of the pregnancy and the delivery over and over again to have such precious boys. The temporary pain I endured was worth it. When we see the results of my pain in the faces of my children, I would do it all over again.

But think about the birth from the twins' perspective. When the boys first entered this world, they left the security and warmth of the womb to be violently faced with the bright lights and cold air of the hospital delivery room. They could only cry, but if they could have talked, I imagine they would have said something like, "What did you do that for? We wanted to stay where we were, warm and happy!"

I wonder how many times I've said that to God?

When we are on the receiving end of pain and can't yet see or understand why we're in such trials, we can find it so hard to trust. But as imperfect mothers and fathers, we often inflict pain on our children for their own good. Whether it is birthing them, giving them their immunization shots, or putting them into time-out so they don't touch a hot stove, we could be seen as the source of their pain, even though we're only doing what is best for them.

So how much more must God, our perfect Father, be doing for us when we're experiencing pain? Like any good parent, God fully understands the pain we feel, and he is with us in it, but he allows us to go through it because he has a greater good in mind.

Can we trust him in that?

It's hard, I know.

But that's also why we place our hope in him. Our hope is that one day the pain will end and we'll live with him in a pain-free eternity, where there is no more brokenness and we are all made whole.

I know there are days in the midst of our brokenness and our trials, when it is so hard to cling to that idea. It feels as though it takes more faith to believe it than we have. Fortunately, God doesn't even demand supersized faith from us. In fact, Jesus says all we need is faith the size of a seed—a mustard seed—smaller than many of the spices in your cabinet. A seed so small it gets lost under a fingernail or stuck in the fold of our palm. That's all we need in order to do what seems impossible.

Jesus said, "Truly I tell you, if you have faith as small as a mustard seed, you can say to this mountain, 'Move from here to there,' and it will move. Nothing will be impossible for you" (Matt. 17:20).

Faith that small.

Because God is that big.

I cling to that thought both as a mother and as a wife. The older I get the more I realize there are few seasons of life that can be labeled "good" or "bad." Right now, I am in a really sweet season of life. Whatever season Martin and I face, whatever new blessings we face, we find new things that rub up against Martin's disabilities and new mourning takes place. The good news is that our mourning often takes place, humorously, in the midst of baby projectile poop, while I am trying to feed the same twin twice because one of us forgot which twin was already fed. (And once again, that "one" is me, not Martin.)

Our life looks much like the life of any set of parents with a newborn baby. Except that we have two babies.

And a two-year-old.

And a husband with a disability.

Okay, so, it probably doesn't look anything like anyone else's life. It probably looks a lot funnier. But that's okay, because it's not about us. If you knocked on my door right now and asked to use the bathroom, you'd likely find there is no soap at the sink and the hand towel is actually a dishrag. The good towels are starting to mildew in the basement in a pile of laundry I have labeled "not yet urgent."

Our dinner menu ranges from "What menu?" to "takeout." When someone wants a snack, I try to give them something healthy. "You can eat the Cheerios under the couch, but not the cheese; it's getting old."

The weekend before our Christmas production at Perimeter, I was at the church on Sunday for fourteen hours straight. Josie was with me. When I was onstage, she was holding my hand the entire time. Some might find that annoying, but I think it is precious memories in the making. That's just what our life looks like.

We were both exhausted by the time we finally left that evening! As soon as we got home and I started feeding the twins, to show her appreciation and contribute to the memories of the day, Josie vomited. That meant another trip out to get Pedialyte and more prayers that no one else in the house would get whatever bug she picked up.

What can you do in a situation like that? You can cry or you can laugh. I choose to laugh and think it could be worse. In a few more years, I'll still be doing the Christmas production, I'll be older and more exhausted afterward, and at that time, I could be bringing home three vomiting kids!

As you've read my story and compared yours to mine, maybe your story is harder or maybe it's easier. But whatever it is, I encourage you to cling to Scripture because that and laughter is what will get you through.

I know people look at our Elvington family and say, "What a mess!" And I'd agree. But despite our brokenness, despite the trials we have endured and will continue to fight through, despite the days when our faith is low, and our patience is lower, we are blessed.

We are blessed by a God who loves us and will never leave us.

We are blessed with the gift of his grace that allows us to spend eternity with him in a place free of trials and free of brokenness.

We are blessed because we have a loving family who gets to serve our great, big God every single day. Whether we are at home or on the road, for us, life is an abundantly beautiful, blessed mess. Despite our brokenness, we wouldn't want it any other way, for it is through our brokenness that God is the hero of our story.

We're all just a phone call away. And when we get that unexpected phone call, we think life as we know it is over. But life as we've yet to know it and how God might use it has just begun.

Share your story.

Give God the glory.

And live a better broken.

ACKNOWLEDGMENTS

FEW THINGS ARE ACCOMPLISHED IN LIFE THAT ARE NOT a team effort. And for my life specifically, I can think of four groups of people that have been invaluable in the writing of this book:

To the amazing team that has worked on this project: Jennifer, you are truly the best writer I have ever met. And it's more than the words you eloquently put on the pages; it's the way you worship. Thanks for the countless hours over cups of coffee and Panera Thai chicken sandwiches. Through much laughter and many tears, we have created something I believe God will use in a tremendous way. To Nicole, I still can't believe you talked me into this. This project never would have happened without you and to simply say thanks seems much too small a word. I so appreciate you, dear friend. To Debbie Wickwire and the team at W, thanks for taking a chance on me and for being more than just a publishing company. It's a privilege to partner in ministry with you guys. To Kathy, Dan, Jim, and the whole team at CT, thanks for all the hard work and for believing in me!

To the gang at Perimeter Church: Thanks for loving our family in the midst of our mess. You guys have consistently been the hands and feet of Jesus to us, and my life is richer from being a part of this community. To my worship and arts staff team, thanks for praying me through this project and picking up the slack when I've needed to be away. You guys are the best. And a special thanks to the Popes, the Woods, and the Wilhelms. The truths I have written about in this book have been taught to me and lived out in front of me by you three couples. Thanks for seeing the story God was writing in my life when I could not and for carrying us through our hardest times. I love you guys.

To team Elvington: Our little family, as broken as we are sometimes, has made my life fuller than I ever could have dreamed. To Josie, Benjamin, and Griffin, for the smiles and giggles that make each day bright. And to Martin, thanks for walking this hard road with me. Through your loss, I believe many will gain Christ. Thank you for never giving up and for always entrusting your life to God's hands.

Last but not least, to you, the reader: To anyone who is willing to pick up this book and spare a few moments to read a bit. Thanks for your time. My prayer is that you will not hear *my* story but *God's* story, experienced through my life. In turn, I pray you begin to ponder what story God might be writing through your brokenness. May my adventure of trusting God be the beginning of a faith adventure of your own.

DON'T FORGET...

MYTH: TRIALS ARE A CURSE.	*TRUTH*: TRIALS ARE AN OPPORTUNITY.
MYTH: GOD'S PRIMARY DESIRE IS TO FIX BROKEN THINGS.	*TRUTH*: GOD'S PRIMARY DESIRE IS TO FIX MY BROKEN RELATIONSHIP WITH HIM.
MYTH: SALVATION IS GAINED BY THE THINGS I DO.	*TRUTH:* SALVATION IS GAINED BY WHAT JESUS DID FOR ME.
MYTH: WHEN THINGS LOOK DARK, GOD IS GONE.	*TRUTH*: WHEN THINGS LOOK DARK, GOD'S LIGHT SHINES THE BRIGHTEST.
MYTH: THE PLAN I HAVE FOR MY LIFE IS MUCH BETTER THAN THE PLACE WHERE GOD HAS ME RIGHT NOW.	*TRUTH*: WHERE GOD HAS ME RIGHT NOW IS THE BEST PLACE FOR ME.
MYTH: THE CHURCH IS A BUILDING WITH SERVICES.	*TRUTH*: THE CHURCH IS THE PEOPLE OF GOD AS THEY SERVE ONE ANOTHER.
MYTH: THE STRENGTH OF MY FAITH IS BASED ON HOW STRONGLY I BELIEVE.	*TRUTH*: THE STRENGTH OF MY FAITH IS BASED ON THE STRENGTH OF MY GOD.
MYTH: I GAIN BY HOLDING ON.	*TRUTH*: I GAIN BY LETTING GO.
MYTH: CONTENTMENT BEGINS WITH UNDERSTANDING WHY.	*TRUTH*: CONTENTMENT BEGINS WITH ASKING HOW GOD MIGHT USE THIS FOR HIS GLORY.

MYTH: I WORSHIP BECAUSE I FEEL GOOD.	*TRUTH*: I WORSHIP BECAUSE HE IS GOOD.
MYTH: GOD CAN ONLY USE MY STORY WHEN THERE IS A HAPPY ENDING.	*TRUTH*: GOD CAN USE MY STORY WHEN I TRUST HIM IN THE JOURNEY.
MYTH: I AM DEFINED BY MY PAST.	*TRUTH*: GOD REDEEMS MY PAST AND GIVES ME A FUTURE.
MYTH: MY STORY ISN'T WORTH MUCH.	*TRUTH*: MY STORY IS MY GREATEST OFFERING.
MYTH: GOD NEEDS MY HELP.	*TRUTH*: GOD WANTS MY TRUST.
MYTH: I MUST WORK TO KEEP MY DREAMS ALIVE.	*TRUTH*: I CAN REST WHEN I RELEASE MY DREAMS TO THE HANDS OF MY LOVING FATHER.
MYTH: GOD IS WITHHOLDING WHAT I WANT BECAUSE HE IS PUNISHING ME.	*TRUTH*: GOD IS WITHHOLDING WHAT I WANT BECAUSE HE HAS SOMETHING BETTER FOR ME.
MYTH: GOD IS INDIFFERENT TO THE DESIRES OF OUR HEART.	*TRUTH*: GOD IS ABLE TO DO ABUNDANTLY MORE THAN WE ASK FOR OR IMAGINE!
MYTH: THINGS HAVE TO GET BETTER BEFORE I CAN GET BETTER.	*TRUTH*: MY SITUATION MAY NOT GET BETTER, BUT I CAN GET BETTER.

"You will know the truth, and the truth will set you free."

—JOHN 8:32

ABOUT THE AUTHOR

LAURA STORY IS A BIBLE TEACHER, WORSHIP LEADER, GRAMMY award-winning singer/songwriter, and bestselling author. "Blessings" was certified GOLD in 2011 and inspired her first book *What If Your Blessings Come Through Raindrops*. Laura's music and writing show God's love and grace intersecting with real life, and serve as a reminder that despite questions or circumstances, he is the ultimate author of our story. She has a graduate degree from Covenant Theological Seminary and has served as the worship leader at Perimeter Church in Atlanta since 2005, but her greatest joy is being a wife to Martin and the mother to Ben, Griffin, and Josie.

Laura Story's music is
available on iTunes.